An Essay in the History of
THE RADICAL SENSIBILITY
IN AMERICA

An Essay in the History of
THE RADICAL SENSIBILITY
IN AMERICA

L. S. Halprin

Skyhorse Publishing

Skyhorse Publishing books may be purchased in bulk at special discounts for sales promotion, corporate gifts, fund-raising, or educational purposes. Special editions can also be created to specifications. For details, contact the Special Sales Department, Skyhorse Publishing, 307 West 36th Street, 11th Floor, New York, NY 10018 or info@skyhorsepublishing.com.

Skyhorse® and Skyhorse Publishing® are registered trademarks of Skyhorse Publishing, Inc.®, a Delaware corporation.

Visit our website at www.skyhorsepublishing.com.

10 9 8 7 6 5 4 3 2 1

Library of Congress Cataloging-in-Publication Data is available on file.

Cover design by Kai Texel
Interior design by Peter Lyons

ISBN: 978-1-5107-6624-2
Ebook ISBN: 978-1-5107-6625-9

Printed in the United States of America

Contents

PREFACE

How do *you* use the word radical? Committed to the progressive? The cooperative? The communal? The equalitarian? Feeling these to go together at the *base* of things? Their fulfillment *our* fulfillment?

Well, in so far (and it is very far) as social, political, and economic power is sought and wielded in malice, just so far is benevolence radical. The history of social, political, and economic power has been mostly the history of malice. The history of benevolence has been mostly the history of radicalism. The sensibility that loves benevolence has been a radical sensibility.

That sensibility came anew to an extraordinarily exuberant energy among American youth of the 1960s and inspirits them now and again since then. Well, many tell the young radicals that they should know more of the past, more of the history of which they, the youth, are only the forward edge. Yes, I suppose they should. The history of the radical sensibility includes a great deal of stumbling into the traps of sentimentality: there is much in their past the young would do well to remind themselves to avoid. And it is said that the young should know their debt to the past. Yes, but the only way properly to pay our debt to the past is to profit from it—to be made wiser by its wisdoms and by knowledge of its follies. The young should know the past not so as to learn a debtor's humility, but to learn still greater and firmer pride: not to constrain youth's gestures of exuberance but to extend them, substantiate them, fill them out, as it were, with the weighty stuff they have inherited.

Ignorance is, I think, often not simply a failure to know but rather an interested defense of malice: it is easier to prey on those in whom we do not recognize ourselves. The history of malice and of the ignorance that defends it is very long. But the history of benevolence and of the love of knowing is also long, and redeems the other. I have

1

delineated here some of the work from the American history of the partisans of a knowing benevolence. Their work is recorded proof of the greatness the species can accomplish: it ought to embolden us with a sense of our possibilities.

My argument is essentially this: that before the middle of the nineteenth century the work of all American radicals was organized to defend some form of sentimental faith in millennial progress; that the work of the great writers of the middle of the nineteenth century was the first to be fundamentally free of the constraints of sentimentality; that despite that generation's accomplishments, the old sentimentalities have persisted, perpetuating the cycle in which illusions designed to make radicalism's chances seem better than they are become the disillusions that make them seem worse.

To be sentimental means, I take it, to make belief subject to wish. The wish for certainty, for faith that some force will make the world certainly to be as we want it to be, is terribly strong. The wish for certainty has made much radical thought sentimental. Faith in the unfettered heart's power spontaneously to create millennium; faith in the universal moral efficacy of economic well-being (whether created by the fettered or the unfettered marketplace); or, bereft of an optimistic certainty, a pessimistic certainty holding that humankind is, after all, only vicious and that therefore history and social change are morally meaningless. These three sentimental reductionisms—the romantic, the economic, and the pessimistic—are, I think, the major forms by which the radical sensibility has allowed its thought to be governed by the wish for certainty, the wish not to see the contingency and conditionality of human possibilities. Though these reductionisms are persistently attractive to radicals (as to others), by the early nineteenth century they had been given classical American formulation—see Jonathan Edwards, Benjamin Franklin, and Ralph Waldo Emerson.

In the works of the great writers of the middle of the nineteenth century—in Poe, Hawthorne, Melville, and Whitman—the

2

reductionisms that had until then constrained the radical sensibility in America were overcome. These writers gave to the love of benevolence and of knowing a sense of history, of human nature, of society, that it had not had before, that it has not always had since, and that, in my view, it ignores only to lose a wisdom commensurate with the beauty of its aspirations.

To unfold something of the contribution of Poe, Hawthorne, Melville, and Whitman to the specific content of the radical sensibility in America, that is the central intention of this book. Since the middle of the nineteenth century, the radical's work has been primarily to accomplish political power. That work and the frustrations of it often leave little energy for the pursuit of a thoroughgoing self-awareness. That is why it seems particularly useful now to remind ourselves of both the sentimentalities and the wisdoms from which we come.

INTRODUCTION

The ambiguous language of popular thought about economic matters probably signifies the popular confusion and its character. We call many things "goods" that are patently evils—as though the only arbiter of value were whether or not a thing would sell—and we label the things of the marketplace goods as though there were no other. These may be merely thoughtless conventions of language, and then again, they may not. Certainly, "making a living" and "earning a living" are strange phrases. Do they suggest the attitude that one is not living while one works? Have we really lost so much of life as to regard the money we may be paid as the only motivation or justification of our work? And is "earning" used in the sense of deserving—as in "he earns our admiration"? Then is it implied that van Gogh deserved a living while he worked as a salesman in a picture gallery, but not when he gave up everything else for painting, though it brought him no money at all? If you can't "earn a living," then do you deserve a dying? To feel thus might be appropriate to the life of the jungle and the cave, but to speak intentionally of "goods" as we do would be ignorant even there.

And we talk of the alternatives, capitalism and socialism. But these, not being similar categories, are not properly alternatives or antitheses. The word socialism suggests a motive for economic action. Capitalism suggests only a method of symbolizing and arranging certain kinds of force. That is, a society at once monetary and socialist would still establish and allocate "capital" and could in this sense be called capitalist. Our socialism versus private enterprise is a nicer terminology. The language suggests a clear distinction between societies asserting the moral primacy of communal motives, communal action oriented to communal well-being, and those asserting the moral primacy of private purpose, individual pursuit of individual well-being. But the language is again misleading. It ignores the irrelevance of *private* enterprise to the necessary scale of contemporary economic action, and it ignores the fact that the characteristic decision of the American economy is the corporate rather than the individual decision.

To get ahead in a huge corporation and to have the power to decide the action of that corporation is neither more nor less a private enterprise than to do the same thing in a socialist bureau. The real distinction between the economic systems of the two societies, then, has to do only with the culturally sanctioned and sponsored goal of individual and group enterprises. In the one the goal is to be advantage to the society as a whole; in the other the overriding goal is to be characteristically the money profit to the entrepreneurs, whether they produce goods, evils, or inconsequentials. Now it is hard to see how in a society expressedly proud of its Greco-Judeo-Christian lineage the name for this alternative to socialism could be anything but clearly and sharply pejorative.

Rarely today is the power to acquire property thought to prove the right to it. Privatism is usually defended for its efficiency and its freedoms. But it is no longer seriously held by serious economists that privatism is by nature a more efficient economic system—rather the reverse. And the proposition of a necessarily positive correlation between the degree of privatism and the degree of freedom is at best ill considered. Freedom for what? The answer, freedom to pursue private money profit, is, of course, circular: it says only that the society that sponsors pursuit of private money profit sponsors pursuit of private money profit. Unless one regards that pursuit itself to be the goal of social life, the essential good, the proper moral object of human endeavors; unless privatism is proposed as goal rather than as instrument, some other freedom must be at issue.

If freedom means, as I suppose it does, opportunity to do what one wants to do, then making it part of the discussion of economic systems is both useful and dangerous. The use is in the implied wisdom—a wisdom more common among common people than among formal moralists—of seeing economic condition as a major correlate of moral condition. A moral import of economic condition is that the amplitude of one's choices is in important degree dependent on one's wealth. In a general way, the poorer one is, the fewer choices—the less freedom—one has. A serious argument for privatism is that it creates and distributes more wealth, hence more freedom, than other systems do. But first of all, there is enough poverty in America now and enough unused resources of wealth to make this an open rather than a closed question. But even putting that problem aside, there is a considerable danger in this argument. It makes of economic action a means only, morally neutral, except for its efficacy in producing wealth, which is its goal. But the fact is that economic action is what most people mostly do or prepare for doing; and further, most people's extra-familial relations are economic relations—the relations between workers, between sellers and buyers, between competitors, between employers and employees, and so on; and the things that as economic actors we make or do are our most important function as members of society. Our economic functions as a rule *are* our participation in our society's purposes: it is when we go to work that we act most directly as citizens.

An economic system, then, is not only a system of means to wealth and to the freedoms that wealth facilitates. An economic system tends to define, indeed to *be*, the moral relations among the members of society, and to be the inherent moral quality and social effect of work. If, as it seems to me, the essential moral goals are benevolence and excellence or mastery and a coherence of benevolence and mastery, then the moral significance of an economic system is in its tendency to facilitate and to sponsor benevolent relations amongst people with mastery in vocation, and a coherence of vocational mastery and the horizons of benevolence in which one lives. Let me say again that economic action ought not to be discussed as if it were only a means to economic condition: economic action *is the moral condition* of most of most people's lives. Hence the danger in defending privatism for its ability to create wealth and thereby freedom is in the tendency of that argument to ignore the intrinsic moral significance, the moral liveliness, of the economic world itself—the fact that economic action is as formidable and fundamental a life process as is anything else. An economic system not only tends to establish the amplitude of one's recreational choices, but of one's creational choices as well.

Only the poor need see wages as the sole arbiter of work's attractiveness. The irony of most present American discourse about political and economic systems is that though we are a rich nation, we talk as if our choices were still the choices of the poor. Perhaps the memory of poverty still constrains our use of the opportunities of wealth. As, for example, it would seem that the memory of poverty's hunger still organizes the lives of the rich when at dinners of celebration they find it attractive to be served many times more than can be eaten.

But though a history of poverty may inhibit our day-to-day aspirations, enabling us to see dignity only in the rudimentary opposite of the rudimentary deprivations of our past, still, the obviousness of the intrinsic moral significance of work ought to be at least conceptually clear, and the defense of privatism as means to the freedom from poverty ought to be understood as only an anachronism amidst the wealth of any highly industrialized society.

The only intellectually substantial argument for privatism as a means to freedom has to do with freedom from institutional authority over what kind of work individuals will do, freedom from institutional meddling with nature's tendency to make coherent social use of individualized acquisitiveness (sellers must acquiesce to buyers' tastes), and freedom from the human tendency to be corrupted by institutional power, to use it at best capriciously and narrow-mindedly, at worst viciously. The first problem for these arguments is in the fact that privatism has tended to create not only enormous wealth, but enormous disparities of wealth. Great wealth *is*, especially when managed by a giant corporation, a form of great institutional social power and authority. And since the giant corporations are now the managers of most of our society's social capital, the work lives of most of our workers, the uses to which our productive resources will be put—since, that is, the giant corporations are neither more nor less than institutional authorities over our economic lives—the defense of privatism for its defense of individual freedom against institutional power is simply an irrelevance.

Secondly, American mainstream politics—American democracy—is based on belief in the wisdom of the concerted majority. I cannot see how to rationalize our believing on the one hand in the majority's competence for political authority, and on the other hand, the majority's incompetence for economic authority; the moral legitimacy of the majority's political will, the moral illegitimacy of the majority's economic will. Indeed, the separation of economics and politics seems itself a mistake. The business of politics is to establish social purpose and to perpetuate particular purposes; economic life is the major form of most people's social purposefulness; hence economics is properly a political subject. To base our political and our economic systems on antithetical views of human nature seems, then, a formidable confusion.

And *that*—our views of human nature—is, after all, what political and economic discourse is all about. What are people's best possibilities, and what systems of social relation are likely to facilitate them? That is the real subject in the history of ideological controversy. The political equation of privatism and freedom seems fundamentally an assertion of the view that opportunities for socially concerted benevolence and mastery are simply not opportunities that people require or find conducive to their happiness; that such opportunities become, in fact, only the breeding ground of corruption, coercion, and stultifying constraint. The best that we can hope for is so to fragment our society by the separation of politics and economics, by the glorification of competitive privatist acquisitiveness, that though we are as a species vicious, social fragmentation will keep our viciousness relatively weak.

Freedom is, of course, a serious concern only when people don't like what they're doing. Opportunities to choose what we dislike are not really opportunities at all. Obligations to persist in enjoying ourselves are not really constraints. The privatist denigration of those political-economic systems that propose especially to sponsor opportunities for benevolence and the power of willful social concert—privatist denigration of such systems must rest finally on the belief that people cannot use such opportunities except by transforming them into opportunities for evil.

To regard this as a closed question seems clearly absurd. Human nature and its relation to social condition and historical process—there is no subject in which we have less final knowledge. And since political controversy is probably the most consequential controversy of our time, there is no subject more in need of clarity, or at least attempts at clarification.

Ideological commitments, of course, have complicated motives in them. An ideology's fundamental postulates, the logic or factuality of them, may be irrelevant to our loyalty. Most people are probably quite unaware of the fundamental beliefs their ideological loyalties engage them to act for. We tend to be attracted by a particular style of compatriot rather than a particular theory of social relations. Ideological discourse is more likely to be inquisitorial than inquisitive, more likely to be a rationalizing defense after the fact of our commitments than to precede them.

It's the image of an attractive social identity rather than the rigorously accomplished coherence of a social philosophy that draws us. That is the ground of the irrelevance of ideological analysis. It is also the ground of its potential force: the older the history of an illusion, the more startling the disillusionment; the older and more entrenched a belief, the more startling the discovery that it's incredible. A critical narrative of the ideas of human nature expressed in America's major ideological points of view (what these pages introduce) may partake only of the irrelevance; but then again, it may even by its errors generate the self-consciousness without which our belligerencies are absurd.

The method of my narrative will be seen to require defense on at least three counts: its abstractness, its dependence on materials from the history of American literature, and its argumentativeness.

As for the abstractness—the treatment of whole periods and philosophies as if they were no more than rudimentary arguments in an unfolding ideological dialectic. I am aware that history is a more complicated process than that. But my purpose is not exploration of historical causality, but clarification of the present ideological argument. If the present ideological argument has any force, any relevance in our wish willfully to affect our lives, then we are entitled to regard philosophies for the first principles of ideology they imply or explain, and we are entitled to regard lines of ideological argument as real participants in historical process and legitimate subjects of analytical concern—not tantamount to the world, but forceful participants in its workings. Furthermore, ideological alternatives are not numberless. A delineation of the essential ones—if the delineation is understood to be tentative and hypothetical—ought to be useful, even though it's wrong, if it elicits arguments that improve it. That need not be so lame a defense as it looks. Public ideological discourse in America now is as a rule so unmindful of itself—so belligerently assertive without being self-conscious—that too reductionist an attempt at essentials might well be more useful than one risking over-complexity for the sake of completeness.

As for the dependence on the materials from the history of American literature. That is in part the result of the accident of my own training. It need not be, however, an altogether unfortunate accident. Human nature is our major writers' major subject. The impressiveness of their images of the first principles of human nature and

11

its dependencies is a large part of important writers' importance. Unlike political writers, whose concern is usually defense of a particular political program, inclusive symbols of humanity are the literary writer's concern. And furthermore, probably no country has so consistently used its literature as repository of philosophical wisdom, hence demanded of its writers that they make inclusive moral purpose their subject. Many people of widely disparate political conviction would nevertheless agree that Melville, say, was extraordinarily wise about human nature. Hence it would seem likely to be useful to try to work out the political implications of Melville's anthropological insights.

As for the argumentativeness of my account of our ideological history. I tend to the view that all ideological history is either covertly or overtly argumentative and has ideological judgment as its object. I cannot see that overt argument and judgment would be more dangerously distortive and prejudicial than the covert and implicit. Rather less so because its principles of judgment are set forward to be seen, to be accepted of course it is hoped, but to be seen in any case.

My account of America's ideological history assumes that history to have been in general a two-sided argument: on the one side, the more or less constant mainstream privatism; on the other, the developing forms of radical opposition to the mainstream. Changes in the history of mainstream privatism and arguments among privatists have been about methodology, not ideology. Primarily, they have been arguments about the degree to which government ought to police the society to ensure equal competitive opportunity to each competitor—about racial, ethnic, and gender discrimination, about equality in education, about antitrust laws, about labor's right to organize, about wage and hour laws, and most recently about the government's responsibility when a history of poverty incapacitates one for the competitive pursuit of wealth—and about the degree to which government ought to succor those competitors who have lost. However consequential the resolutions of these arguments have been for individuals, and however radically changing have been the situations to which these arguments apply, commitment to the politico-economics of competitiveness and to the anthropology on which it is based has been the constant of mainstream ideology. Fundamental argument and radical developmental change in conceptions of human nature and morality's necessary conditions—that has gone on primarily, if not only, among the radicals. Which is not to suggest that the developmental changes in radical ideology have always been fortunate, have always proceeded toward a more adequate complexity and coherence. In fact in many instances it has been rather the reverse. But that argument is my subject.

One more prefatory remark. In trying to get a clear sense of the central terms both of the radical sensibility's objects and of the diverse ways in which it has understood the place of those objects in the world, I've looked at materials that have quite different relevancies to the life of the radical sensibility today. I've written about these materials in ways suggested by the forms of their relevance. What I take out of the period from the beginning of the Renaissance to the early settlement of North America (Chapter 1, Part I) is its definition of the modern radical sensibility's defining preoccupations: the relation of individuality to community; the relation of the ideal to the actual; the relation of the conditional to the essential. Because what the radical sensibility accomplished in this period was the very rough roughing out of its modern concerns, the broadest synoptic terms seemed appropriate. What I take out of the period from the early English settlement of eastern North America to the middle of the eighteenth century (Chapter 1, Part II) is the early immigrants' preoccupations that have tended to persist as rudimentary foci of American life. Time wears ideological inheritance to the bone. Only slightly more particularized terms seemed necessary for what we still draw on of the early immigrants' thought. What I say of Edwards, Franklin, and Emerson (Chapter 1, Parts III and IV) is a little less cavalierly assertive, but

only a little. My preoccupation with what I take to be their fundamental sentimentalities comes from my reaction to those who draw
more richly from them *because* of their sentimentalities. Readers who
have not themselves been involved with these secondary materials are
especially unlikely to be interested in what I say about them.

In the chapters on Poe, Hawthorne, Melville, and Whitman, my
argument is much more concretized because I find in their works the
particular insights that it seems to me misfortune to lose hold of.

In the last four chapters, the argument is broadly synoptic. My
concern in reviewing American radical politics of the last hundred and
fifty years is to support what seems to me most substantial by making
clear the ways of thinking that are less so. And from the beginning to
the end, this book is intended not as a history of the radical sensibility
in America, but as an essay *in* that history.

CHAPTER ONE

Early American Certainties

I

To begin with, it is important to remember that modern privatism began as part of a radical reform movement, as radical as modern socialism was later to be. The early privatists, in rebellion against what we may call medieval institutionalism, asserted three things radical to the societies they wanted to change, the long tradition from which they wanted to depart. They asserted individualism, naturalism, and what we might call activism or instrumentalism.

By their individualism the privatists rebel against medieval institutionalism, rejecting two views in which people had for a long time been reared: first, that there is some single all-embracing and established truth and a single universally applicable model of perfection; second, that an institution, the church-state, knows the truth and holds the responsibility for seeing that human society conforms to it.

It is centrally important here that in pre-individualist society the truth and the idea of perfection both deal with the universal community as the rudiment of order, as the single important organism. This view of truth and of the ideal follows from the belief in a single morally unified creation for which some inclusive institution holds the plan and administers the will. The institution's function is to whip into place the various parts, to their comfort if they are amenable, to their discomfort if that is made necessary by rebellion against the plan and its overarching moral necessity. The point is that individuals are significant only for their places in the plan of unification, as any part of any unified or organismic structure has its form, its meaning, and its value only by its relation to the overall structure within which it has its being and that is the rationale of its being. The primary individualist insight is that even if there had been a single morally willful creation and an overarching moral principle and plan and a perfect model for each part, people know them not and human institutions know them not: rather, the institutions seem more the instruments of myriad sufferings than of joyous unanimity. Given the failure and the corruption of the social structure, the failure of the organism successfully to sustain the organ, the individual is left only with the sanctity, the autonomy, the unsubsumedness of his individuality. Each part, each person, must find his own way, and that way is toward the satisfaction of his own nature, not his social place. This insight is as much the basis of Locke's psychology or Montaigne's as of Roger Williams' radical politics or Calvin's theology. Individualism proceeds from the insight that the truth is lost to the institutions that were supposed to know it. It may follow that the whole truth is nonexistent, or an impossible ideal, or that truth is to be discovered again only piecemeal, or that truth is really only a subjective proposition anyway, being, for people at least, never more than a description of relations seen from some individual point of view. Such ideas of diversity and uncertainty can be either depressing or elating, depending on whether or not one can tolerate complexity and can give up hankering for a universe organized by a single absolute moral will. Some forms of this idea can, as we know, be kept with, rather than instead of, the old absolutism simply by one's believing that man has only lost touch with the absolute (though he may be redeemed to it) rather than that he has discovered the unlikelihood of there being any absolute at all. In any case, the switch from an institution to one's own individuality, the appropriate arbiter of choice was the primary revolutionary doctrine of which many movements, among them privatism in economics, partook. Had there been in the Middle Ages an expression like "Look out for number one," it would have been written "number One" and it would have had to do with obeying God. The meaning of the phrase today represents one of the forms of the privatist revolution. Perhaps revolution is a misleading word here. It suggests a concentric turn. What happened was a change of centers. Individuals came to be seen as the centers of their worlds, and the world itself became no longer uni-centric or mono-centric, but a multi-centric world, having as many centers as it had individuals. Individuals were left to concentrate, as it were, on themselves. This was a radical shift rather than a revolution.

The second major change wrought by the rebels against medieval institutions had to do with the sense of time, the temporal unit with which one was to be especially concerned. The shift here was parallel with the shift from the absolute to the individual: the absolute's time is eternity, the individual's time is local and immediate and pressing—irrevocably consequential. The lived event had been thought mediate only, subsumed and demeaned by God's eternity and one's fixed place in it. Given and believing an image of some infinite eternal stasis, how could a merely local pain or pleasure really matter? But if the character of eternity becomes vague and the roads to it, heretofore rigidly prescribed, are thrown in doubt, then this moment's "anxious walk with God," an exploratory experience rather than a traditionally defined obedience, becomes the crucial religious event, and this moment and this life become the crucial secular ones. If eternity seems vague, one's mortality gains importance, and the definiteness of this life in all its immediacy can be conscientiously turned to. (Boccaccio's gardener in the nunnery is in a way no less than Francis Bacon an empiricist testing the transcendent vision.) Naturalism seems as good a name as any for this turning toward absorption in temporal experience.

The third major challenge is closely related to the others. It is the rejection of Greco-Christian asceticism. We are familiar with what is called the "business" man's anti-intellectualism. This is an inappropriate name. He is not against using the brain, against understanding relations, against thinking as hard as he can to solve problems he takes seriously. What distinguishes him is the ranges of experience he believes in thinking about and those he refuses to think about. It is the kind of thought, not rigor of thought, that is at issue with the philosophical beginnings of modern privatism. Let us assume that the mind works in this way: given some purposes not automatically satisfied, we perceive relationships that seem to contain the problem. We may then exert ourselves to rearrange those relationships to our satisfaction. The mind is that faculty by which we comprehend (grasp together) the relationships in which we are engaged, and plan, and direct force. Religion has been said to be the postulate of an ultimately satisfactory plan. It often seems that the grander the plan, the further it is from being satisfactorily effectable. If we are unable to tolerate a continued disparity between the ideal and the actual, we may reduce the plan, change the purpose, and disparage our "idealism." Or we may try somehow to ignore our ineffectiveness by proposing to be satisfied with the plan itself, satisfied with contemplation of its perfection as image, the art for art's sake in it. Whether or not it was because the Greeks gave little status to "work" and great status to "ideas" and the exclusively contemplative life, and though the apostle James said that faith without works is dead, an eminent Christian tradition has held it supremely righteous to forsake this world for contemplation of the next, the ideal idea of heaven. This I would call intellectualism or asceticism and devotion particularly to contemplation of the ideal and more or less disdain for instrumental action. Or, to be directly pejorative, the belief that fantasy should absorb and satisfy all one's best purposes. To be sure, such Christians held to the instrumental effectiveness of asceticism—it promised an eternity of bliss. But in terms of this world, their aestheticism was also the purest asceticism. The Christian idea that for sin at least the wish is tantamount to the act suggests both a frightening morality and the extent of Christian

18

asceticism (conventionally called spirituality).* The new movement was not anti-intellectual but anti-ascetic. The asceticist tradition said that one was to be judged by one's intentions. The anti-asceticist said that one was to be judged by one's actions and admired only for one's accomplishments, one's success in making the environment conform to one's will.

* * *

Having learned to honor their individuality and the immediacy implied by its mortality, people turned conscientiously and with assertiveness to their mundane environment to see how they could make it serve them *now*.

Under the economics of medieval religion, the body was to be spent to save and nourish the soul. This view was replaced by the radical discovery that for people, if not for angels, the soul and body are inalienably united and that the soul is more likely to be liberated and empowered when the body is satisfied than when it is debased. Jonathan Edwards came to assert that salvation must be understood to include the "utmost felicity of both body and soul."

By the eighteenth century, privatist ideology had been a long time growing and had come to the maturity in which its beliefs could be formulated with the economy of aphorism—hence Benjamin Franklin, or at least Poor Richard. And though God's will was still cited as the authority for a proposition in morality, as in Franklin's "One serves God by serving men," the kind of service authorized had

---

* It is also a self-contradictory morality. When the Christians assert that one's morality is the character of one's choices, then they contradict themselves in defining a morality, at times exclusively, by the character of one's wishes, since choice amongst wishes and desires is as much a moral action as any other. In fact, it may be *the* moral action. Choice of objects determines the choice of a course of action, and choice of objects is first a choice amongst desires and only secondly a choice as to which object will most satisfy the already chosen desire. The first is the moral problem, the second, only an analytical or empirical or methodological one.

changed. One served God not primarily by devout meditation but by devout industry in the economy of this world. For some, asceticism was replaced by the new science; for others, by technology and trade. Exploiting the wealth of the East could become at least as attractive a crusade as the opportunity to conquer the heathen.

Privatism in economics was but one avenue in the general movement that carried the new beliefs in individualism, this-worldliness, and anti-asceticism. It was part of the radical reform movement asserting that one's *own* well-being, not the well-being of king or church, is the justification of life and work. From such a belief it was not long until one could assert with pride the *unalienable* right to life, liberty, and the pursuit of happiness, and, assuming the right, could demand the opportunity. The concentration on business, wealth, and the sanctity of private property was but one of the new directions. Taking it, people could express their individualism, joy in the immediate, their valuing this life's life, their will and their power to make this world yield now to their demands.

II

Among those who settled North America were the new religionists who needed a new continent so that they might walk uprightly unmolested with their God, and the new secularists who found the Old World no longer able to accommodate their desire for adventure and wealth.

Captain John Smith not only spoke to the dominant style of the secularist spirit but embodied it in his description of the virtues of migration to America.

> Who can desire more content, that hath small meanes; or but only his merit to advance his fortune, then to tread, and plant that ground hee hath purchased by the hazard of his life? If he have but the taste of virtue, and magnanimitie, what to such a minde can bee more pleasant, then planting and building a foundation for his Posteritie, gotte

from the rude earth, by Gods blessing & his owne industrie, without prejudice to any?

In this passage from Smith's "A Description of New England" (1616), we get a sharp sense of the secularist's feeling for the Old World's failures and the New World's promises. The sanctity of old authorities had been dispelled and had made room for man's swelling sense of his own merit, his own deserts, not arbitrarily inherited but inherent in himself. And the New World gave him ground, limitless ground, to try his merit, as the Old World, where "meanes" had already been distributed—arbitrarily, now it was clear—did not. In the Old World the "rude earth" was already divided up, not as God's blessing, but merely by privileged descent. By the combination of hereditary oppressions and the possibility of change, the Old World had generated the impulse to liberty, to assertive individuality, to freedom from an encumbering history, to an adventurous taking of a new claim.

But disdain for the past did not altogether undo its effects. If inherited authority lost some of its honor, inherited wealth was still wealth and an enormous advantage in the new competitions. The accidents of inheritance still prejudiced the condition of the present generation. But in the New World there was more new verdant land than even the most lavish fantasy could settle. Indeed anyone with the time's spirit in him could make for his own posterity and thereby for himself the place and honor that the Old World's history had withheld from him. And there, of course, is the irony. In his lyric to the New World's opportunities, Smith does not so much reject the old system of inherited privilege and prejudice as he asserts the right to a new chance, a new competition so that he too may command the honor of his contemporaries and his progeny. For Smith the New World's promise is not that the adventurer and his posterity will be freed forever from the arbitrary advantages or disadvantages of inherited social condition. The New World's promise is the adventurer's opportunity to get the advantages for his own posterity. America is to be the new chance, but for the old prize. But if Smith announces an equivocal social morality—honor for individual industry, to which the reward will be one's children's inherited advantage—the equivocation was obscured by the New World's size. There seemed room to privilege everybody's posterity; the honoring of individual industry did not have to imply competitions in which some lost and thereby condemned their progeny to a prejudiced beginning.*

The secular adventurers and many of the Puritans were enemies from the start. In part because the secularists' only partial break with the Old World's system of social and economic stratification was paralleled by the Puritans' only partial break with medieval social and religious tradition. We might even say that the Puritan colonies in America tried to establish in small the old institutionalism that had failed them. In many ways they were closer to the medieval church than they allowed themselves to believe. The Puritans still held to communitism and the proper authority of the church-state. Though many Puritans might have been ambivalent about it, they still hoped to value this world's transience as no more than mediate to the next world's

---

* We see prefigured here the period two centuries later when under Andrew Jackson, the first president from the people, the corporate charter was made no longer a grant of privilege but a universal right. In England and in colonial America, the corporate charter was the state's guarantee of monopoly on some enterprise—a bridge, a road, the Indian trade—that the state needed done. The grant of monopoly on that enterprise was the state's inducement to some group of entrepreneurs to undertake the work. To Jackson's populism it was clear that if a monopoly is a good thing, then everybody ought to have one. The creation of a corporation came to require only formal application to the state: hence the state's loss of power to grant privilege and at the same time its loss of power to initiate economic enterprises designed for the public good. By the 1880s competition amongst corporations had again created monopolies. Hence a new round of legislation—of which the Sherman Anti-Trust law is the most famous—again designed to give him "that hath small meanes; . . . or but only his merit to advance his fortune" a fresh and fair start in the competition. Government, seen only through memory of it as instrument of privilege, impossible to conceive as positive instrument of concerted social purpose, is constrained to be merely the policeman of the private competition, inhibiting inheritance of advantage from the old competitions—exactly the role that Smith had ascribed to the New World's untapped natural plenty. (See Oscar and Mary Handlin, *Commonwealth: A Study of the Role of Government in the American Economy*, New York, NYU Press, 1947.)

eternity—contemplation of the next world being the most moral action in this one. The Puritans' break with medievalism was not over the existence of the church-state but over the size of the church-state. If Puritans argued among themselves whether the masterable unit was one congregation or several, they did not doubt that the integrity of the community was of more consequence than the integrity of any individual. More than that, they believed individual integrity ought to be diffused by its place in the communal order—one should be the sign of the other. Smith's view that the Old World's failure was its inhibition of individualism—to the Puritans this view was absurd. To them the Old World's failure was precisely its inability to enforce obedience to the final moral truths from which only the vicious would want to be free. And most people are vicious. John Winthrop, first Governor of the Massachusetts Bay Colony, put it this way:

> There is a twofold liberty, natural (I mean as our nature is now corrupt) and civil or federal. The first is common to man with beasts and other creatures. By this, man, as he stands in relation to man simply, hath liberty to do what he lists; it is a liberty to evil as well as to good. This liberty is incompatible and inconsistent with authority, and cannot endure the least restraint of the most just authority. The exercise and maintaining of this liberty makes men grow more evil, and in time to be worse than brute beasts. . . . The other kind of liberty I call civil or federal, it may also be termed moral. . . . This liberty is the proper end and object of authority, and cannot subsist without it; and it is a liberty to that only which is good, just, and honest. . . . This liberty is maintained and exercised in a way of subjection to authority. . . . If you stand for your natural corrupt liberties, and will do what is good in your own eyes, you will not endure the least weight of authority, but will murmur, and oppose, and be always striving to shake off that yoke; but if you will be satisfied to enjoy such civil and lawful liberties, such as Christ allows you, then will you quietly and cheerfully submit unto that authority which is set over you, in all the administrations of it, for your good. (John Winthrop, *The History of New England*, 1645.)

Smith is preoccupied with economic condition, with a history of subservience to wealth independent of individual merit, with a social situation that constrains his eager industriousness and insults his aspiration to economic well-being, dignity, and power. He needs freedom from the past's hierarchies and freedom for his own expansive energies and pride.

Winthrop is preoccupied with the degenerate and presumptuous libertinism of both the emergent classes and the dissolute aristocracy. Winthrop has the established gentry's sense of responsible local authority, the sense of having inherited the knowledge of justice, decorum, decency, restraint, and the responsibility to administer dictates to those threatening from below whose inheritance has been only the licentiousness of poverty and ignorance, and to those threatening from above whose inheritance has been only the licentiousness of capricious power. To the poor man the law had been his oppressor; to the king the law had been his will; to Winthrop the law had been his guide and his responsibility.

Winthrop does not defend prerogatives; he defends justice. He cannot defend freedom or tolerance, for the dictates of justice are known and to tolerate divergence from them is practically complicity in evil. To Winthrop, the economic subservience of the poor is but a correlate of their morally necessary subservience to the just. Removal to the New World is not escape to freedom, but escape from the freedoms of people and crown that made the dominion of the just impossible. The New World is opportunity to establish their dominion and through them, God's will—again. It is the opportunity to establish at once the unity of church, state, and social authority—small at first but as a "beacon on a hill" that would illuminate God's will for all the world to see. Unlike Smith, Winthrop does not describe removal to the New World as an exciting adventure. Winthrop, to Groton Manor born, trained in the law and practicing it successfully, foreswore much to come away to the wilderness. What he gained was a chance midst the radically shifting social forces of his time to establish for his class the social authority of inherited economic stability and moralistic gentility that in England was endangered on every side. Full citizenship in the Massachusetts Bay Colony was defined by loyal church membership and property ownership. When new communities were established, citizenship in them granted the right to use undivided public land—the "common"—and went to those who owned private land, were loyal church members, and accepted subservience to the central General Court, by whose dictates the people were freed from the vicious inclinations of their nature. Though the American Puritan communities could not hope to have in their power a holy international empire, they did not thereby propose to tolerate a local liberty of the community's expansion beyond the masterable horizon of the church's authority. Nor did they propose to forsake the commonwealth for the private wealth. That is to say, the early American Puritans stood for a closed society, which, while making its way to heaven, held the commonwealth—defined by clergy and gentry—to be the preeminent arbiter of social action.

But the early American businessman, with or without the counterpull of a Puritan church allegiance, wanted an open society. He wanted the fastest possible land expansion, though it would be faster than the church authority could keep up with and control. And he wanted trade and prices regulated not by the interest of the community but by what the traffic would bear. The businessman wanted private-wealth, the church-state wanted commonwealth. Representative of their antagonism was the fight over the church-state's right to regulate prices. The individualist ideal had been preempted by those for whom it meant hardly more than opportunity for private acquisitiveness. The commonwealth ideal had been preempted by those for whom it meant static, hierarchical, orthodox authoritarianism based on conviction of most men's final moral incompetence.

The businessman won. In the 1630s, John Winthrop, speaking with the authority of the church-state, told the businessman and the religious heretic what the General Court would make them do or let them do. By 1700 the Puritan divine had given up hope of governing the economic activity of the community; like Cotton Mather, in his "Essays to Do Good," he had been obliged to change the tone of command to the tone of persuasion; he could now only plead with the businessman to fill with private conscience and kindness (to be paid for in otherworldly bliss) the vacuum in public morality left when church authority was deposed. The pattern remained the same for a long time. Those devoted to the expansion of economic power were the businessmen; and though their motive was money-gain above most if not all things, by their elaboration of economic power they did indeed liberate more and more people from the drudgery and penury of economic self-dependency. The future, they felt, was theirs. Those devoted to a benevolent public morality and to the idea that man is something more than an economic animal who finds total satisfaction in a secure economic luxury—these were left to plead to private conscience and to preach a return to the old days before man had the economic power to make so many miserable. As the Puritans had learned to fear the oppressive power of the international and even the national church-state, and could trust a power no greater than that over the contracted church community, so the radical reformers of the next century and a half had learned to fear the power of the expansive national and even international economy, and could hope that a return to a bygone economic weakness would facilitate a new moral strength.

It is now a truism of our history and need not be described that the secularists took over the wilderness and made America theirs. That they did so with protestations of the religious sanction of their work is interesting and important, but not to the point here. The point is that in taking over, the philosophical basis of their radical secular entrepreneurialism underwent a profound reduction and rigidification. Individualism, naturalism, and instrumentalism became, in their hands, privatism, localism, and what is usually called materialism.*

Perhaps popularization depends on oversimplification and rigidity; these being easier, until one pays for them, than complexity and viability. The easiest rebellion takes its course by simple polarity. For medieval absolutionist communitism and indifference to individuality, the business ethic substituted privatism and indifference to community; for the old preoccupation with the next world and eternity, the business ethic substituted not the full complexity of this world's human experience, but preoccupation with no more than this moment's profit (as Henry Ford said, "History is bunk," and "Let the

---

* This is another ambiguous name. It means to suggest preoccupation with what is just as ambiguously called "goods," but it has also been used to name the philosophy that refuses a spirit-matter dualism and holds instead that what we call spirit is simply one of the characteristic functions of particular organismic relations of matter. If the American business ethic takes the name materialist to itself, then it suggests a false distinction, leaving those who honor other than business values to appear as spiritualist, a distinction many do not want at all. Further, I don't think it is true that the business ethic is really so much preoccupied with acquisition of the kind of matter called goods. For one, they are very much interested in services, which economists generally distinguish sharply from goods. But more, it seems that what is especially honored is money. Wouldn't an American millionaire who lived most ascetically be just as much honored as one who lived lavishly? Indeed, it is a characteristic American term of high valuation not that a thing is good, or beautiful, or useful, but simply that "it cost a fortune." Conspicuous waste is, we all agree now, a characteristic of American life, and waste does not suggest materialism, or the coveting of certain kinds of matter. Honoring money above "goods," we seem to be honoring a symbol of power (our relative indifference to the way in which money is acquired suggests that for us money is the symbol not of past accomplishment but of some possible action in the future), perhaps honoring a symbol of the liberated, the empowered, will. This is in a way spiritualism in the old sense. It carries also a major idea of the revolution we have been describing, the discovery that instrumentalism can liberate will here and now from the brute striving for survival. Its error, its reductionism, is especially that there is so puny an idea of what the will can be liberated to. But its importance, from the point of view of the radical reformer, is that the populace, in its love of opulence, is not expressing an exhaustive preoccupation with "things," but with a symbol of the liberated will. American radicals' disillusion with the wisdom of the populace has been misplaced. The populace in its love of the absurdly elaborated luxury of cars is thought to express merely its need for things. In fact, it seems to me, it is expressing its love of symbols of power—power of many kinds, to be sure—and it expresses an excess of "spiritual energy," however misdirected, more than it expresses an exhaustive materialist gluttony. The now much-discussed American malaise demonstrates surely that Americans are not satisfied by cars and such, and have moral energy beyond that. The trouble with cars as the objects of American aspiration is not so much with their being tawdry *things* as with their being such tawdry symbols, capable of only so puny an integration of human action, expressing aspiration to so childish a power.

future take care of itself"); for the old asceticism it substituted *not* the instrumentalism believing that we can accomplish physical well-being and security and thereby be liberated *to* engagement in a larger and larger world of ideas, and ideals, but the belief that in an elaborated luxury, one is then liberated, one has in fact arrived. That is to say, action was admired especially or even only as it produced "goods," and money. Altogether, the dominant business ethic held to a most severe limitation of the world in which we live, and should propose actively and sympathetically to live. There was contraction in all but one area. Economic action was extended and integrated as never before. Especially in the nineteenth century, when industrialism became the primary business phenomenon, it grew progressively clearer that the logic of industrialism was not only toward enormously increased productivity, but also toward extending the province and unifying the direction of economic action. The logic of unregulated, competitive industrialism soon appeared to be monopoly and the nationally and even the internationally organized economy.

III

The business ethic and its institutions have, of course, had opposition from the beginning. The opposition saw and was appalled principally by business's effective if not avowed denigration of benevolence as a primary motive of social action, the narrowness of the lives of the business ethic's followers, but most of all, the extensive savage poverty that the business ethic sponsored and on which it even thought itself to depend, and that it heightened by contrast to its own accomplishments of wealth. The opposition began when business was still pretty much a local and personal affair. The reformers' concern was to restore to, or to create for, the businessman a personal morality based on benevolentism rather than privatism and to establish or maintain an unbusinesslike environment in which greed was supposed to wither.

Reformers saw business as a tool of greed alone: eliminate one and you go far toward eliminating the other. Hence the unbusinesslike economics of artisanry and subsistence farming was looked on as the adequate antithesis of business and social corruption. Perhaps in part because the reformers did not see that business, especially as it became industrialism, was an enormously expansive as well as a contractive force, their antipathy was irrelevant to its growth. They never met it on its own ground or dealt with the most obvious appeal in what it was doing. Capitalist industrialism is a system for organizing a whole society's economic power, and by the middle of the nineteenth century it was creating not only unspeakable slums of degraded life: it was also creating the instruments of unprecedented economic power and was capable of creating unprecedented economic felicity. But at least until the middle of the nineteenth century, the business community that directed capitalist industrialism was opposed only by benevolentist pastoralism and the individualist Christian ethic. Benevolentist pastoralism, while it was a scheme for organizing a society's economic action, was so obviously regressive in terms of the power with which it would deal, that it was clearly irrelevant as an alternative and could soon be proposed (e.g., Brook Farm) as no more than an isolated retreat (in both senses of the word) of which the epitome was Thoreau alone at Walden Pond. The individualist Christian ethic is not a socioeconomic program, and though it might enhance the benevolence of an individual industrialist, it is in no sense an alternative to capitalist industrialism, privatist or otherwise. For the most part, the business ethic was practiced most flagrantly, powerfully, and dangerously in capitalist industrialism. The two—the ethic and the tool its devotees had created—were mistaken to be one. Their simultaneous destruction was thought by reformers to be indispensable to a moral society. The reformers were without significant force. Their beauty—the beauty for which they are now revered as we revere no industrialist early or later—was that, despite the irrelevance of their social programs, which were the consequence of their ignoring the great progressive force of industrialism, they did refuse the contraction of human life into the pettiness and brutality of privatism.

The instrumentalism they dealt with and proposed to master was in one area inadequate to contemporary possibilities and in a way less than that of their opponents and the mainstream. But their benevolentist individualism, their sense of extended temporal continuity, and their ideals of excellence and mastery in extra-economic action were great and hardly less radical today than when argued more than a century ago.

The reformers' mistake was to argue political economy when they meant to argue philosophical anthropology. They said that human nature is such that it cannot be expressed adequately within the confines of the business ethic. If a morality is a way to self-consistency, to the integrity without which there may be local pleasure but no fundamental happiness, they said that the business ethic was no morality adequate to people, certainly not to some, probably not to most. People have a sense of communal identification not expressed in privatism, a sense of temporal continuity not to be satisfied by devotion to this moment's business, and they have needs and talents not necessarily engaged in what will make money or be satisfied with what money will buy. People, they said, are not creatures whose public life need be no more than a business life, whose private life need be no more than securely luxurious. Most of all they said that only the depraved could condone private wealth at the expense of mass poverty. Theirs was not a new tradition: by its benevolentism we make its beginnings the beginnings of Western civilization. But in privatist industrialism they had a new enemy, an enemy of unprecedented power. Not until the middle of the nineteenth century did radical reformers realize that retreat from this power was not the only alternative, but that it could be mastered and made an instrument of civilization.

Before that breakthrough, the essential positions in the argument about the necessities and possibilities of social life can usefully be seen as a dialogue between Jonathan Edwards, Benjamin Franklin, and Ralph Waldo Emerson. The question was—and is—the relation of human nature to the social immorality that every moralist sees.

IV

Benjamin Franklin spoke for the mainstream. He said that the human problem—an extension of the problem for all animal life—is that our desires are many and often not compatible, our environment is complex and rarely arranged for the spontaneous gratification of our desires. But we, unlike other animals, have reason. By our reason we are made master of our desires and of our environment. Under the discipline of reason we can defer gratification of any particular desire, the better to synthesize the gratification of all desires. And by our reason we may see through to the forces of nature, and so seeing, govern them. The other animals are dominated, tyrannized, by the world simply as it is and by necessary obedience to the passion of the moment. By being able to experiment with the environment and to influence our desires, we can become the master of both. Social well-being will follow simply from individuals in rational pursuit of private well-being. The whole is simply the sum of the parts: all the parts are in a simple additive relation. The moral and orderly society waits only on the extension of education (by which method will be taught), the liberation of discourse (by which reason's dictates are shared, clarified, and refined), and the progress of technology (by which nature will finally be mastered). Franklin's advice to Britain at the time of the colonial movement toward revolution typified the working of his utilitarian calculus. No issue of political principle beyond the rudimentary will to survival and power is raised. Britain acts against no ideal of liberty or equality; it acts only against the clearly rational course by which it might keep its colonies. Significantly, *all* the errors of which Franklin accuses Britain are errors in money matters—taxation, freedom of trade, and so on. The reductionism of Franklin's utilitarian calculus is not in the utilitarianism but in that he calculates with so little, he seems to see so little of the uses to which people may be committed. The only future to which his prescriptions are directed is a world of rationally coexisting economic competitors, each pursuing no more than private economic ease and security. Benevolence is no fundamental motivation or ideal. It is merely the obvious expedient by which each has a better chance to survive. And should a people be incapable of that rational restraint and industry by which mastery is assured? Franklin says in the *Autobiography* that alcoholism may indeed be beneficent nature's way of wiping out the Indians. They are capable of no more than alternations of indolence and drunken frenzy; when they are gone the diligent white man may at last put to use the lands otherwise lost to progress.

Jonathan Edwards would agree altogether to this definition of human nature, to this description of human aspirations, to the natural appropriateness of privatist business enterprise as the system of human relations, to degree of power as the human distinction, and to survival of the fittest as the law of human intercourse, the law by which the Indian's disease and self-destructiveness can be seen as a boon to progress. But for Edwards this description is no more than the definition of original sin, of the essential depravity of the human heart, of all that stands in the way of beauty, of all that generates the ugliness of human history. For Edwards, benevolence is not a device, an expedient for private safety or increased power. For Edwards, benevolence is an essential, ideally *the* essential motive if human action is to have any true virtue, any true progress, in it. Benevolence is the goal of progress, not its instrument. To be sure, all action, all acts of will, of choice, are—by definition—directed toward the gratification of the actor. The horror of human nature is not its hedonism—hedonism or selfishness means no more than that one wants to do what one wants to do. The horror of human nature is in the ugliness of human desires, their malevolence, their indifference—it is not because we want, but what we want that damns us. The preponderances of evil in human history, the hegemony of the very principles of the Franklinian view of human nature and its consequent theory of society: these are enough to prove the preponderant evil of the human heart, enough to prove the impossibility of any man-made progress except toward some tawdry animal contentment, the impossibility of there being anything inherent in human nature on which the moralist might depend.

Anything, that is, except fear of personal suffering: hence Edwards' most famous sermon, "Sinners in the Hands of an Angry God." There, though in it he contradicts the very basis of his definition of virtue— that virtue inheres only in love of benevolence, not at all in obedience through fear of punishment, subservience to laws arbitrarily commanded, alien to the human heart—in the "Sinners" sermon Edwards has no recourse in his passion to influence human society, no recourse but to fabulous threats of the extrinsic legal consequences of moral failure—an eternity of hell, the retribution of a vengeful God. If nothing in another's aspirations is consonant with one's own, then coercion is the only action that makes sense—coercion or pessimistic resignation and final alienation. Edwards was shocked that coercion wouldn't work, that people would persist in immorality despite the hell that it would surely bring, and despite the eternity of heavenly bliss that obedience to divine command would ensure.

Edwards was also a chiliast. He believed that the time would soon come when under Christ's rule on earth, all human hearts would be turned toward benevolence; grace, the virtuous disposition of the heart, would be given to all. Perfect progress toward the perfect world is the necessary corollary of God's benevolence and omnipotence. But until the entrance into human affairs of that perfection of will now altogether alien to the species' total depravity, nothing that we can do can alter our condition or make a significant moral difference in society. 'Til then those few whom the bestowal of grace has already transformed must live as victims of society's unalienable animality.

America's profoundest moral sensibilities have shared Edwards' revulsion from the dominant social philosophy of American life. And many have shared his anthropology, the conviction of the horrible but inviolable appropriateness of that social philosophy to human nature. But most such moralists did not share his chiliasm, his faith in a moral omnipotence that would transform the species and create the millennium by one fell swoop of grace. Most such moralists were left with only the pessimism that characterizes so much of our literature, that has kept so many of our most formidable minds committed to belief in the inutility of any social action that might positively engage the society in the work of a humane civilization. Twain in *Huckleberry Finn* has no recourse but to "light out." Ezra Pound came at last to trust only the coercive power of Fascism. T. S. Eliot sees nothing for this world but its whimpering end. Faulkner's fiction contains nothing so much as an image of the moral way to freedom and honor and decency paralyzed by a history of custom and the Snopes' animal greed. Hemingway's heroes have no fate but alienation and a death that can save only some private symbolic honor, some proof of brave constancy despite the inevitable doom and failure.

It would of course be wrong to suggest that the only tradition appropriately generated by Edwards' philosophy is a pessimistic determinism based on an overpowered moral sensibility, the only out some faith in an extrinsic redemption, a saving incursion of divine forces. As Perry Miller has demonstrated, Edwards moved out of or beyond Newton and Locke to formulate the bases of what were—one hundred and fifty years later—to be established as naturalism, pragmatism, organicism, and radical empiricism. The important point for present purposes, however, is that Edwards' anthropology, like Franklin's, believes there to be no essential complexity in human nature, nothing of what we now call ambivalence, nothing that a society directed to cooperation not as expedient but as fundamental gratification could elicit into prominence, and in most people no internal aspiration antithetical to the morality of private contentment. According to Edwards' practice as a preacher, only coercion has social relevance. Only threat of violence can establish reform or maintain decency. The nature of the social order can make no significant moral difference to the nature of human choices or the moral quality of human action. Though Edwards was probably the finest moral sensibility of eighteenth-century America, and though he was a preacher, by profession a public moralist, his public exhortations contain no reference to the morality of social institutions. His particular admonitions—as distinct from the general exhortation to benevolence toward all beings— have only to do with abstemiousness, coveting not one's neighbor's wealth, and, interestingly enough, loyal obedience to spiritual and secular authority. If the absence of attack on the *institutions* of privatist economics is inconsistent with belief in the essential immorality of these institutions, it is consistent with the theory that holds to the irrelevance of moral social institutions to the individual's moral life, that holds to the homogeneous depravity of human nature, and hence to the impossibility that anything we do can have significant influence on the moral quality of the human will. If Franklinian political and economic institutions, if Franklinian privatism burgeoned into what was to be called "the American way" without ever stopping to reckon seriously with Edwards' morality, it may be in part because Edwards' anthropology never led him to make American political and economic institutions his subject. The Edwardsian Christian ethic simply does not take part in discussions of political-economic institutions or their instrumental force, and is in that sense simply not an alternative to any one of them.

Emerson changes nothing in Edwards' condemnation of the privatist ethic. What he does change is the view of the relation of that ethic to human nature. The enormity of human discontent is precisely, Emerson says, in the incongruence of privatism and essential human desires. All our hearts yearn, not as Edwards says they do, but just as Edwards says they should. This is proved by the desperate sense of dislocation expressed in the anxieties of social life. Yet society has somehow imposed on, somehow come to stand in the way of, essential human nature. The social order does not manifest human nature, it impedes it. In "The American Scholar," Emerson says that when the moral hero—man thinking—shall have penetrated the mud of custom to the truths of his heart, he will discover the brotherhood of all men. This is the fundamental postulate of Emersonian anthropology: that the moral hero, he whom Edwards would define as having the grace of gracious affections, is by his graciousness human. The few good people have been alienated from most people not *by* fundamental difference but *from* their fundamental identity. The good have openly what has been repressed in the many. The brotherhood of man is neither an expedient for mutual aid among reasonable and diligent entrepreneurs, nor a generic guilt for a generic sinfulness: it is an essential benevolence, a passion for universal community integrated by benevolence that makes of human life without it a depression and a remorse. Edwards said that if most people were allowed to obey the dictates of their hearts, the world would be set on fire, fire that only a second flood could put out. Emerson said that only if we were freed to obey our hearts would the viciousness of history be transcended.

The Emersonian breakthrough was in postulating integrated community as appropriate to human needs. The difficulty remained in explaining the historical dominance of fragmentation, aggression, repression, and the hardly impeded emergence of the business ethic. If Franklinian monistic anthropology left too many passions unaccounted for and made a society that all knew to be less than lovely, if Edwards' anthropology could account for the tawdriness but not the discontent with it, Emerson's equally monistic but antithetical anthropology could not explain the obeisance to custom, repression, and the gods of greed in the first place, could not explain how there ever came to be a need of radical reform. Though Edwards and Emerson could never settle for the Franklinian entrepreneur as an image of human dignity nor tolerate a society in which man's poverty and the extinction of weak or weakened would be the legitimate price of entrepreneurial success; though Edwards and Emerson refused both the jungle and the anthill as prototypes of moral human community, they did not reckon as Franklin did with the positive relevance of the environmental situation to the condition of human morality. Though Franklin did not have an anthropology that was more adequately complex, his concern with instrumentalism, with manipulation of the environment so as to create the situation, the power, and the opportunity of extended human choice, was consonant with a more adequately complex anthropology. The logically appropriate influence of Edwards' anthropology was exhortation arguing its own uselessness for any significant moral regeneration. Emerson's anthropology, since it did not reckon with the source of opposition to his morality, had much of its influence in movements of escape. The social environment had somehow imposed on people, made them servants to enemies of their nature.

Since business industrialism was the obvious tyrant, to Brook Farm transcendentalists the answer seemed clearly to be a return to a precedent incorruption, a pastoral community morally grand but economically, that is, instrumentally, primitive. Emerson himself saw even that scale of social integration as menacing or abandoning the potency of the individual. What the Brook Farmers had to learn, he said, is "that one man is a counterpoise to a city—that a man is stronger than a city, that his solitude is more prevalent and beneficent than the concert of crowds" (*The Journals of Ralph Waldo Emerson* ed. by E. W. Emerson and W. E. Forbes; Boston, Houghton Mifflin, 1911)—that one man saying truth could redeem the whole society.

However slight Franklin's ideals, he saw that primitive instrumental-ism of ideals unsubstantiated by economic means made the moralist a social irrelevance and kept most people the servants of their grossest needs. Emerson saw economic specialization as the corollary of social fragmentation. Franklin saw it as the way to unprecedented power, the city its symbol, which would, by the wealth it created, free people as it freed Franklin himself—to their public life. Economic animal and public citizen were two different beings: if Franklin could not make them into one person at all, Emersonians could make them into one person only by retreat to little oases of rural, economically self-sufficient farming communities that, as Hawthorne said, strengthen the back, but exhaust the mind. If they integrated a community, taken as a general social-economic program they would fragment the nation and return the world to primitive isolations. Modern subur-banism with its geographic fragmentation of home, work, govern-ment, school, store, and so on, could reasonably be seen as heritage of popularized Emersonian romanticism in the world of Franklinian economics.

I have said that Franklin, Edwards, and Emerson proposed monist anthropologies. Though each did propose a single characteristic or power as *the* human quality, each, of course, implies a dualism: for Edwards, natural depravity against the divine benevolence, which is grace; for Franklin, rationality against thoughtless animal gluttony; for Emerson, the transcending heart against whatever vulnerability to social custom it is that impedes the heart. Both Edwards and Emerson believed that the world had been begun perfect, that the dangerous part of human nature had somehow become dominant, and that the problem was to return to a primeval perfection. But Franklin had a thoroughgoing distrust of the primal and primitive. For Franklin, primitive means brute exhaustion in the unthinking struggle for sur-vival. Progress is not in the return of grace or the autonomy of the heart, but in liberation from primitive preoccupations and the primitive's contracted horizons. For Edwards and Emerson the hope for progress is in transcendence, the leap above that which restrains the good. For Franklin the hope is in systematic gratification; in a sense, satisfy the evil to liberate the good. The strangeness of Franklin's character—we expect formidable minds to have formidable sensibilities—is that he could look with such equanimity on the evil attendant upon satiation and that so slight an idea of humanhood could be a satisfying image of liberation. Perhaps a greater moral sensibility lies imbedded under an imposed calm. Perhaps he simply could not let himself believe that an easy reasonableness would not make all things right. Perhaps he restrained his aspirations lest a hard reality make success impossible. Perhaps the most formidable Franklinian self-discipline is to want nothing that you cannot rather easily have. And perhaps it left him not really satisfied very much with what he actually got. Perhaps the *Autobiography* is not only to explain to his son the road of his success, but to reassure himself that he had after all been a success. And perhaps Emerson's transcendentalism, like Edwards' faith in universal regeneration that would come from some source utterly outside human action—not an integration of the complexities of human will but sudden reformation of it into simple virtuousness—perhaps these, too, manifest incapacity to tolerate disparity between aspiration and accomplishment, the world between what one wants and what one may have. Yet, reduction of the spectrum to monisms or dualisms, to black and white, as the cliché has it, eliminates not only the ambiguities of gray, it also eliminates all that we call color. It is interesting that in descriptions by their contemporaries Franklin, Edwards, and Emerson are repeatedly accused of too great a coldness, too colorless a discipline of mind and body, too numbing a self-restraint. Yet surely these three men were among the most formidable of their generations. The question is, I suppose, whether the only alternatives are the polarities of maximum moral concentration at the cost of austere self-disciplining evasion or the average person's loose tolerance that blunts with condoned ignorance the moral insensitivity presumably dignified by the name of work-a-day realism.

In any case, whatever the psychological correlatives of reductionist anthropology, neither monism nor dualism could master the crash of forces that make American society. No monist or dualist was capable of integrating an adequate sense of history with Franklin's perception of the liberative significance of industrial power and the great moral imperatives that are the heart of Edwards' and Emerson's preaching.

To summarize, let me put it this way. If we assume that we are by nature complicated, that we are at every moment a very complex relation of desires and powers and convoluted perceptions, that any act has for us many significances, that any moment may find us synthesized in any of a great many ways, that there will be in a great many greatly disparate situations something to which we can organize satisfactorily—at least to ourselves—all of which we mean when we say that our species is a very adaptable species. Then a great deal of what one is depends on where and when one is, and a great deal of the quality of a particular human nature depends on that human nature's particular situation. This insight is probably fundamental to the long transcendentalist tradition (which included, for instance, the stoics) as it is to the environmentalists. Seeing the enormously diverse situations to which people are vulnerable and seeing the moral misfortunes so often produced, the stoics, like all transcendentalists, hoped to give stability to a desirable human possibility by persuading people to be indifferent to their situations, to rise above them, adapting not to the complex pulls of the moment of place and time, but to a fixed, simpler, and more manageable ideal of character, more easily approximated when one ignores the various attractions of one's multifarious situation. In this sense, Edwards, with his doctrine of extrinsically delivered grace, is no less a transcendentalist than Emerson. The alternative to transcendentalism, if one wants to elicit a particular quality of character, is to manipulate the environment so that it will tend to facilitate the synthesis one admires. Now, transcendentalists, of course, must always live and act within an environment. Few are able to wait altogether on some force utterly independent of their wills. Unless one can, or unless one believes that the transcendence on which alone hope depends is not forthcoming, one must try to establish that situation in which the transcending leap is most likely. The situation Edwards committed himself to was "The Great Awakening," where a religious ecstasy induced by images of human jeopardy under divine wrath might be the instrument as well as the sign of grace. Emerson committed himself to public art and discourse on individual dignity and self-respect, which alone would liberate our essential fineness from its subservience to false custom. Only Franklin among the three committed himself to the social and economic environment. But he committed that environment to too little of himself. To be sure a society's symbols of humaneness, the categories of thought and feeling it deals with and administers to its people, these are among the forces by which a situation makes actual the myriad human possibilities. Such symbols as Edwards and Emerson made were simply weaker, less imposing than they could have been had they reckoned with and proposed to master more of the powers of which the society was capable. It yet remains to be seen whether in the long run the mainstream acceptance of Franklin's environmentalism, tied as it was to his contracted moral aspirations, will prove a final misfortune or prove the appropriateness of a pessimistic anthropology, or whether by its commitment the mainstream will have indeed assured the creation of the instruments necessary for an unprecedentedly moral civilization. If automation, for example, is a particularly pressing contemporary problem, our history of Franklinism has made it so. And the problem that automation has most importantly given us is its obligation for whole societies to have to decide how they will live their lives. Jonathan Edwards, in his famous *Treatise on the Will*, argued that all that freedom of the will could really mean is opportunity to choose. Poverty, like other constraints upon the will, is a misfortune not unmixed with blessing. It gives us the obligation to organize our lives by our simplest desires, and hence it removes from us the obligation to choose in terms of the larger possibilities of our humanity. Wealth is so often damning in part because then we can see what one will do with freedom. Our Franklinian instrumentalism has created for many the possibility of an unprecedented freedom of the will. The instruments are there. It remains to be seen what we will do with them.

The mainstream's faith in the beatitude of wealth—time made good by pursuit of wealth, work given honor that gains wealth, people given dignity who have wealth—this has been a force defining much of American history. The faith may be no more than a confusion of instrument and goal (when an instrument is critical and potent, it seems radiant), it may be no more than the human form of the animals' exhaustive occupation with individual or familial physical survival. But since there have always been people who did not so order their lives, and because as preachers such people have always been at least sabbatically listened to by most people, and because when we succeed at wealth we do not get the contentment we expected, we know that though we are economic animals, we are not only that. The weakness of an Edwardsian pessimism is in its seeing people as self-aggrandizing economic animals only. The weakness of the Emersonian romantic optimism is in its having to believe that we are not really that at all. The weakness of the Franklinian mainstream is in its belief that for virtue's sake, economic animal is all we have to be.

V

With Edwards, Franklin, and Emerson we are at the heart of American anti-politics. Belief in politics depends on belief in a diversity of human possibilities and belief that social morality depends on the creation and direction of social institutions whose business is the conscious moralizing of social relations by creating social conditions conducive to the morality one admires. But in America as in Europe, belief in politics went almost always with belief that the species is finally divided into two groups: the many who will act morally only if they are coerced to it, and the few—the well-born, the rich, the faithful to the true faith—fated by their inherent virtue to the boon or burden, but in any case the moral necessity, of coercing the many. Belief in politics, that is to say, had almost always been belief in aristocratic politics, and had included the crucial assumptions that between aristocracy and commonality there is no continuity of interest or sensibility, and that the signs of the division—birth, wealth, race, creed—are final and absolute index of moral nature, exceptions but proving the rule. From Winthrop to Alexander Hamilton, this was the dominant political orientation. It drove to the opposite pole, to anti-politics, those repulsed by aristocratic politics' presumptuous fragmentation of the species. It drove them to believe that politics could only be an instrument of arbitrary privilege, more or less hypocritically disguised. It drove equalitarians like Benjamin Franklin who were preoccupied with economic condition and the oppressive conditioning of poverty to see "Laws and Ordinances of Kingdoms and States" as tending always to produce advantage for "private persons or bodies in the State who procured them," and *at expense of* the rest of the people, "the Commonwealth." (*The Writings of Benjamin Franklin* ed. by A. H. Smyth, 1905; IV, 243–244.) It drove those like Jonathan Edwards who were devoted to the ideal of universal benevolence and preoccupied by the universality of selfishness under all veneers of social distinction whatsoever to see all environmentalist social action as a moral irrelevance—all that people "depended on for peace and safety, were nothing but thin air and empty shadows." ("Sinners in the Hands of an Angry God.") It drove those like Emerson who were devoted to the ideal of individual creativity and preoccupied by the universal urgencies and self-denials under all formal social differentiations and obeisances to custom to see nothing in social institutions but impediments to individual integrity and its power.

Though in their anti-political equalitarianism Edwards, Franklin, and Emerson express revulsion from aristocratic presumption, they are no less pushed than the aristocrats are to find faith in a simple, automatic moral resolution of social diversity, discord, and discontent. Anti-politics is the other side of the aristocrats' political reductionism. Aristocratic politics proposes arbitrary discontinuities of interest and moral competence; anti-politics, whether optimistic or pessimistic, says there are really no discontinuities of interest and moral competence at all. Both sides depend on and serve belief in the world's utter simplicity. One of the things people need is belief in the world's moral coherence, belief that what is and appears necessary is just. So great is the need that unless alternatives are obvious and look gallingly available, even the radically disadvantaged usually acquiesce to philosophies justifying their misfortunes. Defense of privilege is not the only motive of aristocratic politics. By believing that some overarching universal will not only sanctions but requires terrestrial aristocratic authority and advantage, most aristocrats and their loyal subjects not only rationalize past and present inequities, they satisfy the less particular but no less urgent wish to believe that the world's moral orderliness is guaranteed and simple and, indeed, easy. Because the indices of aristocratic distinction—birth, wealth, race—are almost always arbitrary, it couldn't be easier to draw them, and then to abandon oneself to the automatic moral coherence they assure, to the work so simply cut out for one. It gives one so neat a lever and so neat a place to stand midst the vast incoherences that threaten our apprehensions. Edwards, Franklin, and Emerson could not tolerate the inequities or the banality of aristocratic pretension, but they were no less in need of a simple guarantee against all incoherence, against any continuing discrepancy between virtue and power. They, too, had to find some simple mode of action by which all the world would surely be redeemed from moral discord, some simple source of power with a universal moral efficacy. Not politics—not contests for power over social institutions that will direct the society's moral purposiveness and establish if they can the social conditions conducive to one's morality—but God's transformation of all men's hearts from simple viciousness to simple benevolence; or one man, "counterpoise to a city," by the vibrance of his exhortation unlocking a universal harmony; or "trade taking its own course" to millennium. All three are radically democratic, radically equalitarian, but though they refuse commonality's acquiescence to an aristocracy, their proposals have a similar psychological thrust. For Edwards, acquiescence to God, who is omnipotent; for Emerson, acquiescence to the heart, which is omniscient; and for Franklin, acquiescence to economic privatism, which is omnivorous, and what the people were doing anyway.

The persistence of these three forms of anti-politics in America is a persistence, I think, of our radical democratism wedded to our inability to believe that the universe does not conspire in our wishes and make their success inevitable by managing our affairs for us, and transforming our adverse impulses into some automatic universal coherence.

CHAPTER TWO

Ready for the Complexities

We come now to a very difficult question. How is it that in the middle of the nineteenth century we get more or less suddenly both a literature and a politics radical not only in the sense of their opposition to aristocraticism or mainstream privatism, but radical in the complexity of the anthropology they propose? From the history of the mid-nineteenth century we may take three facts obviously important to the present study: the creation of a truly modern American literature—the works of Edgar Allan Poe, Nathaniel Hawthorne, Herman Melville, and Walt Whitman; the established success of the industrial revolution; and the beginning of a modern radical politics, traditionally radical by its moral commitments, modern by its commitment to industrial society as the key instrument of social action. The question is, how do these three facts fit together? It may be that industrial socialism is not only a necessary consequence of the industrial revolution, but also a political corollary of the new literature.

* * *

From the time of the breakdown of the medieval worldview to the middle of the nineteenth century, a constant characteristic of the otherwise most disparate schools of thought was a search for a force, *the* force, that could be counted on to do what medieval theo-politics had failed to do: support the faith that the world has moral unity at its center and the moral unification of our species as its certain destiny. It seems that we needed not only the assurance of a certain future—a tensionless beatitude surely to come—but also a faith that there is a single avenue to that beatitude, a single mode of action on which all depends, if not in this world, then in the next. So our history has swung from faiths in the omnipotence of the mind to faiths in the omniscience of the heart, from faiths in a perfect God to faiths in the perfectibility of the people, from faith in science to faith in poetry, from faith in monastic poverty to faith in worldly wealth, from faith in individuals to faith in states. And we have done battle with one another to protect our certainties, even if the certainty we hold to is the omnipotence of love.

It is easy to see why our own contemporary philosophies characteristically asserting diversities, uncertainties, heterogeneities, are generally also philosophies of anxiety. It is nevertheless hard to know why it is that in the nineteenth and twentieth centuries serious thinkers came more and more to accept—at last, one might say—being's fundamental complexity, the mere particularity in nature of human ideals, the precarious relation of those ideals to the complexity of human character. I think part of the reason may be that the enormous increase in the power to manipulate nature—to deal willfully with the environment—at once emboldened people to look more and more directly to see how complex an affair the environment is, and at the same time it obliged people and gave them the self-respect to see the humbling, indeed often the humiliating, implications about ourselves in the purposes to which we put the power we had always craved. When our jeopardy in our physical environment is very great, it is not surprising we have little energy for psychology or the niceties of social relations. We imagine that bliss is just on the other side of our immediate problems. But if one has gone far in creating the instruments of physical security and finds life still not blissful, then one may have both time and energy and the need to look inward to see if the source of one's life's disorders may not be there. It may even be a general rule that the least optimistic philosophies come at times of the greatest wealth, the greatest economic success.

Thought, it seems, is generated by disorder—by discontinuity between desire and condition—and is one of the instrumental devices by which we would make our environment yield to our will. Reason is the will's agent. But we endure frustration badly, and when the environment is overridingly frustrating, thought does its work by imagining some magic way to success. When reason fails, we rationalize—more or less fantastically, depending on our sophistication. We mask with fantasy of the will's magic potency the vacuums in our arsenals of power.

It is true enough to say often that for most of human history we have been necessarily preoccupied with getting sustenance and in competing for it. Hence thought has been preoccupied with the problems of sustenance and with rationalizing failures to secure it. It is also true, it seems to me, that our species has been preoccupied by what appears to be a commanding need for universal harmony, the need to believe that all the world's interests somehow combine to make moral order. Hence all ideas of justice, which are simply assertions of the feeling that a competitor's interests *ought* to be compatible with one's own, and that the competitors' failures at what they think they want are really proper for them and necessary to their coherent place in a just world. (Even "the survival of the fittest," when put as prescriptive rather than descriptive law, carries the implication that since a sound world and a healthy species is everyone's final good, even the death of the unfit is ultimately to their own best interest and they ought to accept it gladly.)

Because we want not only security but harmony, not only private well-being but the feeling of the world's assent to our having it, the necessity of competition for sustenance has also been necessity to construct a belief that the competition is not antithetical to the proper interest of even the loser. Hence all the philosophies proposing discontinuities in human nature that make the loser's loss, the servant's servitude, the subject's obedience, the pauper's poverty, the woman's subjugation, compatible with their best interests, if not, indeed, the very ground of their happiness. Most of formal generalizing thought has had this double foundation: fantasies about the world's regard for and promise of success for our sustenantial wishes (if not in this life, then in another); fantasies about the nature of the species as ultimately joined by identical compatible interests (e.g., the lion lying down with the lamb), or by a morally perfect antithesis of interests gloriously resolved in some superman's destined synthesizing victory (e.g., the survival of the fittest).

Now, our economic history (the history of our sustenance-getting) has been the history of greater and more widespread success. Economic success has reduced the need for dependence on fantasies of supernatural resolution of our natural problems. Also, by reducing the need for economic enmities, general economic success has reduced the need for fantasies of discontinuity between members of the species. It has made opportunity to discover in the likenesses of aspiration throughout the species the possibility of equalitarian harmony. Scarcity of what we all want tends to make us enemies and to make us see in others' likeness of aspiration the very basis of their nefariousness, their threat to our well-being. Abundance, or enough of it to make for the mutual efficacy of cooperation (though we may be incapacitated for perception of abundance by an overbearing memory of want), facilitates the feeling that likeness of aspiration is the basis of sympathetic harmony, our mutual virtue. In any case, the history of generalized economic success and the extension of the species' economic power seems to have paralleled the rise of democratic, equalitarian politics.

It is also important that modern American history was begun at a very advanced stage of this process. The first principle of our nationality is the assumption of people's adequate self-dependency and the equality of the species. The liberal American mainstream's commitment to the ideal of universal freedom is based on the view that it is precisely the historical constraints of the will that are responsible for past evil, the liberating and empowering of the will that can moralize the world. Though in the twentieth century economic privatism implies a pessimistic view of human nature that constrains our communal impulses and the potentials of power inherent in cooperative enterprise and at the same time contradicts the optimistic anthropology of our democratic political theory, in the eighteenth century it did not constrain or appear to contradict. In the eighteenth century the people were so dispersed and the scale of our political institutions so radically incommensurate with the country's economic opportunities that privatism was a logical correlate of a benevolentist's belief in individual freedom and the moral efficacy of the species' expansive power.

With the view that the deprivations of our European political history—and nothing in our own nature—were responsible for social evil, the American entrepreneurial spirit undertook the opportunities of the New World. But, though by the middle of the nineteenth century free men had created unprecedented instruments of economic power and unprecedented distribution of wealth, economic power was used too often as of old—as a weapon by which the rich could coerce and oppress the poor. When American freedom produced the city slum, rural poverty, and an imperious economic aristocracy, the New World began to appear no different from the old and the history we'd hoped to escape. A great deal at issue in the period is to be seen in the fact that the southern slaveholding aristocracy, frankly Anglophile and reactionary, could argue with some cogency that the chattel-slave of the South was better off by far than the wage-slave of northern industrialism: the chattel-slave owners had to be interested in their slaves' health and longevity; the wage-slave hirers couldn't care less and had no need to—immigration supplied them with endless cheap fodder for their machines.

Freedom and power, then, were not the guarantors of virtue we imagined them to be: human nature—the constant, presumably, under the changes in social condition—must be more complicated or at least something other than our now obviously naïve hopefulness had imagined it to be. The death of one illusion often generates its opposite—we swing between equally sentimental optimisms and pessimisms—but it also often generates a new order of thoughtfulness and inquiry. Medieval pessimism about the species' moral nature (in part a rationalizing of its economic weakness) was replaced by faith in its uniform *a priori* virtue as moral guarantor of Renaissance expansive economic success. The moral failures of equalitarian power led many to see power itself, then, as the source of corruption (the idea of corruption implies, of course, a primal purity), it led others to the view that history can be no more, after all, than cycles of catastrophe, with a universal explosion, perhaps, at the end. (See, for example, James Fenimore Cooper's late novel, *The Crater* [1847], in which the population of a new world, this time a Pacific paradise, merely repeats, as America had, the turning of a wilderness into a moral chaos of factions and predatory selfishness.) But it led some to reconsider the question of human nature and its relation to social condition in a way quite extraordinary to that point in American history: the reconsiderations were not governed by an *a priori* assumption of humankind's simple homogeneity or of history as single-stranded certainty.

Why? No doubt some extraordinary psychological strength and poise made it possible that Hawthorne and Melville, for example, should be able to give uncertainty, complexity, our precariousness, and our moral diversities an essential, organizing place in their thought. But even if we could find the psychological base of Hawthorne's or Melville's ability to express the complexity of experience, even if we could make substantial psychological analyses—which we cannot—our question would still be unanswered. Surely there must have been many eighteenth-century Americans with an adequately similar psychological power and poise. Assuming that, our "why" is primarily a matter of "when," and our question must occupy itself with the particularities of the time in which a given psychological orientation would accomplish this particular intellectual success.

First of all, the simplistic guarantors of moral order—Christian pietism, eighteenth-century rationalism, early nineteenth-century romanticism, liberal economic privatism—all had been abraded raw by experience. Each had proposed the universal moral efficacy of some single source of power, some simple way to the integration of the complexities of human nature and the human situation. But God either failed or forsook us. Antitheses of inclination and interest boggled the mind and then embittered the heart. The freedom to which we were empowered by extraordinarily extensive wealth became opportunity merely for history's reiteration of our nasty vulnerability to greed. Mid-nineteenth-century thinkers could see the naïveté of earlier faiths because history had tested the faiths and had made their naïveté obvious as earlier it could not or need not have been obvious.

But beyond that, it seems a crucial fact that it was less the failure of these *isms* than their success that proved their vanity. Each had been successful in two ways. First, each had had its day and had gotten the institutional instrumentation it had thought both necessary and sufficient for its purposes. America was made free for all religionists to proselytize to their heart's content. Franklinian rationalisms had accomplished for Americans more free public education than ever before in the history of the world. The politically enfranchised men were free at last to express the wisdom of their hearts. And the liberal economic privatists had, of course, made American enterprise free of practically any authoritarian constraint whatsoever. And each of these movements had succeeded in a second sense. A crucial motive of each is, after all, some form of benevolent equalitarianism. The fact is that if in America in the middle of the nineteenth century people did not seem so very much better than they had ever been before, they were, at least, very much better off. It was from this double eminence of success that in the middle decades of the nineteenth century people had opportunity to reconsider the meaning of their failures.

The presidential election of 1840 dramatized the confluence of these several issues. It came in the midst of the terrible depression to which the economy had plummeted after the astonishing boom of manufacture, agriculture, and transportation before 1837. To equalitarian reformers, the issues were wonderfully clear. Van Buren represented unambiguously the interests of the masses, William Henry Harrison the interests of the rich. The reformers' opportunity was great. The moral significance was dramatized by the depression, the electorate was more broadly based than ever before, free public education had made enfranchised men literate to a new degree, and intellectuals had newspapers and journals in which to broadcast, as never before, a thoroughgoing and clear delineation of the issues. And Harrison's managers, implicitly acknowledging the clarity of the issues, decided their only chance was to run the campaign without reference to them. Instead they mounted America's first great "public relations" campaign. Their answer to all questions was simply this: Van Buren was rich, a champagne-drinking New Yorker; Harrison, military hero against the Indians at Tippecanoe, American of Americans, was born in a log cabin and drank hard cider. (Though he was the son of a prominent Virginia statesman, it was Harrison—rather than Lincoln—that first made humble log-cabin beginnings the famous political symbol.) For equalitarian reformers the election of Van Buren was to be the great demonstration of the masses' clarity of mind and goodness of heart and of their moral use of economic freedom. Harrison won in a landslide. All the forms of equalitarian hopefulness had now, it seemed to many, been proved simplistic dreams. Therefore human nature *had* to be reconsidered. My point (the cumbersomeness of the way I've put it so far makes me put it again) is that some, at least, could reconsider it in ways less dominated by panic for panaceas because the power equalitarian man had gotten was the source of the pride, the confidence, with which alone the moralists who identified with equalitarian man could undertake the rigors of a critical examination of equalitarian anthropology. Past accomplishments both expose the naïveté of our old dreams of bliss, and make the plateau of self-confidence from which we have the pride to survey our frailties. Past accomplishment, if I may change the figure, is the thread of confidence with which like Daedalus we dare try the labyrinth of our complexity.

One more related speculation. The wealth and freedom had another effect that facilitated the newly formidable understanding of human nature we find in the mid-nineteenth-century writers. Theirs was the first American generation of writers for whom writing could be a primary profession. Until then, our writers were by occupation either churchmen or statesmen and wrote to serve these primary professions. Edwards, Franklin, and Emerson are representative. And it seems a telling fact that each of them assumed not only a single line toward universal salvation, but also that his own profession, perhaps even his own work, was the essential and adequate instrument of its accomplishment. Edwards thought the minister chosen by God to excite the Great Awakening to the truths of religion would be the usher to the millennium. Franklin thought the same about the statesman who could instate *laissez-faire* economics and equalitarian politics. Emerson, though he left the church, remained a preacher, albeit a secular one, and though he changed the substance of Edwards' sermon, he kept the view of the preacher's instrumental efficacy.

The fact that an adequate intellectual confrontation of complexity and uncertainty comes at a time when intellectuals can be free from an institutional profession's commitment to a particular kind of social action—free, that is, for the intellectual's primary business as an intellectual, the contemplation of the meaning of experience—it may be that that confrontation depends on that freedom. It was not until the nineteenth century that American society could support the writer simply as writer, could give him opportunity to describe life and prescribe for it in a way free from immediate obligations to a social institution's programs. When in the course of his day's work

Edwards met people, he met them as parishioners, as subjects, or as objects, perhaps, of his preacherly skills and intentions. His work obliged him to define people in their relation to it: simply as those whom he had or had not succeeded in saving by their conversion to piety, and he saw conversion as the ultimate accomplishment. The same with Emerson, though he defined salvation differently. And so with Franklin: as entrepreneur and later as statesman representing the entrepreneurial point of view, he saw people almost exclusively in business and political roles as economic animal, and he saw economic success as the ultimate accomplishment.

But the writer of poetry or fiction is not, or not directly, in any case, the agent of a social institution. Writers' work is first of all to stand back, to look at the diversity of experience. Writers are first of all observers, observers of all the diversity they are equal to. To be sure, their work is also to find and give image to the representative, as that will be defined by their moral sensibility, their point of view. It is the clergyman's job to concentrate on people's religious motives and functions. It is the statesman's job to concentrate on people's political motives and functions. It is the writer's job to see the diversity of motives and functions by which people live their lives, to see them in all their roles and the relationships of them. That is perhaps part of the reason why—as Alfred North Whitehead and others have pointed out—works of fiction and poetry and drama often express a more sophisticated, a more adequately complex, a sounder sense of life than do the more formal, abstracter, system-making disciplines. The formal disciplines of science, ideology, and philosophy have the professional obligation to isolate particular kinds of data. The writer's professional obligation is the synthesis in concrete images of the full flood of daily experience. The danger for writers, of course, is that their preoccupations may be merely crotchety, that their freedom to get meaning by connotative implication gives their crotchets free rein. It is also the danger that even their wisdoms remain implicit only, that their discipline does not require them to work out in explicative detail the systematic application of the fruits of their labors. Indeed, the novelists' novels may know more than they do—of which *War and Peace* is the classic example: its epilogues of explicit philosophy of history so sadly incommensurate with the astonishing richness of the novel itself. But that discontinuity illustrates my point: representation in art requires a catholicity and intensity of observation that often generates an extraordinary order of knowing, an order often beyond the explicational disciplines of even the artist's own explicational competence. And my point is also that both the arts and the explicational disciplines will be disadvantaged by the constraint of perception in the degree to which they are oriented by institutional obligations—the degree to which the observer is churchman or statesman (or whatever) first, and contemplative observer—that is, intellectual—second. Perhaps I ought here to say that the question is *not* whether disaffiliation is the condition of intellectual accomplishment. The question is whether intellect ought to be the agent of one's *a priori* affiliations, or one's particular affiliations the accomplishment of one's intellect, one's comprehensive synthesizing understanding of one's inclinations and one's situation, one's rational appraisal of the forces amidst which and by which one lives. Intellect is the faculty by which we undertake the rational appraisal of our intentions and the resistances to them: intellectuals are those who make that work, rather than a more particular kind of problem-solving, the business of their lives. This requires the distinction between the intellectual statesman, say, and the intellectual as political scientist, between intellectual as adjective and intellectual as noun, as when we make the distinction between an artistic work of craftsmanship and a work of art. The distinction ought, of course, to denigrate neither. A world without either defeats both. Each is pathetic in a world without the other, like science without a scientific technology, like art that accomplishes no extension of sensibility, like the moralist who makes nothing moral, like the philosopher from whom no one learns clarity, or coherence, or reach of understanding. And as a world without scientists or without artists or without moralists or without philosophers will in time embarrass each of them, pressing them to work they cannot do, and hence to pathetic pretensions of a universal adequacy.

But putting these generalizations (or generalities, as they may be) aside, my point is this. Many major innovations in our understanding of human nature have appeared first in our literature. This was because America's mid-nineteenth-century accomplishments of wealth created an audience for literature, hence opportunity for American intellectuals to make the contemplation of experience their work in a way particularly substantial because unencumbered by obligations as professional agent of a social institution. Further, mid-nineteenth-century literature is extraordinarily rich intellectually not only because literature was newly and particularly available to intellectuals as a profession, but also because the literary disciplines require and depend at once on intuitional freedom, confidence in one's intuitions, and extensive concretizing of one's intuitions, and because such disciplines are necessary and likely to be particularly fruitful in a period when traditional certainties no longer make sense of the world, hence a period particularly requiring intellectual innovation.

And though intellectual innovations generated by disillusionment are as likely as not to be regressive—attempts to recapture the gratifications of an earlier, simpler coherence of life we think we remember—the feeling of potency that was habitual to the American character and the accomplishments of power characteristic of mid-nineteenth-century life made the need for intellectual innovation an opportunity to reconsider the relation of power to moral excellence in a newly integrative rather than a regressive way. The liberation of energy that had been characteristic of American life and America's revolutionary place in the world had been in part a consequence of the view that in an equalitarian society benevolence and potency are correlates; benevolence properly seeking to empower the species; and only the common people's socioeconomic impotence that keeps them from acting with benevolent effect. It was the equalitarian prideful-ness inherent in this view, heightened by America's accomplishments of power, and inherited by the mid-nineteenth-century writers, that made them able to reconsider the relation of power to benevolence and, when old hopes were, like balloons, burst or blown away, to see in an unprecedented way the heterogeneity of the species, the com-plexity of individual inclinations, the sociohistorical conditionality of character and its social effect, the immense diversities of cause amidst which our self-dependent inclination to fraternity and individual dig-nity must uncertainly and anxiously make its way.

Power is simply the ability to get what one wants. The distinctive quality of American life, the quality defining its break with European tradition, is the American common people's assumption of the moral legitimacy of their desires, their confidence in what they want, hence their internal freedom to go get what they want and their demand for social opportunity to go get it. Given also America's virgin wealth of natural resources (the impulse and the opportunity were mutually rein-forcing), the common people's pursuit of power was unprecedentedly successful: and this made possible the range of occupations in which intellectuals could consider human nature in a way unencumbered by an employing institution's demands. Motivated now by a background of pride in the knowledge that people in an equalitarian society could *be* powerful—more powerful than nature or kings—the intellectual motivated by the equalitarian ideal no longer needed to assume the common people perfect in order to protect them from the humiliation in an aristocrat's gestures of condescension or contempt, in order to assert the common peoples' equal right to well-being against the aristo-crat's pretension to a morally warranted desert of privilege.

It should be said, too, that the mid-nineteenth-century writers had also inherited the accomplishments of their predecessors, and no longer needed to go over that ground again. Edwards had dispelled the class pretensions to virtue in the Puritan aristocracy by both his equalitarian pessimism about humankind's moral nature and his faith in an equalitarian redemption. Franklin had dispelled belief in the political sanctity, social efficacy, or entrepreneurial competence of inherited wealth. Emerson had turned Edwards' anthropology around to make its basis of attack on the complacency of an establishment orthodoxy an equalitarian pridefulness rather than a universal humiliation. Together they made it possible for the heirs of their equalitarianisms and their victories over particular aristocratic defenses to consider at once the truths of Edwards' preoccupation with human selfishness, Franklin's preoccupation with the moral significance of economic condition, and Emerson's preoccupation with the compatibility of individual integrity, creativity, and social fraternity.

The radically equalitarian intellectual had to reexamine the old simplistic equalitarian anthropologies because the common people had in acquisition of power betrayed the simplistic confidence in their spontaneous goodness or their spontaneous badness. Radical equalitarian intellectuals could reexamine the old simplicities in part because they had already been given classic exposition, but more importantly, I think, because equalitarian society's success at wealth gave them time to do it, gave them freedom from the need for defense of the common people's deserts against aristocratic pretension, made the common people themselves rather than an economic aristocracy the intellectual's potential audience and therefore the subject of the intellectual's inquiries, judgments, and exhortations, and gave the ambience of equalitarian accomplishment in which to assume the possibility of success at a higher order of purpose, the need to define that purpose, and the confidence to inquire into the now apparently internal resistances to it. All of which may be taken to suggest that if wealth is properly not a goal but a means to development of extra-economic talents and desires, to understanding and aspiration and moral sensibility free of the narrowing melancholy or the fright or the meekness of the squint by which the hungry animal must see all the world, then the existence of the writers of what has been called the American renaissance proved that the American mainstream's preoccupation with the pursuit of wealth had been in no insignificant degree a success—Edwards' pessimism, Franklin's narrowness of aspiration, Emerson's pastoralism, all these to the contrary notwithstanding. Even though the mainstream itself would not know its successes from its failures, and in so far as it was aware of them at all, would revile the real heirs it had nurtured with its wealth.

I have said all this in a cumbersome, convoluted, and repetitive way. But I let it stand because I seem unable to say it better and because its substance seems to me important. First of all, I assume few will dissent from the view that the writers of mid-nineteenth-century America constitute a very high order of our culture's accomplishments. That warrants our asking, even if awkwardly, why they came when they did—what general social conditions were propitious for them. Since these questions are not very often asked, even rather loose, speculative answers are worth setting down.

Secondly, these issues seem important to me because in the twentieth century the American radical moral sensibility has often seen the scale and power of the technology of wealth as its major enemy, whose force in the world makes pessimism necessary, and activism for the sake of the radical moral sensibility an absurdity. But if, as I've argued, the technology of wealth was a condition, perhaps a necessary condition, for the generating of an American "renaissance," then the technology of wealth is not a monovalent force. It is not merely capricious to say that the morality, the positive commitments, inherent in the radical's pessimism is itself no less the product of the society and the historical process the pessimist abhors than are the subjects of that abhorrence and that pessimism. Of course the pessimists may be right. The final product of the technology of wealth may be the military obliteration of everything. But even then, or at the penultimate moment, rather, we should have to wonder if pessimistic resignation, as well as romantic evasion or direct complicity in predatory economics, had not been a contributory cause. But be that as it may. What I want to insist here is that the radical pessimists (and the romantic escapists) must include themselves, their morality, their self-consciousness, the sense of their own dignity and integrity, the ambience of discontent that defines their audience and to which they speak, and the growing number who have opportunity to discover the demands of their particularity as these writers have discovered theirs—the radical pessimists must include all these as constituents of the world they describe and judge. Which is not to suggest, of course, that we give ourselves up to entrepreneurial authority or the entrepreneurial passions. It is to suggest that the alienation from the technology of wealth is less appropriate than the turning of the technology of wealth toward a greater consistency with the radical ideals of benevolence, mastery, self-consciousness, and social integrality, the extension of which the technology of wealth itself particularly facilitates, even though only ambivalently or inadvertently.

Which is why I said that industrial socialism is a political corollary of the new literature and a necessary consequence of the industrial revolution.

CHAPTER THREE

Poe: Politics and Nature's Perversities

In the four chapters that follow I am going to talk about the political implications in some of the works of Poe, Hawthorne, Melville, and Whitman. I am aware of the danger of politicizing everything, of reading lyric poems as political tracts, of reducing a rich literary fabric to merely the political thread in it, of capriciously translating the most various modes of discourse into political metaphors because one's preoccupations allow no other perception. Still, the questions we are dealing with here seem to me to make the politically oriented reading legitimate. If a new order of political and literary sophistication (consciousness of reality) emerges at the same time, it would seem silly to ignore the relation of literary to political consciousness. Secondly, the point I want to make is that one's politics are no more and no less than the application of one's knowledge and the way one thinks to the particular problems of communally organized life. If one's poems have truths in them, then one's politics ought to be at least consistent with one's poems. And indeed there are some poetic truths by which one's politics ought to be directly informed. If, as Archibald MacLeish said, poems do not mean but be, one of the things the poems we like seem to us to be is true. Take, for example, Poe's poem "Israfel" (1831):

And the Angel Israfel, whose heart-strings are a lute, and who has the sweetest voice of all God's creatures. —KORAN.

In Heaven a spirit doth dwell
   "Whose heart-strings are a lute;"
None sing so wildly well
As the Angel Israfel,
And the giddy stars (so legends tell)
Ceasing their hymns, attend the spell
   Of his voice, all mute.

Tottering above
   In her highest noon,
   The enamored moon
Blushes with love,
     While, to listen, the red levin
     (With the rapid Pleiads, even,
     Which were seven,)
Pauses in Heaven.

And they say (the starry choir
   And the other listening things)
That Israfeli's fire
Is owing to that lyre
   By which he sits and sings—
The trembling living wire
Of those unusual strings.

But the skies that angel trod,
   Where deep thoughts are a duty—
Where Love's a grown-up God—
   Where the Houri glances are
Imbued with all the beauty
   Which we worship in a star.

Therefore, thou art not wrong,
   Israfeli, who despisest
An unimpassioned song;
To thee the laurels belong,
   Best bard, because the wisest!
Merrily live, and long!

The ecstacies above
   With thy burning measures suit—
Thy grief, thy joy, thy hate, thy love,
   With the fervor of thy lute—
   Well may the stars be mute!

Yes, Heaven is thine; but this
   Is a world of sweets and sours;
   Our flowers are merely—flowers,
And the shadow of thy perfect bliss
   Is the sunshine of ours.

If I could dwell
Where Israfel
   Hath dwelt, and he where I,
He might not sing so wildly well
   A mortal melody,
While a bolder note than this might swell
   From my lyre within the sky.

Of course it has no directly political subject matter. But the subject matter it does have and its tone hold meanings of which no politics ought to be unaware. It begins for the first six stanzas as if it were a conventional, one might even say orthodox, romantic poem, evoking in a conventional romantic's idioms the whole system of beliefs condensed around the idea that to be perfect is to be perfectly in tune with nature; the idea that the artist is not maker but instrument, and that his greatness is not in the forms he imposes on experience, but in the degree to which he can let nature's ultimate truths and beauties be played on him or through him. Israfel is like the Aeolian harp, the stringed instrument of which the romantics were so fond because it was played by the wind, as they wished they themselves could be played, and thus in its sweet hum sounded the very soul of nature's wisdoms.

Then suddenly it's clear that Poe has spoken the romantic conventions only to embarrass them. The heart's melodies may be sweet and whole and pure, a perfection of harmony in some dreamed heaven, but here, where people live, the heart's songs are likely to be discordant and harsh with the pains of mortality and loneliness.

Emerson says (in "Nature") that, "1. Words are signs of natural facts. 2. Particular natural facts are symbols of particular spiritual facts. 3. Nature is the symbol of spirit." The wisdom of this triad is in its implication of the operational theory of language—that words define events of human purposiveness, that words stand not for things in themselves but that things as our words know them are "emblems of our thought," that our words stand not simply for things in themselves, but for the way we think about things, and our thoughts are always about what we would do with the world we perceive. But Emerson takes all this his characteristic step further. Words are not only the creatures of *our* purposive minds, they and the things or events they point to are the creatures of God's mind as well. Not only is the Earth properly (though only partially) defined as what we stand on: our having a place to stand was the reason of its creation and existence. Hence to know the proper word for a thing is to know "the will of God," his purpose for all the world: "the laws of moral nature [the proper uses of things] answer to those of matter as face to face in a glass."

To which Poe says, so may it be for Israfel. The songs of *his* heart's desire and heaven's anthems may be one; but *our* world is a world of sweets and sours: our flowers are—merely flowers. Flowers are not emblems of God's will to delight us, but living things, surviving as they can, not more often succored by life than ruined. Or if they are emblems of the "laws of nature," they are not more so than are weeds, disease, and death. People must make their way as they can, not as nature's beloved, but merely people, surviving and dying as flowers and weeds survive and die, one not more central to the world than another.

Poe's "Israfel" is important in part because it is among the first works in our literary history to have at its core the sense of our species' mere particularity in nature. As such, it takes part in the intellectual ambience that makes possible a new order of political sophistication.

On its surface Poe's poem has rather a joking tone—the tone that punctures pretension by looking at it archly, hence denying its power to command. But under that tone there is another. Toward its end, the poem's tone is more and more melancholy—with the wish that people *could* sing so wildly well, that the stars *did* attend, and with the sense of human loneliness and fragility. That tone is at the opposite pole not only of presumption but of indifference. That melancholy is, at times at least, a necessary consequence of compassion. And compassion is not only the source of a humane politics, it is humane politics' object. Of course compassion is not a new literary subject or accomplishment. Nor is melancholy or recognition that we are not omnipotent. But the bringing of them together—compassion made melancholy by perception of all life's and each life's mere particularity in a universe whose only order is in the amoral laws of the relations of force and matter—*that* begins with Poe as a new American literary preoccupation, a new foundation of sensibility. One has only to name the names of the earlier poets from Anne Bradstreet and Edward Taylor to Freneau and even Bryant and Longfellow and Whittier to make the point.*

And it is a sensibility with political implications. It would seem to make a considerable difference to the way one will act if one thinks that the essential moral problem is simply the unlocking of all people's immanent compatibility with one another and a benignly attendant universe or if one thinks that the moral problem is the welter of antithetical purposes in each of us, amongst us, and in the universe itself. Aristocracies have made the second view plus the assumption of their own divinely ordained excellence the justification for the pursuit of authoritarian power over the grubbily contentious many. If the sentimental equalitarians' mistake has been habitually to confuse their wishes and reality—to assume that all people are as the radical sensibility wants them to be—it is a mistake to which the demands of opposition to aristocraticism have pushed them. But if there is on both sides of this disagreement about unities and diversities an equalitarian benevolence—a moral sensibility that finds human misery a source of

---

* Longfellow's melancholy is always primarily a mere yearning back for a fantasied primeval Arcadia, where "The nights shall be filled with music/ And the cares that infest the day/ Will fold up their tents like Arabs/ And silently steal away." These are lovely lines, but like all American poems before Poe's, they face the world's disorder only through the fantasy of escape from it to some past or destined God-promised beatitude.

pain, human happiness a source of pleasure, and the human capacity for a concerted benevolence itself perhaps the highest pleasure of all—that is, if both sides share the radical moral sensibility—then the difference is between the liberal and radical in politics. The distinction between liberal and radical is often hard because theoretically at least they share the radical moral sensibility. Let me take a minute to try to define it, or at least to list its major constituents.

Central to the radical moral sensibility is the view that we, as human beings, are properly prideful. The proper source of this pride is our capacity for willful (that is, chosen rather than merely dutiful or unself-consciously instinctive) sympathetic identification, the extent of which and our ability to act self-consciously (that is, on the basis of perceived consequences rather than in merely instinctive response) for its sake are properly the basis of the degree of our pride. The heroes of the radical moral sensibility are those who act courageously for the sake of fraternal purposes, and especially those who act to extend the universe of sympathetic identification, to extend the circle of those with whom sympathetic identification is possible, to obliterate impediments to the perception of fraternity, to discover the arbitrariness or superficiality of boundaries within the species' identity.

Two things here may need emphasis. First, that the radical moral sensibility is a motive that has itself as its object. It is the equalitarian benevolence that seeks a general well-being, but seeks an equalitarian benevolence itself even more. If it had to choose between a general well-being and the extension of equalitarian benevolence itself (between a contentment universal but mechanical and a world in which equalitarian benevolence must struggle, even tragically, to extend itself), it would choose the latter. Secondly, though self-conscious equalitarian benevolence is *as a unified whole* the radical moral sensibility's object, the world rarely accomplishes that unity. Instead it imposes the necessity of choice between values that one would want all to be primary. Self-consciousness is not incompatible with selfishness, nor knowing with viciousness. Benevolence may readily be slavish and mindless. When experience imposes the necessity of a choice between self-consciousness and benevolence, the radical moral sensibility usually identifies with the benevolent, though if it had to choose forever between them, it probably could not choose at all.

Liberal and radical disagree not about the moral ideal, but about its place in nature and historical process, and hence they disagree about the forms of social action appropriate to the moral ideal and necessary to its accomplishment.

I think the essential disagreement is this: the liberals feel that the radical moral sensibility is not merely the accident of their own natures but the fundamental aspiration of all nature: that all resistance to it is only some form of ignorance or disease, and that all history is the inevitable evolution toward knowledge and health by which at every moment nature unfolds its essential purpose.

Political radicals, however, tend to feel that the radical moral sensibility is in more or less constant danger—because of the small number who share it and the large number who hate its menace to their narrower contentments and identifications, because nature is no more conducive to it than to its enemies, because, in fact, unless there is a revolutionary break in the historical continuity of people's predatory contentions, our species by its progressive sophistication of the technology of belligerence will destroy itself.

Because they share elements of the radical moral sensibility, liberals and radicals can on occasion make common cause, a united front. Because they do not share a view of the place of the radical moral sensibility in nature and historical process, liberals and radicals are often enemies.

The liberals' inclination is to evolutionary compromise that they believe necessarily progressive because fundamental compatibilities of interest underlie all contentions—hence contention is always on one or both sides a mistake that reasoned compromise resolves. The radicals' inclination is 1) to the revolutionary overpowering of those whose interests are antithetical to the radical sensibility and 2) to the creation of those environmental conditions that impede the development of mutually exclusive interests. To the liberals our true nature is revealed in the moments and the work of compatibility. To the radicals our true nature is revealed no less in viciousness than in benevolence, no less in war than in peace, no less in cruel power or subservience than in equalitarian cooperation. The radicals' preoccupation is the socially cooperative development of so extensive a wealth that competitions for sustenance and ease and freedom need no longer be the natural determinants of our character. In the eighteenth century in America, liberals and radicals had hardly to differentiate themselves. In the eighteenth century, the first work and the great accomplishment of the radical sensibility was the codification of its own ideals. It had to break the hegemony of inequalitarian theories of human nature, the theoretical justifications of inequalitarian social institutions and political systems. Whatever complex of changes in the conditions of life makes possible an urgency to a new order of ideals, whatever hints to the possibility of a new order of well-being, the conceptual formulation of the ideals, the formal justification of the emboldened hopes they express, seems a necessary early stage in their development if they are to become a social movement. It was to this stage in the work of modern radicalism that the eighteenth-century thinkers of the radical sensibility had to address themselves. They did so with an exaggeration of the virtues of their claimants, an exaggeration characteristic of all movements to defend or acquire power and probably especially necessary to movements of radical reform for the sake of the previously underprivileged. Aristocracies had always defended their desert of power and privilege on grounds of either superior reason and reasonableness or superior moral inclination. Equalitarians, too, needed a general justification for their aspirations, a justification beyond the simple fact that life would be nicer for the common people in an equalitarian society. They, too, needed a justification defending no merely special interest but promising advantage to all society, all humanity, indeed all the future. So, radicals of the Enlightenment assigned to all a perfectibility of reason; radicals of the Romantic Movement assigned to all a perfection of spontaneous inclination. These assertions were necessary to the radicals of the eighteenth and early nineteenth centuries. But by the middle of the nineteenth century they had done their work. For the common man, at least, legal equality had been accomplished. Reiteration of belief in people's underlying homogeneous excellence became the work merely of the sentimental and those liberals whose investment is in the belief that legal equality is the final accomplishment, obviating all other radical antitheses of interest and all other fundamental meddling with the status quo. Eighteenth-century equalitarianism's success had other consequences that the radicals had not expected. Instead of initiating a society of fraternal cooperations, legal equality had initiated a society of equalitarian pursuit of private wealth (and private wealth is, after all, the real base of aristocratic privilege). Hence, by the middle of the nineteenth century, reiteration of the doctrines of eighteenth-century radicalisms became innocuous to established power, offering the aura of its merely remembered radicalism, a sheep in wolf's clothing, thereby an offense to the radical sensibility.

It is in this context that Poe's story "The Tell-Tale Heart" was written and has its thrust. To the once radical but now merely liberal faiths in universal reason and/or inclination, Poe tells the story of a marvelously lucid madman whose passionate inclination it was to murder an old friend because the man's eye was somehow hateful to him. The murderer defends himself against the accusation of madness by describing the wonderful care and restraint of the murder, dismembering, and concealment: the crime would have been perfect, the madman says, if the dead man's heart had not beaten so loudly that the police, merely pretending ignorance to torment the murderer, could not help discovering the hiding place of the dismembered corpse.

Even without reference to its innovational originality, "The Tell-Tale Heart" is an impressive story for its convincing image of a madman's consciousness—especially the awful mix of awareness and delusion.

> No doubt I now grew *very* pale;—but I talked more fluently, and with a heightened voice. Yet the sound [of the dead man's beating heart] increased—and what could I do? It was *a low, dull, quick sound—much such a sound as a watch makes when enveloped in cotton.* I gasped for breath—and yet the officers heard it not. I talked more quickly—more vehemently, but the noise steadily increased. I arose and argued about trifles, in a high key and with violent gesticulations, but the noise steadily increased. . . . I paced the floor to and fro with heavy strides, as if excited to fury by the observation of the men—but the noise steadily increased. O God! What *could* I do? I foamed—I raved—I swore!

But "The Tell-Tale Heart" is especially impressive, I think, for its contextual significance. In a time when intellectual life is organized by faiths in universal reason or universal conscience as the sure and easy means to spontaneous millennial progress, Poe initiates the American literature of the dark abysses of the mind from which rise the terrible impulses by which our lives are sometimes governed. We are quite used now to a dark psychology much more informed than Poe's.

We ought not therefore to lose a sense of how startling Poe's concerns were and how radically important to general ways of thinking about the world. Part of Poe's importance is that he began the American literary exploration of the darkness our sentimental political and anti-political philosophies had habitually ignored.

To be sure, let me say again, stories like "The Tell-Tale Heart" have no directly political substance. But what needs to be said is that political theory ought to know the complexities of human motivation that Poe's stories delineate: political theory that does not reckon with the factuality of such motivations simply has to be incommensurate with the actions it means to describe and organize. That needs to be said not because society must arrange for asylums or penitentiaries or hospitals for the aberrant, but because political theorists must reckon with the obscure motives that may organize large-scale social affairs and national contentions no less than they impel individual lives and disasters.

And what needs to be explained is that these stories of Poe's feel like political gestures. In so far as they carry rejection of the simplistic generalities of political theories or movements that do not face the complex conditionality of political phenomena, these stories *are* political gestures, gestures especially by which the nineteenth-century radical sensibility expresses both its passage beyond the certainties of eighteenth-century radicalism and its disdain for the evasions inherent in the equanimity of nineteenth-century liberalism.

Poe's stories of madness and mystery, of irrationality and obscure passions, are addressed to the conventional temper of his times—a temper epitomized in Emerson's saying "Undoubtedly we have no questions to ask which are unanswerable. We must trust the perfection of the creation so far, as to believe that whatever curiosity the order of things has awakened in our minds, the order of things can satisfy. . . . Let us interrogate the great apparition, that shines so peacefully around us."

And what Poe's stories say to that temper is that truth is often dark, often too complicated and too terrible to be clear, and that, as in the "Fall of the House of Usher," decay, madness, and evil have a history no less real and commanding than do sweetness and light.

I suppose the essential vitiating quality of nineteenth-century liberalism is its evasion of the realities of power. Perhaps because of its submissive identification with the powerful, the realities of power are what liberal ideology is at its greatest pains to deny. Power matters when there are antitheses or discontinuities of interest resolvable only by conquest. In the eighteenth century, denial of the essentiality, of the irreducibility, of such antitheses was an act by which one opposed aristocratic pretensions to a right to rule, a right to unchecked power over the many. In the nineteenth century, denial of such antitheses meant in effect complicity in the tyranny of those who had won power in privatism's equalitarian but still vicious competitions. In the nineteenth century, the function of liberalism's protestations that we are all brothers was to obscure the fact that many of us are Cains, and that some social systems and situations tend especially to empower this Cain in us and the Cains among us. Poe's stories dispel the base of righteousness around liberal equanimities by exploring the brutalities the equanimities obscure.

Of course Poe's stories can be and often have been taken most to heart by the radical sensibility that sees his evocations of the essentiality of evil as demanding (or defending) disaffiliation from *all* categories of action that have social progress as their object. With equal legitimacy, both political and anti-political radicals read Poe as their own. The compounding of our knowledge of the dark, of the disjointed complexities of cause our actions ignorantly serve—increasingly in the twentieth century this has made the simple social logic of benevolence seem absurdly irrelevant to our species' social possibilities. Though political radicals may see in Poe's work the manifestation of their own point of view, so may anti-political radicals, and by concentrating on the same things in the work. Poe's heroes, for example, are very easily seen to cut both ways.

The American fiction of anti-political radicalism can be said to have begun with Poe, and among the most enduring of Poe's innovations in that literature is the figure of the hero who stands not at the apex of some great human enterprise, not superlatively at the head of the battalions of virtue, but apart and alone, his excellence either anonymous or the object of public derision, distaste, and enmity.

The dwarf in the story "Hop-Frog" and Dupin in the detective stories are representative.

Hop-Frog is a dwarf, ugly in his resemblance to an ape. Trippetta is also a dwarf, but exquisitely beautiful and a dancer. She and Hop-Frog are slaves in the court of a vicious king, rare gifts to him from one of his conquering generals. They are a delight to the court, she for her delicate beauty, he for his value as wit to be laughed with and crippled dwarf to be laughed at. The story tells quickly of the king's pleasure in tormenting the two dwarfs: for example, "He knew that Hop-Frog was not fond of wine; for it excited him to madness; and madness is no comfortable feeling. But the king loved his practical jokes, and took pleasure in forcing Hop-Frog to drink and (as the king called it) 'to be merry.'" The rest of the story describes the dwarf's revenge, the grotesqueness of which (the king and his equally vicious counselors are burned alive) is, ironically, an invention of the wine madness to which the king has forced Hop-Frog, first by making him drink and then by striking Trippetta when she begs that Hop-Frog be let alone.

Dupin is, of course, the first of the long line of detective story heroes. He is also the archetype of Poe's all-knowing heroes whose brilliance makes their aloofness from all other people inevitable because the others simply cannot understand them. In "The Purloined Letter" we get the key to Dupin's brilliance and his necessary separation from most people. The Prefect of Police, public official, representative of society and representation of it, cannot solve the crime of the purloined letter because his attempts depend on tracing the course *he* would have followed if he were the criminal. Dupin solves the crime rather easily because he first finds out just what sort of a man the criminal is, and then by imagining himself such a man can follow the course such a man would have followed. The Prefect's ignorance, his commonality, is his inability to perceive heterogeneity, hence the necessity of seeing himself as the model of the world's order. The Prefect imagines his own point of view to be the world's because he cannot conceive another. Dupin's excellence is his own complexity and his awareness of it, hence his ability, indeed, his freedom, to perceive the world's complexity and the multifarious forms of particularity within it. G. B. Shaw said some place that we should not necessarily do unto others as we would have them do unto us: they may not like what we like. This axiom applies as much to one's relations with one's friends as it does to one's relations with one's enemies. It applies as much to politics as it does to more immediate kinds of personal relations. Poe's stories, like the axiom, commend the political theorist to define sharply the interests he must oppose and to define too the heterogeneous modes of life the society he proposes must somehow integrate.

Poe's appeal to anti-political radicals of pessimistic disaffiliation lies in his images of the hero as isolated by his excellence, living a life of solitary privacy because most people, the public, the society for which the Prefect stands, cannot understand the hero or the world. They cannot be the hero's equals; they cannot even understand him well enough to want him for a leader; he would not in any case want to lead them any place they are capable of wanting to go.

But the stories' implications for an anti-political radicalism do not exhaust them. Their delineation of the heterogeneity of the species as rudimentary fact and perception of that heterogeneity as the rudimentary quality of intelligence give the stories particular critical bite in the context of sentimental radical equalitarianism. These delineations also make the stories representative of and a contribution to the intellectual substance of the radical politics emergent in the middle of the nineteenth century—a radical politics that makes the perception and moral management of people's differences rather than the rhetoric of an idyllic universal concert the subject of its theory and the object of its actions.

Dupin and Hop-Frog and Trippetta together represent the emergent perception that excellence is not more the essence of all people than it is the essence of an established aristocracy, but that it is an oddity of nature, sometimes grotesque in its appearance, occurring where least expected, and responded to by most with the contempt of incomprehension.

The relation of this perception—that excellence is peculiar rather than representative—to radical equalitarianism and to the radicals' sense of the accomplishments they can expect from their reforms and the social system they would establish if they could: those issues are no less aggravatingly open today than they were in the mid-nineteenth century when Poe and the other intellectuals—but the writers especially—began to raise them.

Activism depends, of course, on the belief that things can get better. Radical activism depends on the belief that things can get better for everyone and in such a way as to facilitate a benevolently oriented individualism and excellence amongst people. Sentimental activism depends on the belief that things will absolutely get not only better but absolutely better. For the sentimental activist, progress to the less than perfect is not progress at all. Poe's delineations of the obscure, intransigent barbarisms of our nature and of the peculiarity of excellence debilitate the activism of only a sentimental radical. What Poe contributes to activist radical politics is grounds for consciousness of the realistic objects of political progress: a society that breaks the instruments of tyranny; that calms, rather than excites—by the forms of social relation it imposes—our predatory propensities; and perhaps most importantly, a society that facilitates the life and growth of the rare, random, peculiarity of excellence as much by eliminating the capricious constraints on it of poverty and the outrage of class hierarchies as by the positive opportunities of knowledge and self-consciousness it can offer.

CHAPTER FOUR

Nathaniel Hawthorne: The Politics of Compassion

When I speak, as I often have, of the legitimacy of delineating the political implications of a poem or story, I am arguing against those who denigrate such readings not primarily, I think, because they want to protect art's richness from reductionist simplifications, but primarily to protect themselves from the social dangers (and/or to save themselves the exertions) of finding specific actions for a generalized sensibility. Vague lyrics to love or art or doom as a rule endanger no one's power. It's only when we announce the socially specific terms of our allegiances that our enemies know who we are. A more or less secret feeling of superior sensibility is the only victory that most dare seek. Like the yachtsman who only sketches himself first a boat and then a glowing picture of the winner's cup.

When it comes to Hawthorne, though, I argue with myself. A book such as *The House of the Seven Gables* is so full of so large and complex and organismically continuous a sense of life that to point to a passage here and there that says something about the meaning of classes or the weight of history seems silly. The particular truths are so many, they illuminate so many categories of experience, that one cannot point to them all, yet it seems silly to do less. And the particulars, however true, cannot give a sense commensurate with the luxuriance of the whole. To talk about it at all, one must ignore too much.

Yet there are two subjects to which I will address myself here anyway: the enormously increased realism of the specific content of the radical sensibility in America in the middle of the nineteenth century and the sentimentality of much twentieth-century radicalism—a sentimentality that vitiates radical energy, that turns radicals away from rather than toward the possibilities of our times, and that makes defense of particular sentimental consolations the basis of gratuitous enmities amongst radicals. So I will simply extract from a few of Hawthorne's works a few particular insights that seem to me to have been of especial importance in extending radical political consciousness, and then go on to Melville and Whitman without further apology. With Melville and Whitman it will be easier: because Whitman devoted much of his poetry to a relatively few directly political propositions; because in *Billy Budd* Melville made a highly compacted summary of his own political anthropology and the relation of it to the major political orientations.

* * *

One of the constants from Jonathan Edwards to Ralph W. Emerson, indeed, one of the constants of all eighteenth- and early nineteenth-century American thought, is the assumption that history need not count, that what will be is not irrevocably bound by what has been, that the future need not continue nor contain the past. Edwards believed that God would come in a moment to put the love of benevolence at the center of every human heart, in a moment to wipe all evil from being. Benjamin Franklin believed that when governments had enough sense to let trade take its own course, the competition would make all tradesmen serve the public's interest, thereby making benevolent effects without benevolence as a cause, a future constantly discontinuous with its past. And Emerson says that when one devotes oneself to the slow historical accumulation of technological, scientific, and economic power, it is "as if a banished king should buy his territories inch by inch, instead of vaulting at once onto his throne" ("Nature"). But how do we vault at once onto the throne of our dominion over nature? Emerson's list of ways includes "religions and political revolutions" to be sure, but moves climactically to "prayer; eloquence; self-healing; and the wisdom of children"—all forces, if such they be, that propose to transcend lines of cause rather than to master them.

It is conventionally understood now that Nathaniel Hawthorne, unlike Edwards, Franklin, or Emerson, was preoccupied by "the weight of history." Students as a rule take that to mean no more than that Hawthorne felt guilty for the sins—the persecutions, the greed, the hypocrisy—of his Puritan forefathers. I do not see in him such a guilt. I sense no *self*-accusation in any of his works. Many of Hawthorne's works *define* his forefathers' sins, expose them. But by the exposés Hawthorne accuses his forefathers and those who are like them; he does not accuse himself. It is precisely the tone of accusation and the substance of his accusations that mark Hawthorne's freedom from his forefathers' natures and the sins inherent therein. Many, perhaps most, of Hawthorne's works are heavy with a sense of the burden of evil all of us inherit with the world we enter. But feelings of guilt are the burden of those who clutch to themselves the evil they disdain. The heaviness of Hawthorne's writing is in the sense of the world's encumbering evils of greed and indifference that he, Hawthorne, unequivocally abhors. Perhaps students accept the view that a sense of personal guilt is the center of Hawthorne's concern with history because that view lets them regard moments such as those when Hawthorne delineates, in his story "The Artist of the Beautiful," for example, "the very perversity of fate that makes human existence appear too absurd and contradictory to be the scene of one other hope or one other fear"—it lets them regard such moments as the data of a merely personal problem in clinical psychology, as merely an emanation of Hawthorne's life, rather than as an insight into theirs.*

---

* I don't mean here at all to denigrate inquiry into the psychological sources of an artist's art. I mean to denigrate only a particular conventional psychologically oriented misreading of Hawthorne.

But perhaps I do mean something more. It seems that at the present stage of psychological insight, we can explain satisfactorily the psycho-biographical ground of an artist's failures of wisdom or craft, but we can do very little to explain the causes of an artist's success—the good fortune that enables or compels one to transform one's misfortunes into vivid wisdom. We know better what turns us away from reality, coherence, compassion, than we know what turns us toward them and the talent to give them image. We are likely, it seems, to find similar rather than dissimilar phenomena in the pasts of those whose work directly extends our own understanding and of those whose work strikes us primarily as the effect of, and index to, the causes of incapacity. This means, of course, that we do not yet know where to look for the ground of the species' best possibilities. It means that for the present we must content ourselves with being grateful for them.

Hawthorne *was* preoccupied by the weight of history. The serious question is not, now, why he was thus preoccupied, but what was the concrete substance of that preoccupation. To say that history is a burden is to say that what has been dictates the terms of what is and will be, that getting what we want or being what we want to be is impeded somehow by the world time delivers to us. The question is, what are the particular forms of the forces of impediment? In Hawthorne's view they are class, social system, and fundamental antitheses amongst human natures. If the first two preoccupations seem trite to us now, it is not because we know of deeper problems, I suspect, but because we are tired of dealing with problems at once so simple, so flagrant, and so intractable. And they are intractable in part, I suspect, because of our ambivalence toward their solution; and certainly in part because of most people's unwillingness to risk the enmity or foreswear the approbation of the powerful who assume themselves to profit greatly by the status quo.

Hawthorne is of course aware of wealth and poverty as physical conditions, so to speak, as conditions relevant to our physical well-being and freedom. But what concerns him is poverty and wealth as psychological conditions, as conditions affecting one's sense of one's self, one's ability to perceive disjunctions of reality and appearance, of fact and conventional belief, one's ability to know one's desires and the internal and external resistances to their success.

The House of the Seven Gables has to do with two families, the Pyncheons and the Maules, both among the first European settlers in New England. The first American Pyncheon was a colonel and Puritan dignitary, the first Maule an "obscure carpenter." Colonel Pyncheon coveted Maule's little piece of land and got it finally by seeing to it that Maule should be "executed for the crime of witchcraft." The story of the subsequent lives of the two families, Hawthorne says,

> if adequately translated to the reader, would serve to illustrate how much of old material goes to make up the freshest novelty of human life.

> Hence, too, might be drawn a weighty lesson from the little-regarded truth, that the act of the passing generation is the germ which may and must produce good or evil fruit in a far distant time; that, together with the seed of the merely temporary crop, which mortals term expediency, they inevitably sow the acorns of a more enduring growth, which may darkly overshadow their posterity.

The novel devotes itself to the Pyncheons and Maules of two centuries later, the ways in which their lives are formed by the histories they have inherited.

The Maules inherited poverty, crept quietly "along the utmost verge of the opaque puddle of obscurity," and "if, at their own fireside, they transmitted, from father to child, any hostile recollection of the wizard's fate and their lost patrimony, it was never acted upon, nor openly expressed."

> Nor would it have been singular had they ceased to remember that the House of the Seven Gables was resting its heavy framework on a foundation that was rightfully their own. There is something so massive, stable, and almost irresistibly imposing in the exterior presentment of established rank and great possessions, that their very existence seems to give them a right to exist; at least, so excellent a counterfeit of right, that few poor and humble men have moral force enough to question it, even in their secret minds.

The issue is not a simple instance of greed, a simple crime for its sake, a question of ill-gotten gains and unfortunate victims. The evil at issue is that when there are rich and poor, both rich and poor tend to know not themselves or each other, but to know only the social forms they inhabit. The terrible thing is that we tend to *believe* our raiment, to feel that we *are* the characters our social histories have dressed us to play. The problem is less that we can't see ourselves as others see us than that we tend to see ourselves no other way. We tend to preen or cringe before our image in the eyes of others as if there alone we see justly what we are.

Perhaps we ought to stop here to say that for Hawthorne the preeminent good is—what shall we call it?—benevolence and creative self-awareness. Abstract phrases for the good are always dissatisfy-ing. They have been too much blunted by callous handling. And even were that not so, the good is to us what it is axiomatically; self-evidently. It is not to be argued. We can point to instances wherein it is embodied and hope that its radiance there will not be such to our eyes alone. But we can name it only in ways that will be abash-ingly bland to our friends and either silly or ugly to our enemies. In "Rappaccini's Daughter," Hawthorne calls it "the height and heroism of love." Hawthorne says—within the metaphors of this story—that in wanting the sympathy and affection of others we are vulnerable to them: because we need them they can hurt us: because they hurt us, we hate them. So, despairing of love, we seek the power by which we would be feared, the power that is at once our vengeance and our safety. Human inanity is in our repetition of the rest of nature's merely instinctual pursuits of private contentment, a pursuit in which others are to us only objects, things of indifference except in so far as they are instruments of pleasure or jeopardy. (Such in "Rappaccini's Daughter" is Giovanni, the callow student, or Baglioni, the professor for whom all others are merely the stepping stones of his reputation.) Humanity's beauty, for Hawthorne, is in the capacity for sympathy, that part of our nature that makes other lives' pleasure our pleasure, other lives' pain our pain. Human dignity is in our power not only to love harmony, not only to wish for harmony, but to know reality and the forces of dissonance and to *make* both the symbols and the circumstances of the harmony that at times it seems all nature con-spires to resist. Human beauty is in our capacity to find sympathy beautiful; human dignity is in those who can be not only the lovers of the beautiful, but beyond that the makers of the beautiful, the artists of it, those who by their intellect and their craft can, as Hawthorne says in the perhaps over-delicately allegorized figure in "The Artist of the Beautiful," undertake "to spiritualize machinery, and to combine with the new species of life and motion thus produced a beauty that should attain to the ideal which Nature has proposed to herself in all her creatures, but has never taken pains to realize."

But most people are neither beautiful nor dignified, however sympathy may find pathos in their misfortunes, their ignorances, in the history of impoverished aspirations that makes their frightened readiness to accept any self-constraining impress of identity or enmity their time may impose on them. Most are pathetic in their misfortunes, but in their success or their dreams of it, they are inane. Should "the artist of the beautiful" conceive that time itself should be made the subject of his art, that he could make each moment's "fall into the abyss of the past" toll less of the harsh dissonances of life "and more of harmony," he will be at best abandoned by most, "that steady and matter-of-fact class of people who hold the opinion that time is not to be trifled with, whether considered as the medium of advancement and prosperity in this world or preparation for the next." They will abandon him because he will seem at best an irrelevance to their aspirations. At best an irrelevance, at worst a menace to their sense of themselves: a menace from which they will fall back to the fortress of conviction that he is mad. "How universally efficacious—how satisfactory, too, and soothing to the injured sensibility of narrowness and dullness—is this easy method of accounting for whatever lies beyond the world's most ordinary scope!" The artist of the beautiful—the symbol of all whose beauty and dignity it is to try to empower sympathy—is either an irrelevance to most people's sensibility or an injury to it. He would make a world that forsakes the assurances they know for the sake of larger integrations that can only frighten most people with a sense of complexity but dimly perceived and therefore fraught with the danger and the humiliation of proven impotence. Perhaps their sensibility is injured especially by the sense of the scale of the artist's world and the dangerous scale of his proud assertiveness in refusing to believe that what is is right, his drive to make the world conform to his will rather than to humble his will for the sake of the certainties of custom. The scale of the great artist's perception and aspiration to mastery makes most people's world seem puny. They call him mad to get at once vengeance for the insult that his very existence trumpets and safety from the demands for the endangering labors of novel thought, novel sympathy, and novel change he would make on them.

They seek the art of complacency, the sentimental assurance of their centrality in a simple world. He injures their sensibility by delineat-ing an extent and complexity of reality beyond their habitual ken, an extent and complexity of aspirations beyond their habitual instruments of power or their capacity for moral identification. If the world he describes *is* real, then they will look foolish to themselves. So they call him mad: by which they say to themselves that he sees not reality but only phantoms.

The inane seek the artist's complicity in ignorance. The artist of the beautiful—whatever his craft—seeks theirs in the extension of know-ing harmony. Everyone's primal wish is for harmony, a universe that identifies with one's own inclinations. Despairing of sympathy; recoil-ing from most people's antipathy, some who have the artist's capacity of knowledge—Rappaccini, Chillingworth in *The Scarlet Letter*—become not artists of the beautiful but artists of revenge. Human inanity is to see others as things. Our beauty is to see others as persons whose feel-ings engage our own. Our dignity is in the capacity for knowledge that empowers sympathy and extends it. Our viciousness, inhering, as sym-pathy does, in the capacity for identification, is in our inclination to revenge, which is pleasure in another's pain—the primal wish for sym-pathy, the capacity for pleasure in another's pleasure, inverted by the thwarting of it. Villainy is in the turning of human power—of which knowledge is the essence—toward the objects of viciousness, toward the pleasures of revenge.

All this seems to me to be the subject of one of Hawthorne's subtlest passages. It comes at the end of "Rappaccini's Daughter." Rappaccini, by his mastery of the arts of medicine—it is his theory that both medicine and poison have the same chemical base—has given his daughter Beatrice the power to kill by her very breath. She sees in this gift of lethal power only her own "miserable doom." Rappaccini cannot understand it.

> "Miserable!" exclaimed Rappaccini. ". . . Misery, to be able to quell the mightiest with a breath? Misery, to be as terrible as thou art beautiful?"

That is Rappaccini's goal: to be at once terrible *and* beautiful, at once desired and feared. To be terrible to one's enemies is the object of mere common sense. It would mean safety and privacy from them. But Rappaccini doesn't want safety and privacy. To be beautiful is to be desired—in a sense to be loved. Rappaccini wants to be desired, but he wants those who love him to cringe in fear and despair of possessing what they love. The perfect—if ultimately pathetic—revenge for him, he who had sought love and gotten enmity, disdain, or indifference.

> "I would fain have been loved, not feared," murmured Beatrice, sinking down upon the ground.

To be truly loved requires that we be known. To be known is to be vulnerable—else knowledge were not power. The heroism of love is in daring to know and to be known and—should love fail—in refusing to make the knowledge on which love depends the instrument of revenge.

All this seems a long way round to talk about the moral significance of poverty and wealth, of social classes economically defined and graded. It has usually seemed enough for the radical to say that class hierarchies necessarily mean a lower or a lowest class, that the lowest class are the poor, and that poverty is an evil that needs no explication.

Yet the radical are likely to agree that one who *chooses* poverty either to take common cause with the poor or when professional integrity requires it—the radical are likely to agree that such a choice is morally grand, even heroic. From which it follows that though poverty is one of the concomitants of classes, there are worse. If one is heroic who chooses poverty for the sake of moral identification with the oppressed, then failures of sympathy are worse than poverty. If one is heroic who would be poor rather than disloyal to the integrity of one's work, then the self-denials of chosen ignorance and conformity to custom and the abandoning of the pursuit of mastery are worse than poverty.

Primitive poverty is an economic condition in which mere survival exhausts practically all of one's capacity for work and in which the scarcity of the stuff of sustenance makes the extension of sympathy amongst peoples a practical impossibility, indeed a danger to survival. But by the middle of the nineteenth century in America, that was no longer what poverty meant. Economic survival was no longer incompatible with the extension of sympathy nor with work of which the intrinsic objects go beyond mere rudimentary physical survival. Yet most people's moral consciousness was organized by a sense of themselves, of one another, and of the meaning of work that was far below the economic possibilities. The economic technology the society had created was capable of producing far more wealth than it did in fact produce. Eighteenth-century America preoccupied Benjamin Franklin by the ways in which economic systems and conditions constrained consciousness. Mid-nineteenth-century American life turned Hawthorne to see the ways in which consciousness, especially class consciousness, had come to constrain progress in economic systems and conditions. It is the weight of the history of class consciousness that Hawthorne delineates in *The House of the Seven Gables*.

If self-knowledge is an essential good (and self-knowledge means knowledge at once of one's particularity, one's likenesses, and of the forces on which one's desires and their fulfillment depend), then social classes and the weight of their impediments to self-consciousness are an evil. For the poor, the weight of a history of class consciousness means "the opaque puddle of obscurity," "the plodding uniformity of common life." Poverty grinds individuality to sameness, sodden and sullen, and class hides it behind façades of plodding uniformity, opaque, though "doubtless . . . the whole story of human existence may be latent in each of them. . . ." The façades of class distinction mask our individualities and our likenesses with such force that for most they become the reality itself; the face behind a mask so rigid and worn so long takes on at last the shape of the mask itself. What was but difference of economic condition becomes moral hierarchy. "There is something so massive, stable, and almost irresistibly imposing in the exterior presentment of established rank and great possessions, that their very existence seems to give them a right to exist; at least, so excellent a counterfeit of right, that few poor and humble men have moral force enough to question it, even in their secret minds."

When the poverty of the poor is imposed neither by nature nor by a primitive economic technology, when there is enough wealth to make poverty technologically unnecessary, when the number of the poor is so great as to imply the political power to end their poverty, then poverty is not so much an economic question as it is a sociopsychological one. What concerns Hawthorne in *The House of the Seven Gables* is the way in which classes add to the physical incapacitations of poverty a moral incapacitation: the tendency for poor people to see their misfortune not as the victimization of their class but as the just consequence of their own moral desert; their tendency to see gross discontinuities of wealth not as symbols and instruments of society's moral ugliness but as all-knowing nature's distribution of justice; not as the outrageous effect of an arbitrary inequality of condition, but as a morally necessary effect of an inherent inequality of character. The crime against the poor is not only their poverty, or, indeed, not so much their poverty, as it is their humiliation: it is the humiliation, after all, that keeps them from realizing the political power by which the poverty could be undone.*

_____

* It must be said that the poor are vulnerable to the crime of their humiliation in the degree to which they too aspire to no more than privatist economic success and, believing the myth of equal opportunity, will see in their poverty, therefore, only their private failure.

And class means the moral incapacitation of the rich no less than the moral incapacitation of the poor.

"The act of the passing generation," Hawthorne says, "is the germ which may and must produce good and evil fruit in a far distant time; that together with the seed of the merely temporary crop, which mortals term expediency, they inevitably sow the acorns of a more enduring growth, which may darkly overshadow their posterity."

The seed sown by the first Colonel Pyncheon was "the highest prosperity . . . , his race and future generations fixed on a stable basis, and with a stately roof to shelter them, for centuries to come. . . ." Two centuries later, there are three Pyncheons: Judge Pyncheon, Hepzibah, and Clifford. The judge has inherited the old colonel's wealth, his class position, and his character—the energies, the talents, and the sensibility of the predator. Hepzibah and Clifford have inherited neither the wealth nor the character: only class, a sense of themselves as defined by their history, a sense of themselves no less morally incapacitating, in Hawthorne's view, than a history of plebian anonymity. For the Pyncheons, the enduring, overshadowing, morally incapacitating growth is aristocracy, whether they have the judge's brutal character or Hepzibah and Clifford's pathetic ineffectuality.

The rudimentary good is, for Hawthorne, self-awareness.

> The Judge, beyond all question, was a man of eminent respectability. The church acknowledged it; the state acknowledged it. It was denied by nobody. . . . Nor (we must do him the further justice to say) did Judge Pyncheon himself, probably entertain many or very frequent doubts, that his enviable reputation accorded with his deserts. His conscience, therefore, usually considered the surest witness to a man's integrity—his conscience, unless it might be for the little space of five minutes in the twenty-four hours, or, now and then, some black day in the whole year's circle—his conscience bore an accordant testimony with the world's laudatory voice. . . .
>
> Men of strong minds, great force of character, and a hard texture of the sensibilities, are very capable of falling into mistakes of this kind. They are ordinary men to whom forms are of paramount importance. . . . They possess vast ability in grasping, and arranging,

and appropriating to themselves, the big, the heavy, solid unrealities, such as gold, landed estate, offices of trust and emolument, and public honors. With these materials, and with deeds of goodly aspect, done in the public eye, an individual of this class builds up, as it were, a tall and stately edifice, which in the view of other people, and ultimately in his own view, is no other than the man's character, or the man himself. . . .

. . . The snowy whiteness of his linen, the polish of his boots, the handsomeness of his gold-headed cane, the square and roomy fashion of his coat, and the fineness of the material, and, in general, the studied propriety of his dress and equipment . . . what room could possibly be found for darker traits in a portrait made of lineaments like these? This proper face is what he beheld in the looking glass. This admirably arranged life was what he was conscious of in the progress of every day. Then might not he claim to be its result and sum, and say to himself and the community, "Behold Judge Pyncheon there"?

. . . A hard, cold man, thus unfortunately situated, seldom or never looking inward, and resolutely taking his idea of himself from what purports to be his image as reflected in the mirror of public opinion, can scarcely arrive at true self-knowledge, except through loss of property and reputation. Sickness will not always help him do it; not always the death-hour!

"A hard, cold man, thus unfortunately situated . . . , can scarcely arrive at true self-knowledge. . . ." There is no irony in the "unfortunately situated." Judge Pyncheon's situation nurtures the worst in him. It nurtures his cruelty and his inanity by so honoring wealth that all acts and all people are but indifferences except as means to wealth. It nurtures his hollowness by teaching him to look for his own radiance in the deference of fools to the glint of his cane and the cut of his coat. It creates in him the need that there be poor and humble, else his wealth would be nothing to him and himself less.

But what would be a *fortunate* situation for such a man? "Loss of property and reputation," Hawthorne says, if self-knowledge is to be possible for him. But for such a hard, cold man is self-knowledge, then, such a boon? What well-being is there in the knowledge that one is hard and cold, in knowing that one is cruel and a petitioner for the deference of fools? The judge and his like, Hawthorne assumes, are

more complicated than on the surface they appear. By their investment in the façade of wealth and class, they foreswear something of
themselves, some desires or pattern of them the gratification of which
promises a more inclusive well-being, a more satisfying happiness.
The arbitrariness of class—the definition of people by things, hence
as things—cuts both ways. Like Beatrice in "Rappaccini's Daughter,"
the judge, too, in some corner of him, wants "to be loved, not feared."
The judge, too, would find greater pleasure in mutually knowing sympathies than in the impersonal dignity of the façades of wealth and
aristocracy. But unlike Beatrice, the judge is incapable of the "height
and heroism of love" and all it implies. That is his misfortune. That
is his vulnerability to the crime his society commits against him. It
plays at once on the cowardice in the weakness of his sense of himself,
the strength of his lust for respect, and the ease for him of cruelty and
indifference; it plays on all of these to elicit his passionate complicity
in the system that denies him his most inclusive well-being. Like a
magnet, the system draws to the surface the desires that make a man
a thing among things, leaving the desires of his humanity to wither
in the dark; murmuring up, perhaps, only "for the little space of five
minutes in the twenty-four hours, or, now and then, some black day
in the whole year's circle," the mournful or grating voice of guilt, the
sense of self-betrayal.

In the short run, it matters little, of course, whether the judge's lust
for a morally ugly eminence is a jot or two short of a perfect expression
of his character. In the short run, Judge Pyncheon is simply the enemy
of everything humane. Hawthorne gives but one sentence of the novel
to the seed or residue of the judge's humanity, one sentence of sympathy for the judge as victim of a social history that did everything to nurture his worst possibilities, practically nothing to nurture his best—the
more in need of nurture for their frailty. Indeed, when the judge dies,
choking on the black blood of his own predatory passion, Hawthorne
only gloats over the death:

And there we see a fly,—one of your common house-flies, such as are always buzzing on the window-pane,—which has smelt out Governor Pyncheon, and alights, now on his forehead, now on his chin, and now, Heaven help us! is creeping over the bridge of his nose, towards the would-be chief-magistrate's wide-open eyes! Canst thou not brush the fly away? Art thou too sluggish? Thou man, that hadst so many busy projects yesterday? Art thou too weak, that wast so powerful? Not brush away a fly? Nay, then, we give thee up!

But though in the short run the judge's whole significance is his enmity to and danger to the good as the radical sensibility conceives it, and though in the short run the only serious question about the judge is how to oppose him, how to wrest power from his hands; still, in the long run the germ or remnant of the radical sensibility in the judge himself—his capacity for pleasure in sympathy and self-awareness and their extension—in the long run that is an important question. If our species survives the sophistication of the technologies of war and environmental exploitation, the chances are good that the sophistication of the technology of sustenance will make such plenty that our lives will no longer be organized by economic competition; degrees of wealth and competence or luck in the competitive pursuit of wealth will have lost their meaning, their power to impose arbitrary—that is, depersonalized—humiliations and honors, their efficacy as instruments of will, their attractiveness as alternatives to self-awareness. Perhaps we will, then, simply define wealth differently—according to some other scarcity—and those such as Judge Pyncheon will seek and protect whatever it is that's scarce with the same predatory passion they now invest in money. But the question is: as society frees us from the lowest, the most depersonalizing, order of our fears, hence the lowest order of our aspirations, are there in those who now accommodate themselves so easily to that order some now-unsponsored inclinations that could become the basis of positive citizenship in a society of which individual and collective self-consciousness, mastery, and effective benevolence were the objects? Or are such as Judge Pyncheon forever the enemies of civilization as the radical sensibility defines it? To what degree must those of the radical sensibility prepare themselves for a perpetual enmity? To what degree must they prepare their society for some people's perpetual incapacity for civilization? To what degree is the work of the extension of individual and collective self-awareness, mastery, and benevolence incompatible with human happiness? To what degree is our inanity, or beauty, or dignity, or viciousness a mutable function of history, to what degree an immutable function of nature?*

---

* The depersonalization of primitive life—that is, the depersonalization by rudimentary insecurities—has two directions: depersonalization of the self and depersonalization of others. We tend to know ourselves by our unfulfilled desires, or, rather, by the needs the satisfaction of which is insecure. When our lives are dominated by insecurities of food and shelter, it is by the body's need for food and shelter that we know ourselves. It is in those needs that we are least individual.

We tend to know others by their relation to our unfulfilled desires. When our lives are dominated by insecurities of food and shelter, it is simply in others' depersonalized roles as cohorts or competitors in the pursuit of food and shelter that we know them.

There are two kinds of socialism: the socialism of scarcity and the socialism of plenty. The socialism of scarcity requires and imposes the homogenization, the depersonalization of human beings. In such a society, all people are necessarily rather homogenized by the necessarily universalized economic preoccupations. Differentiations are according only to rudimentary economic specializations and simple hierarchies of competence. The society's survival depends on a depersonalized (or an only rudimentarily personalizing) conformity to rudimentary economic roles.

It is in the socialism of plenty—the socialism of universal economic security and well-being—that people will be free of the necessary preoccupation with the relatively non-individuating economic needs and for the unfrightened inquiry into and expression of the individuality of their characters. And it is in the socialism of plenty that opportunities for community will depend less and less on the impersonal coincidence of economic work, condition, and interest; more and more on the sympathy generated by the discovery of coinciding individualities of aspiration and integrality.

Those who fear the increasing sophistication and integrated scale of economic action for their assumed threat to individuality are wrong, I think, because they mistakenly see industrialism's necessary socialization of labor according to our experience with the socialism of scarcity. That is the wrong model. Those who see the repressive anti-individualism of Russian and Chinese socialism as the figure of what American socialism would be and as the proof of socialism's fundamental incompatibility with the radical democratic sensibility, they, I think, are making the same error. Russia's and China's pre-industrial economies gave opportunity only for the socialism of scarcity. America's relative wealth and the ease with which that wealth could be enormously increased—that would make socialism here an altogether different matter, a matter for which we have not yet an historical model. For the radical sensibility, the theoretical model, however, bodes only good. Marx's error was not his prediction that the socialist revolution would mean unprecedented freedom, unprecedented liberation to discovery of individuality and individuating community; Marx's error was in predicting that the socialist revolution would come in the most industrialized rather than in the pre-industrialized society.

No one is more aware than Hawthorne is of the profound disparity in people's capacity for civilization. But unlike Jonathan Edwards, who saw that disparity as proof of the moral meaninglessness of history's social and political processes, Hawthorne sees that disparity as the very basis of the profound moral importance of social and political process. History counts *because* of most people's vulnerability to the attractions of ignorance, indifference, and viciousness. That is precisely why social and political processes must be directed to the attractions of knowledge, interdependence, and sympathy. It is only if we were invulnerable to the attractions of uncivilization that we could afford to be indifferent to the moral effects of particular social and political processes. It is because we are vulnerable to the attractions of uncivilization that history carries so heavy a burden to us and from us.

It is this view of the weight of history that Hawthorne concretizes in *The House of the Seven Gables* and *The Blithedale Romance*, the two novels in which he deals explicitly with political issues. It is precisely by our vulnerabilities to the attractions of ignorance, indifference, and viciousness that our class divisions and our economic system get their force and make their mark. Classes make mountainous impediments to our knowing ourselves; our economic system—private enterprise, privatism, capitalism, call it what you will—heightens nothing so much as it heightens the chances that we will know one another as objects only, and that what we will know of ourselves is our danger— hence our capacities for anger and indifference to others—in a world of impersonal objects insecurely contending for survival.

It is not America's economic system but its wealth that is the base of the relatively high degree of individualized freedom that we have. The economic system is, rather, the greatest constraint on the extension of individualized freedom. Not only because of the poverty, the extensive poverty, that is no longer technologically necessary, but because the economic system still imposes on us the definition of ourselves as economic animals primarily, defines excellence only according to competence in marketplace competitions, and defines others to us either as economic enemies and victims or according to inanely depersonalized divisions of economic class.

A little passage at the beginning of *Blithedale* gives, in Hawthorne's characteristic quietness of tone—his liking to find in the casually transient moment the most inclusive issues—his sense of the meaning of our economic system. In the midst of a February snowstorm, four young men have set out for Blithedale, the experimental socialist community. Full of the spirit of youthfully hopeful adventure, they ride "fleetly and merrily along. . . ."

> Sometimes, encountering a traveler, we shouted a friendly greeting; and he, unmuffling his ears to the bluster and the snow-spray, and listening eagerly, appeared to think our courtesy worth less than the trouble which it cost him. The churl! He understood the shrill whistle of the blast, but had no intelligence for our blithe tones of brotherhood.

There are two quite distinct ways in which an economic system organizes a society and the lives of its people: an economic system establishes the ways in which a society as a whole plans the use of its sustenantial resources, and an economic system establishes the ways in which individuals will understand themselves in their relations to others in the universal business of survival and well-being. When we think of "capitalism," it is usually when we are thinking about the whole society's way of allocating economic resources. When we think of "private enterprise," it is usually when we are thinking about economic relations amongst individuals. Capitalism means that the primary decisions about what will be produced and how—the primary planning of the society's economic life—will be made by those individuals who happen to have the money to buy labor, the place of work, and the necessary materials. Private enterprise means that the motive of an individual's participation in the economic system should be money-profit to oneself, and that one shall stand toward others as competitor for economic well-being.

Hawthorne does not deal with our economic system at the level at which it leaves decisions about what will be produced and how it will be produced to whoever it is that can get the capital to initiate production. He deals, rather, with the ways in which our privatism organizes the everyday lives of everyday individuals, the ways in which it teaches us to understand well "the shrill whistle of the blast," but dulls whatever intelligence we have for "the blithe tones of brotherhood." But the motives organizing both levels—the social and the individual—are the same: to talk of one is to talk of the other.

For Hawthorne the good is clear. It is, he says in *Blithedale*, to seek

> our profit by mutual aid, instead of wresting it by the strong hand
> from an enemy, or filching it craftily from those less shrewd than
> ourselves . . . , or winning it by selfish competition with a neighbor; in
> one or another of which fashions every son of woman both perpetuates
> and suffers his share of the common evil, whether he chooses it or no.

It is not that privatism knows no truths. It knows well the meaning of the wintry blast of poverty. It knows well the humiliation, the misery, the tyranny of poverty, and it knows well our vulnerability and our rapacity. But it knows these truths so well that it can hardly know another. It turns us so toward the truths of our insecurity that we have at last no intelligence for the truths of our fraternity.

We are not, as a species, the mere agents of privatism Jonathan Edwards describes us as being. Nor are we the simple conduits of a universal benevolence the Emersonians imagine. Our nature is complex, our characters focused by our histories, our circumstances, from many possibilities, many "essences" inherent in us. We see people's history in their character no less, and perhaps more, than we see their character in their history.

One of Hawthorne's most telling delineations of the weight of history, the ways in which our economic system gives weight to our malevolent rather than to our benevolent inclinations, is in *The House of the Seven Gables* in a little speech of Uncle Venner, a minor character in the novel. Hepzibah Pyncheon, spinster, her share of the Pyncheon fortune gone, is reduced at last to opening a store in one of the rooms of the now decayed Pyncheon mansion. Uncle Venner, the kindly old handyman of the neighborhood, comes in to see how things are going and sees that Hepzibah, her myopic's scowl intensified by anxiety and humiliation, needs advice.

> "Give no credit! . . . Never take paper-money! Look well to your change! Ring the silver on the four-pound weight! Shove back all English half-pence and base copper tokens, such as are plentiful about the town! . . ."
>
> And while Hepzibah was doing her utmost to digest the hard little pellets of his already uttered wisdom, he gave vent to his final, and what he declared to be his all-important advice, as follows:—
>
> "Put on a bright face for your customers, and smile pleasantly as you hand them what they ask for! A stale article, if you dip it in a good, warm, sunny smile, will go off better than a fresh one that you've scowled upon."

Like *The Blithedale Romance, The House of the Seven Gables* also has what we could call the classic speech declaring the morality of radical economics. When Holgrave, young radical and hero of the novel, sees Hepzibah's distress with her new store, her new equality, he exhorts her in the radical's now-traditional rhetoric.

> "I look upon this as one of the fortunate days of your life. It ends an epoch and begins one. Hitherto, the lifeblood has been gradually chilling in your veins as you sat aloof, within your circle of gentility, while the rest of the world was fighting out its battle with one kind of necessity or another. Henceforth, you will at least have the sense of healthy and natural effort for a purpose, and of lending your strength—be it great or small—to the united struggle of mankind. This is success,—all the success that anybody meets with."

Here Hawthorne characterizes the proud grandiloquence of youth, the sweeping gestures of the young intellectual; he also asserts his own view that aristocracy in its way deprives the aristocrat as well as the plebian; and he gives the radical sensibility's feeling for "the united struggle of mankind" as itself a radiant goal rather than merely the unfortunately necessary means to the pleasures of privacy.

But it is in Uncle Venner's speech that Hawthorne most tellingly characterizes privatism and its historical effects. First of all, Uncle Venner assumes himself and Hepzibah to be surrounded by cheats. Uncle Venner's world is a world of petty predators, of people seeking their petty advantage in another's disadvantage, another's petty defeat. The pellets of Uncle Venner's wisdom all imply the stance toward others that his experience has taught him to take—a perfectly impersonal distrust, suspicion, and watchfulness lest he be the victim of everybody else's equally impersonal and petty marketplace machinations. Most of us are so habituated to all this that we have hardly any sense of the moral misfortune in the style of life necessary on even the homey scale of Uncle Venner's socioeconomic relations. We are so used to it all and to fear of misfortunes far worse than short change or counterfeit pennies that we can hardly be aware of alternatives to an economic life of petty deceits, petty insecurities, and a constant, impersonal misanthropic suspiciousness. We are so immersed in insecurity for the lowest order of our well-being that Holgrave's lyric to "the united struggle of mankind" will seem callow ignorance and irrelevant bluster.

But more significant still is Uncle Venner's concluding piece of "all-important advice": "A stale article, if you dip it in a good, warm, sunny smile, will go off better than a fresh one that you've scowled upon." The crucial issue here is that Uncle Venner is a very kindly man. The issue is that economic privatism is not, or not only, a direct expression of our species' essentially predatory character. Uncle Venner has given Hepzibah good advice, kind advice, in her circumstances. The issue is that economic privatism tends to turn the good and kindly into predators, too. For them, too, a smile, the symbol of kindliness, must become the manipulated device of economic competition, the device, indeed, by which one can unload "a stale article" on the unwary. The point is that our economic system and circumstances are not so much the effect of our misanthropy as the cause of it, or of its preeminence. Our economic system and circumstances make an effective misanthropy the necessary means of our survival and of the survival of those we would befriend. We are not dealing here with the history that informs and is informed by Judge Pyncheon's lust for power and prominence. Judge Pyncheon's history has to do with the ways in which a particular socioeconomic system directs and expresses the lives of those whose inclinations and talents are for large-scaled predatory contests, for large-scaled power and the pursuit of it, those for whom dominance is a primary pleasure, its specific content and particular objects a matter of indifference. The crux of our socioeconomic system is that it makes economic dominance the object of Judge Pyncheon's life, and that it tends to make those with talents like his the most powerful in our society. But Uncle Venner's history has to do with those whose propensity is not to power but to kindness, not to dominance but to small-scaled harmonies of affectionate regard, those who take the impress of their time rather than make it, those who will be the subjects of a system rather than its willful agents. And what the system makes of Uncle Venner's propensity to kindness is another suspicious dissembler in a world of suspicious dissemblers. The means it gives him to protect himself and those who inhabit his anxiously circumscribed world of moral identification is the pathetic wisdom of the experienced victim of petty depredations who has learned that survival, even on the small scale of his minimal aspirations, depends on his being something of a predator, too.

Something of a predator, but not much of one, of course. The point is not that privatism turns Uncle Venner into a ravenous beast of prey. The little evil to which the weight of Uncle Venner's history directs him hardly signifies at all. But the great evil signifies a great deal. It is the ambience of suspicion in which our system makes us necessarily to live that keeps us from what are, simply, the nicer possibilities of our natures. It is not that privatism turns such as Uncle Venner toward the delights of greed. For Uncle Venner there probably are no such delights. It is that privatism turns such as Uncle Venner away from the coherent expression of their tendency to kindness and walls in rather than extends its reach. And it is the irony, the pathetic irony, in the fact that the very means our history puts into the hands of Uncle Venner's kindness are the tricks of sly suspicion and a petty chicanery, means that depend on depersonalizing all others for the sake of those few whom the accidents of neighborhood have led him to know as persons and thereby to befriend.

* * *

We must say, of course, that though Hawthorne adds to the specific content of the radical sensibility in American literature a careful attention to the moral debilitations inherent in privatism and class hierarchies—or, to put it in more general terms, adds social and economic systems and their historical effects as principal concrete categories of the literary delineation of reality and moral drama—and that though these became the central preoccupations of radical politics and the literature of radical politics, they are not what we might call the center of gravity in Hawthorne's sense of the weight of history. For Hawthorne the center of gravity is the travail inherent in all people's discordancies of inclination and the travail inherent in discordancies of character and inclination among us. We yearn to be at one with ourselves and one another and the world we inhabit, but we are not. Our selves and our world are populated with more forces than most can hope to master or bear to see; more, indeed, than most can see at all. And those few who can know much and whose inclination to know is undeflected by fear, and whose inclination to sympathy has not been deflected toward revenge—those few come especially to know the ugliness of the vengeful, the pathos of the passive victims, and the tragedy of the grand aspirations.

Aristocraticism has always defended itself by believing in moral homogeneity within classes, moral heterogeneity between classes.

American radicals before Hawthorne contended against aristocraticism by seeing homogeneous moral excellence throughout the species.
Hawthorne introduces into our literature of the radical sensibility not
only the sense of the randomness of excellence or madness that had
preoccupied Poe, but also the sympathetic delineation of the fundamental discontinuities of human inclination and perceptiveness that
are the very basis of our tyrannies, our pathetic passivities, and our
tragedies as human beings. If we were all like Judge Pyncheon, we
could be simply another species of competent and contented predator. If we were all like Uncle Venner or Hepzibah, it is easy to see us as
rather like the grazing species, making way now and again as we have
to for a predator that has singled out one of us, then returning to the
contentments of grazing and the herd. If we were all like Holgrave,
there's no telling what we would be like or could do as a species.

At least since Moses, the great question has been: how to make
sense of people's disparate capacities for civilization. Most thinkers
have tried especially to persuade themselves either that the discontinuities are only superficial and inconsequential and are somehow soon
to be obliterated, or that the discontinuities are people's own fault
and will be integrated into universal justice by the avenging agents of
God or Nature. Hawthorne's divergence from these views embodies,
I think, his most important contribution to the maturation of the
radical sensibility in America. His stance toward the distress inherent
in our complexity as a species and as individuals informs the essential
tone of all his work. No particular passage gives the feeling of the
whole, but what Hawthorne says about Clifford Pyncheon, in *The
House of the Seven Gables*, makes the essential position clear.

Clifford is the sort of man whose highest pleasure is in what are conventionally called beautiful things, things of delicate construction, pleas-
antly harmonious sound, color, and smoothness, things conventionally of
a sweet, sentimental prettiness. He is not a maker of such things, but
a lover of them, able to endure nothing of their opposites, though

easily made happy if surrounded by things of the kind he loves. But Clifford, too socially ineffectual to prove his own innocence, had been twenty years in jail for the murder actually committed by Judge Pyncheon. Though it would seem that Clifford's sensibility would be least able to survive life in prison, still, when released and again in the presence of the beautiful, though muddled in mind and crabbed in body, the simple happiness of which he was capable would flicker up again in him.

> That gray hair, and those furrows,—with their record of infinite sorrow so deeply written across his brow, and so compressed, as with futile effort to crowd in all the tale, that the whole inscription was made illegible,—these, for the moment, vanished. An eye, at once tender and acute, might behold in the man some shadow of what he was meant to be. Anon, as age came stealing, like a sad twilight, back over his figure, you would have felt tempted to hold an argument with Destiny, and affirm, that either this being should not have been made mortal, or mortal existence should have been tempered to his qualities.

The crux of this passage, it seems to me, is that Hawthorne's sense of Clifford's incompatibility with the world he must live in—the necessary discontinuity between the conditions of his happiness and the conditions of his life—this perception impels Hawthorne to argue with Destiny. We all see the random multiplicity of human natures, the miserable thwarting of one necessary to the well-being of another. It impels some of us to construct delusive logics of justice: either retrospective justice, as if beings chose to be born and bred as they are and therefore somehow deserve whatever they get; or prospective justice, as if every local failure were the necessary means of some larger and inevitable coherence (in either case to evade immediate reality by giving moral weight only to past or future). Some are impelled to sentimental faiths that every misfortune is simply a mistake, to be rectified forever when we uncover the unanimous compatibility underlying beings' superficial, merely misguided enmities. Most manage one way or another to evade the injustice of reality by faith in some Destiny, some universal power, that will accomplish the harmony that we want enough at least to pretend to ourselves that we'll get it. Of those who do see plainly the impossibility of justice when the law of our natures requires that the cost of some inclinations' success must be other inclinations' failure—many who do see this are not led thereby to an argument with Destiny, but only to a plaintive or somber remorse, a remorse of which the essence, perhaps, is the feeling that if we can't trust Destiny to guarantee our dreams, we can't believe in anything at all.

The crux of Hawthorne's passage is first of all the sympathy, the benevolence, that is the foundation of the sense of injustice. Second is the pride, the self-assent, that is turned by perception of injustice to argument with Destiny, an argument with the forces of being, rather than to brute competition for the spoils of injustice or to the at once presumptuous and humiliated alternatives of sentimental faith or exhausting remorse—presumptuous with the sense that our wishes must be Destiny's preoccupation, humiliated with the sense that if they are not, we are impotent. To argue with Destiny is to know that one's wishes are particular only, and not universal; it is also to be proud with the feeling that one can contend forcefully for one's wishes amongst the forces that oppose them.

Thirdly: crucial to Hawthorne's stance is the reach of intellect, the power of perception, to see alternatives, to see that what is could be otherwise, that Clifford could have been different or that "mortal existence" could be "tempered to his qualities." Without the intellect for perception and construction of alternatives, of new logics of existence, there is no choice but resignation to what we have.

Fourth, it is crucial that Hawthorne's argument with Destiny proceeds not only to reject, not only to dissent from the circumstances, the forms of life amidst which he finds himself: Hawthorne's argument proceeds also to "affirm," to assert his own will to "temper" "mortal existence," his intention to impose his own will upon Destiny rather than merely to judge Destiny or to endure it.

Let me try to put now in a unified proposition the crucial qualities joined to make the central impulse of Hawthorne's radicalism. They are: benevolence empowered by pride and reason to construct circumstances in which people's diverse and often frail capacities for benevolence, pride, and reason will be nourished rather than thwarted, and in which people will be saved in so far as they can be from malice, humiliation, and ignorance, their own and one another's.

But this gives neither the specific political content of Hawthorne's radicalism nor the tone—practically constant in his works—established by his sense of the tragedies inevitable for his ideals in the long processes of history. The specific political content is, I think, easily to be assigned: it is the socialism of Holgrave, in *The House of the Seven Gables*, and of Miles Coverdale, in *The Blithedale Romance*.

The tone is in the recognition that though the future may have less of injustice than the past, though benevolence, pride, and reason may be more and more empowered than constrained, still, the world can never be theirs alone. The tragedies inherent in our capacities for malice, indifference, and ignorance are as inevitable as each toll of suffering they take is final, leaving the miserable and the maimed and the murdered no less miserable or maimed or dead for the fact that our own trivialities or rapacities of will are the source of our undoing, or for the fact that one day our capacities for virtue will have better luck. It is this double sense—the simultaneous sense of hopefulness for our best possibilities and melancholy for the strength and consequence of our worst—that makes Hawthorne smile at Holgrave's youthfully untroubled enthusiasm.

> Man's own youth is the world's youth; at least he feels as if it were, and imagines that the earth's granite substance is something not yet hardened, and which he can mould into whatever shape he likes. So it was with Holgrave. He could talk sagely about the world's old age,

but never actually believed what he said; he was a young man still, and therefore looked upon the world—that gray-bearded and wrinkled profligate, decrepit, without being venerable—as a tender stripling, capable of being improved into all that it ought to be, but scarcely yet had shown the remotest promise of becoming. He had that sense, or inward prophecy,—which a young man had better never have been born than not to have, and a mature man had better die at once than utterly to relinquish,—that we are not doomed to creep on forever in the old bad way, but that, this very now, there are the harbingers abroad of a golden era, to be accomplished in his own lifetime. It seemed to Holgrave—as doubtless it has seemed to the hopeful of every century since the epoch of Adam's grandchildren—that in this age, more than ever before, the moss-grown and rotten past is to be torn down, and lifeless institutions to be thrust out of the way, and their dead corpses buried, and everything to begin anew.

As to the main point,—may we never live to doubt it!—as to the better centuries that are coming, the artist was surely right. His error lay in supposing that this age, more than any past or future one, is destined to see the tattered garments of Antiquity exchanged for a new suit, instead of gradually renewing themselves by patchwork; in applying his own little life-span as the measure of an interminable achievement; and, more than all, in fancying that it mattered anything to the great end in view whether he himself should contend for it or against it. Yet it was well for him to think so. This enthusiasm, infusing itself through the calmness of his character, and thus taking an aspect of settled thought and wisdom, would serve to keep his youth pure, and make his aspirations high. And when, with the years settling down more weightily upon him, his early faith should be modified by inevitable experience, it would be with no harsh and sudden revolution of his sentiments. He would still have faith in man's brightening destiny, and perhaps love him all the better, as he should recognize this helplessness in his own behalf; and the haughty faith, with which he began life, would be well bartered for a far humbler one, at its close. . . .

It is this sense of the weight of history that is, it seems to me, Hawthorne's most important contribution to the radical sensibility. It is a failure to accomplish this sense of history that so often turns the aspirations of youthfully exuberant radicalism into the bitter vengefulness or numbed despair of disillusioned age.

Hawthorne's story "Young Goodman Brown" is about the failure of a man who cannot bear the fact that even the most decorous and tender of human beings can have red-eyed lusts in their souls. When Goodman Brown comes to know that there are moments when sin is everyone's heart's desire, he does not see that therein lies the glory of virtue; to Brown it means only that all virtue must be a lie. The ground of Brown's embittered pessimism, Hawthorne says, was the wish to believe that the simple purity of his wife Faith's desires would be sign and guarantee of the world's moral order, the medium of his own redemption, the parentally overarching coherence that would make his own adventures in abandonment to the lusts of the "Devil's communion" inconsequential and innocuous to his future or the world's. " 'Well, she's a blessed angel on earth,' " Brown says, as he sets off for the rituals of the forest: " 'and after this one night I'll cling to her skirts and follow her to heaven.' " Brown has to believe in the absolute and simple purity of Faith—and the purity also of all the dignitaries of the town—so that in his dependence on their purity he can be free from the need to contend with the complexity of his own desires. When Faith asks him to stay with her, not to keep him from his infidelities but to help her dispel "dreams and thoughts" of her own, Brown can only hear an implied accusation against himself. When he sees not only Faith but all the dignitaries of church and state at the Devil's communion, when he sees that all contend with antitheses of desire no less dangerously mixed than his own, that no source outside our confusion of inclinations will free us from the consequences of an impulsive license: when he sees all this, Brown can only turn toward an all-denying misanthropic gloom.

"Young Goodman Brown" seems to me to be among the profoundest of Hawthorne's psychological allegories. It suggests that those who deny the species' complexity or their own (to see discordancies of desire in others but not in oneself is only the obverse of Brown's evasion) may do so not only to support sentimental certainty for the future, but also to rationalize impulsive license in the present.

Hawthorne is always about the fact of moral vulnerability, the fact that life is hard, happiness difficult to get or maintain, that all beings are in constant jeopardy. Part of the meaning of the fact that life is hard is the fact that there are fundamentally vicious human desires, for instance the lusts described in "Young Goodman Brown," or Judge Pyncheon's greed, in *The House of the Seven Gables*. Life is a chaos of weaknesses and graspings and failures and of unresolved fragments of accidental beauty; most people turn toward revenge or cruelty or isolation or ignorance or brute power to protect themselves against the jeopardy of their lives; some few heroes undertake by the power of their sympathy and love and art to establish the order of which nature is otherwise incapable.

Hawthorne reintroduces into American literature the Edwardsian sense of the fundamentalness of moral disorder, of jeopardy for everything, of the fragmentariness of beauty or happiness in the complex randomness of nature's pushings. But Hawthorne goes beyond Edwards by his acceptance of life at once without bitterness and without sentimental faith in some sudden necessary universal moral unification, some divine redemption from the complexity of our nature, the complexity of which tawdriness is a part. Edwards confronts the fact of disparity in people's capacities for love and art, but tries to rationalize its tragedies with the doctrine of grace (the doctrine that God is somehow right so unequally to have dispensed virtue). Hawthorne simply accepts the fact, the tragic fact, of the disparity, makes it and the insecurity of all people's contentment the basis not of retribution but of compassion and of commitment to the art by which people make at least symbols of a world better than was given to them. If the world is to be better, we must make it so. But we may fail to make it better. Between the symbol and the social transformation lies the ground of tragedy, which is the disparity between great intentions and actual possibilities, the tragedy inherent in the fact that life, that all action, is consequential, hence evil is, hence all the wisdom and virtue that history has generated must contend with and perhaps be overcome by the forces the past's evil impels from each moment into its future. If our view of life is not informed by the sense of tragedy, by the sense that beautiful resolutions may not be among being's possibilities, by the sense that our natures and our situations may have in them finally destructive incompatibilities, killing our best dreams by no fault but being's nature; if instead we imagine the perfections of moral unity to be inevitable once we who are its instruments have exorcised those nefarious impediments to the design, then we are likely to have an arrogance that will at first warrant brutality to others, and then be brutal to ourselves when, as they must, our certainties turn to ashes in our mouths. Unfortunately, the world is such that the ways of virtue require heroism. Heroism is the wisdom to be uncertain and the courage to risk tragedy. Action from certainty only is pomposity: inaction because there is uncertainty, that is pathos. Sympathy, without which radical politics is morally meaningless, is perhaps first of all the recognition of our mutual vulnerability. Such, in *Blithedale Romance*, for example, we may, I think, properly call Hawthorne's first proposition in political theory.

There are two kinds of tragedy: the classic tragedy proceeding from the great man's crucial flaw, and the tragedy that proceeds from the incompatibility of great desires and the world in which they must but cannot be fulfilled. Terror before virtue's grueling defeats at one another's hands and nature's, that is at the heart of Hawthorne's works.

Until the middle of the nineteenth century, no American literature or politics reckoned with the tragic possibilities inherent in the complexity of human nature: all assumed a destined moral perfection. But the tragic is inherent because, as the history of religions seems to prove, it is part of human nature to crave universal moral unity— universal harmony—yet each person's life is a dissonance of desires, between people there are irreconcilable differences as to what moral beauty is; and being is such that life must prey on life; and life is real— by which I mean that a tree grown crooked will not be straightened by wishes, that an arrow launched is not turned from its mark by a change of the marksman's heart, that a person or a society is reformed by force and changing circumstances, not by regrets or the knowledge that we should have done differently; that if viciousness has bred poverty, and poverty viciousness, it will not be spontaneously undone by the discovery that poverty breeds viciousness, for viciousness will find its object.

But if life must have tragedy in it, that does not mean that it cannot have progress. The foundations of one are indeed the foundations of the other. The dissonances, the complexities of human desires make it possible that people should find gratification in those situations that tend to elicit kindness; the human craving for harmony makes it likely. Our species' power to extend our dominion over nature, our extraordinary power not only to survive but to luxuriate, reduces the necessity of enmity and extends the possibilities of harmony. The disparities in the ranges of harmony that people hear mean not only that the greatest, like the least, must suffer the failure of their wishes; it means also that as evil has its force, so do the heroic whose work is to inform human actions by the images of extended moral continuity, and to make those situations that substantiate those images.

This is not all that Hawthorne gave us to embolden us for life's work, but it is a lot of it. And I am grateful to him for it.

CHAPTER FIVE

Herman Melville: The Politics of Pride

I

The wish for respect is such for many that the particular ground of respect is an irrelevance. Many will do whatever promises respect from whoever or whatever seems more powerful. Not many prescribe the grounds of the respect they seek. Though we all want to be respected, to be thought worthy of affectionate regard, to be thought attractive, few are free enough of the fear of humiliation to see respectability in anything but security within established hierarchies of power; few have so firm a view of the particular qualities they themselves admire that they will seek respect for no other.

There are few discussions in which the accomplishment of truth is not an expendable object if it is thought to endanger approbational regard from whatever is thought to be the locus of power. Discussions are often either ritual reiterations of the respectable or contests for respectability—games, in which winning is the appearance of greater power, no matter for what, and in which winning is all. As with discussions, so with relations between individuals, groups, peoples, nations.

It often seems that what distinguishes those of the radical sensibility is the seriousness with which they take the particular grounds of respect, the particular qualities of character and accomplishment for which they seek respect. We know that those of a radical sensibility characteristically endanger their entrance into a conventional respectability, characteristically devote themselves to works and manners unlikely to get them conventional approbation. It is silly to say that they have not the talents for conventional power, conventional success (as it would be silly to say that Socrates had to teach radical moral philosophy because he couldn't succeed as a teacher of conventional rhetoric). It often seems that what distinguishes those of the radical sensibility is pride, a self-respect, a self-assertiveness, that precedes the search for community and dictates the terms of community that will be sought.

There are, of course, many kinds of individuality, many styles of inclination, that get asserted despite their social unconventionality. Some individual assertiveness is mere rebelliousness: the wish to take power from those who have it, but no particular wishes about the specific uses of power. In political discourse, however, what we call the radical sensibility distinguishes those who make people's rightful pride in themselves a political principle, a cardinal political object. The political radicals assert that the creation of the conditions that will facilitate prideful individuality is properly society's primary work. And against those who say that prideful individuality would mean social chaos, political radicalism asserts that the social sponsoring of prideful individuality is the very ground of social harmony: a) because we are such that conditions of respect for us heighten our capacity for respect for others and benevolence toward them; and b) because our capacity for benevolence toward others and for mastery that serves that benevolence is at once the characteristic that makes us worthy of respect and the characteristic that makes society organized to express and extend benevolence and mastery not only compatible with our individuality, but the necessary condition of our most inclusive well-being.

What distinguishes the political radicalism emergent around the middle of the nineteenth century is perception of the relativity and historical conditionality of all moralities and their sociopolitical substantiation. The difference between Hawthorne's belief in the sociohistorical conditionality of the benevolent impulse in human nature and Jonathan Edwards' belief in its unconditionality is a fundamental difference, suggestive of the profound differences that character, time, and place can make in the specific content of the radical sensibility and the thrust of its actions. I say this to emphasize the distinction between that which is continuous in the radical sensibility and that which isn't. And I say this to emphasize the view that once the radical sensibility comes to accept the conditionality of its aspirations, its great work is to uncover more and more of the terms of conditionality, the particular conditions of expansive benevolence and mastery amongst people. It is the specificity of knowledge that defines the particular greatness of the great writers of the mid-nineteenth century in America.

And I say all this by way of introduction to the discussion of Herman Melville's contributions to the radical sensibility. First of all, because what we might call the politics of pride was for Melville a constant preoccupation. Secondly, because his inquiry into both the acceptance of conditionality and the substance of conditionality was formidable and innovative. Thirdly, because the particular distinguishing impulse of Melville's radicalism seems to me a fundamental one.

The defining constant in the history of the radical sensibility is its ideal. Developmental change in the radical sensibility has been in radicals' understanding of the place of their ideal amidst the forces of being, and hence, in their understanding of the ways to act for the sake of their ideals. That change tends to proceed generationally, in so far as shared situation tends to establish common preoccupations, a constancy at least of subject in the specific content of a generation's politics. But even when the radicals of a generation are joined by their ideals and by the specific content of their politics, there are still differences, of style, perhaps we should call it, that are fundamental—not divisive, necessarily, but fundamental.

Early in *Moby Dick*, Ishmael speaks of the pain for him that he must tell the collapse of Starbuck's bravery under the power of Ahab's will:

> That immaculate manliness we feel within ourselves, so far within us, that it remains intact though all the outer character seem gone; bleeds with keenest anguish at the undraped spectacle of a valor-ruined man. Nor can piety itself, at such a shameful sight, completely stifle her upbraidings against the permitting stars. But this august dignity I treat of, is not the dignity of kings and robes, but that abounding dignity which has no robed investiture. Thou shalt see it shining in the arm that wields a pick or drives a spike; that democratic dignity which,

> on all hands, radiates without end from God; Himself! The great God absolute! The centre and circumference of all democracy! His omnipresence, our divine equality!

The theological terms are equivocal: the terms of the radical political sensibility are not. They are the terms by which Melville announces his identity within the whole history of that sensibility.

Lest we misconstrue the religious terminology, lest we forget that it is not some transcendent divinity but "that immaculate manliness" that is its subject, lest we forget that it is under "the permitting stars" that man's immaculate manliness must bleed and be abased, lest we think that man's misfortune is but his failure to grasp connection with a redeeming universal purpose, Ishmael tells of his own revery in the soft pantheistic sky at the whaleship's masthead.

> Lulled . . . by the blending cadences of waves with thoughts . . . , at last he loses his identity; takes the mystic ocean at his feet for the visible image of that blue, bottomless soul, pervading mankind and nature. . . .
>
> There is no life in thee, now, except that rocking life imparted by a gentle rolling ship; by her, borrowed from the sea; by the sea, from the inscrutable Tides of God. But while this sleep, this dream is on ye, move your foot or hand an inch; slip your hold at all; and your identity comes back in horror. Over Descartian vortices you hover. And perhaps, at mid-day, in the fairest weather, with one half-throttled shriek you drop through that transparent air into the summer sea, no more to rise for ever. Heed it well, ye Pantheists.

No, our fancies of universal unity, humanity under a loving sky above a loving sea—such dreams are our species' own affair, matters dependent on our powers, such as they be, alone. Human identity includes the dream of unity. It includes also our vulnerability to the sea's identity, which is not least its power to drown, or to gravity's identity, which is not least its power to dash us, dreams and all, from the perch where dreams are made.

So saying, Melville announces the defining accomplishment of his generation's greatest radicals. Assimilating the truth of human particularity, they could turn with unsentimentalized concentration to see the realities on which human dignity depends. Knowing the precariousness of our perch, they could seek for our best hopes something besides dreams to hang on to.

But if in this passage Melville announces a defining insight of his generation's radicals, he does it in a tone more particularizing still. Ishmael is lulled into a dream that the world's all one in love and peace. That is, after all, a lovely dream. Not the least noble of us have dreamed it. That it's only a dream could be put as the essence of our misfortune. The more so that, like Ishmael, dreaming it may kill us. Such truth could leave a bitter enmity in the soul. But from his misfortune Ishmael wrests not only a truth but a joke. At the moment of recognition of the truth, Ishmael laughs. To laugh is sign and substance of one's pleasure. By his joke he wrests a pleasure from his misfortune. Of course, he can afford to: it was recognition of the truth that saved him. I suppose it is in part pride in the power to be saved by truth that is the source of his pleasure. But we might also say that it is his capacity for this pleasure that is the source of his pride. It is this convoluted relation of pride and pleasure that seems to me to be at issue in the particular style of Melville's radicalism.

The human dream of universal love and peace makes humankind radical amongst nature's beings and nature's ways. If most people had no such wish, there would be no ground for guilt—by which we manifest our confusion of inclination; no ground for hypocrisy—by which we hide it; no ground for sentimentality—by which we let our wishes expurgate all facts that belie unity. But most are guilty, hypocritical, and sentimental. Which is why any thinker's close attention to the facts of life is felt as radical, no matter what the thinker's politics. Any close attention to the facts of life is felt by most people to be exposé: it will illuminate some form of their betrayal of the radical dream.

Benevolence has two directions: it loves pleasure; it hates pain. Betrayal has two directions: it impedes pleasure; it makes pain. The particular forms—the concrete, historically specific terms—of one's society's betrayals establish the terms of a radical's attack. An unusual fidelity to the radical dream is the essence of radicalism, but it seems that that too may be concentrated in two directions: a radical defense of prideful pleasure, or a radical attack on the forces of pain and humiliation. An essential difference in the thrusts—or better, the centers of gravity—of Hawthorne's and Melville's radicalism seems to be here. It is the victimizing of pitiful Clifford Pyncheon, demented by his misery, that impels Hawthorne to his "argument with Destiny." Hawthorne is made radical by his compassion for human suffering—our lonely, humiliated, weak resistance to the forces of our degradation. Melville's argument with destiny—his "upbraidings against the permitting stars"—is impelled by the sight of a "valor-ruined man." It is for the sake of man's "august dignity," for "that immaculate manliness we feel within ourselves," that Melville is made radical. The radicalism of Hawthorne's art is in the image of Clifford Pyncheon—"that gray hair, and those furrows,—with their record of infinite sorrow so deeply written across his brow, and so compressed, as with futile effort to crowd in all the tale, that the whole inscription was made illegible. . . ." The radicalism of Hawthorne's art is that it would soften us toward one another with the perception of our mutual vulnerability. The radicalism of Melville's art is that it would harden us to do battle for the sake of our dignity and the community of those who could share it, against whatever force—person or system— that would demean our wills, our immaculate manliness, our right, what Ishmael calls "our divine equality." Hawthorne's radical pride is in his compassion for the suffering and in his refusal to accommodate established power by denigrating compassion. Melville's radical pride is in his capacity for pleasure and in his refusal to accommodate established power by denigrating pleasure.

A persistent radicalism requires an unusual self-respect. Hawthorne respects himself for his capacity for compassion, hence becomes partisan of the radical politics of compassion. Melville respects himself for his capacity for pleasure, hence becomes partisan of the radical politics of pleasure.

That essential tone or thrust of Melville's radicalism is beautifully evoked in "The Grand Armada" chapter of *Moby Dick*. The whalemen have been dragged by a harpooned whale into a huge "lake" made by vast herds of thrashing whales ranged in a circle three miles across to protect within the young and the mothers with nursing infants. The sailors gaze into the tranquil depths at the center. Ishmael says:

> Some of the subtlest secrets of the sea seemed divulged to us in this enchanted pond. We saw young Leviathan amours in the deep.
> And thus, though surrounded by circle upon circle of consternations and affrights, did these inscrutable creatures at the centre freely and fearlessly indulge in all peaceful concernments; yes, serenely reveled in dalliance and delight. But even so, amid the tornadoed Atlantic of my being, do I myself still forever centrally disport in mute calm; and while ponderous planets of unwaning woe revolve round me, deep down and deep inland there I still bathe me in eternal mildness of joy.

Melville is made radical by his joy and his pride in it. It is in the dalliance of young leviathans that Ishmael sees himself. The scale of the leviathan and his delights is the symbol of the "immaculate manliness," the "august dignity," that Ishmael feels "centrally . . . , deep down and deep inland . . . ," that is to say, essentially, in himself.

But why must this be radical?

Those who wield social power usually use their power to defend privilege, to defend, that is to say, extraordinary opportunities for pleasure of one kind or another. Among the devices for defense of privilege is the denigration of the desert of pleasure in those who are not privileged. Traditionally, establishments use such instruments of public opinion as press and pulpit to depress the commonality's aspirations by generating the view that some inherent meanness of lower-class character makes their unprivilege both individually just and socially necessary, since the pleasures of the mean could only be mean, destructive pleasures.

And sometimes establishments of privilege must add to their denigration of the commonality the general denigration of pleasure itself—they must add the view that all people are too mean to enjoy anything but vice, and that power and privilege are not pleasures, but onerous duties that depend on somber virtues of self-denial. Probably when the privileged classes are least secure, they are moved to keep their pleasures secret, lest in broadcasting and thereby honoring them, they further excite the unprivileged with a sense of what they are missing. Melville's prideful lyric to the sanctity of his essential desires—to the essential joy of which he is capable—is radical first of all because he identifies with the commonality, and in so far as the commonality feels its equalitarian desert of delight—in so far as it honors its own pleasures—it will refuse humble submission to a system dedicated to the inequalitarian distribution of privilege. And in so far as establishments defend privilege by the pretense that power is not pleasure but self-denying, onerous duty, Melville's lyric honoring delight will be radical in a second sense: if delight is beautiful, then self-denial isn't, those who preach it as a virtue are at best pitifully deluded, certainly not the proper bearers of power; and a system devoted to self-denial and the power of those who are virtuosos of self-denial—such a system even if honest is awful. But of course we know that aristocratic pretensions of self-denial are generally a fraud, a public screen for private gratifications. What such pretensions tend to mean, in fact, is a simple segregation of public and private moralities, designed at once to quiet the masses and, in so far as the privileged believe in the virtue of self-denial and in privilege as reward for that virtue, to quiet their sense of guilt, and to protect their guilty pleasures from the glare of publicity. Melville's public lyric to pride and delight, and thus to the synthesis of public and private moralities, is radical at once for its refusal to see justice in the humiliation of the commonality, for its refusal to see virtue in self-denial, and hence for its assertion that when the privileged practice the self-denial they preach they are wrong and deserve no privilege, and when they do not practice the self-denial they preach, their pretensions to desert of privilege are fraudulent even on their own terms.

To honor sexuality as Melville does in honoring the dalliance of the leviathans is to assign fundamental dignity to the impulse that privileged and unprivileged are understood to share. In so far as the privileged do share the sexual impulse and in so far as they imagine desert of privilege to inhere in unsexuality, their privilege will seem to them an arbitrary advantage rather than just reward for a fundamental difference of character. It is in part, I suspect, to preserve the sense of particularity—hence of particular desert—that gentility commits itself to decorum—that is, de-emphasis of fundamental human impulses—in general, and to anti-sexuality and the compulsive secrecy about sexuality in particular. The price of decorum and the pretense of unsexuality is, of course, guilt; guilt at once for one's sexuality and for the injustice of one's social privilege, since class difference corresponds to no fundamental difference of nature. The price is willingly paid, as a rule. It seems less to pay than abandonment of social privilege: and though guilty sexuality may be less gratifying than prideful sexuality, it is a great deal better than no sexuality at all. The sense of guilt made inevitable by the pretense of unsexuality and the view that the pretended unsexuality warrants privilege—that guilt becomes itself in fact a positive value, a bargain price for the preservation of antithetical pleasures, a positive good compared to such alternatives as abandonment of any fragment of gratification in a world in which few have been given reason to believe that happiness is compatible with truth, that our fundamental desires are honorable, hence deserve synthesizing gratification rather than the veil of secrecy and incoherence. And besides, if only sin is universal, then guilt is the sign of such virtue as we can have, the positive sign of desert of privilege that anti-sexuality was trying to rationalize in the first place.

But we must account also for the ironic fact that Melville's lyric to delight will seem darkly radical not only to those of established power whose privilege it endangers; it will seem just as dangerously unsettling to the commonality for whose sake Melville means to speak.

For one thing, when the commonality, the unprivileged, publicize their desert of delight, they waken the wrath of the powerful whose pleasures of privilege a demanding commonality would endanger. Extraordinary demands from the unprivileged are likely to mean no more than extraordinary repressions by the privileged. Commonality means social anonymity; which is to say, individual invisibility, which means safety from the focus of some extraordinary repression on oneself. Further, the radical's prideful publication of demands brings not only the danger of extraordinary repressions, it endangers the pleasures that the commonality has accustomed itself to eke out of the status quo in secrecy and by secrecy. Like the aristocracy, the commonality accommodates itself to the pubic denigration of pleasure by keeping pleasure private, secret, furtive.

And in so far as the commonality finds pleasure in the approbation of the powerful, the desires Melville honors will be the source not of their pride but of their guilt, and to publicize them will seem to be betrayal of themselves. And still further, because there are degrees of unprivilege and hierarchies among the unprivileged, and because the desire Melville honors is a universal one, implying thereby an equalitarian desert of honor and well-being, he endangers that self-regard amongst the unprivileged that depends on there being someone more unprivileged still.

Melville's radical pride is inherent in his refusal of accommodation to established power. Inherent in that refusal is the public honor he feels appropriate for his fundamental desires, hence for himself. Obviously there is also in that pride some kind of confidence or optimism, some sense that he has or is in league with a power adequate to the accomplishment of his desires. It seems that this confidence or optimism, this sense of power, is a psychological precondition of radical assertiveness rather than the consequence of a rational appraisal of the radical's prospects of success. I take this to be the meaning of the fact that when rational prospects are not good, radicals are likely either quite irrationally to populate the heavens or Nature or history with fantasied forces that are in fact no more than symbolic projections of the feeling of power; either that or they are likely quite arationally to persist in their radical assertiveness under the more or less conscious feeling that the persistence itself is success, hence proof of adequate power. Radicalism is generated by confidence that the most inclusive demands can be satisfied. When it appears that they cannot be, radicals either construct metaphysical fantasies to guarantee them anyway, or they relocate satisfaction, finding success not in accomplishment of what had been the specific *objects* of the radical desire, but in the persistence of the radical desire itself despite the external victory of the forces opposed to it. It is in transition from fantasy of external unities to confidence in internal unity that is at issue in the scene of Ishmael at the masthead. Fundamental to Ishmael's competence for that transition is the pride he has in his own delights, the pride expressed by his identification with the dalliance of the leviathans. He is distinguished by the fact that "deep down and deep inland" he assents to himself whether or not the world assents to him, and he finds in self-assent enough delight to prove he has the power to warrant the pride of self-assent that impelled him in the first place.

II

It is conventional to suppose now—and I see no reason to disagree with the convention—that those whose sense of themselves is unusually independent of the world's judgment are so because the microcosmic world of their infancies pronounced (in the complex forms of that pronouncement) them worthy. It is not that our sense of ourselves is not conditional, but that the relevant conditions are those of infancy and childhood, and that their effect is practically irrevocable. The degree of homogeneity in early conditioning is the degree to which its effect in pride or humiliation is irrevocable.*

---

* The degree to which the conditioning forces were heterogeneous or confused—and their effect, hence, revocable—is the degree of the potential effectiveness of politics (the business of which is to establish conditions that will do the most possible to moralize human nature). Since most people have been raised in confusions of affection and denigration, since most are neither irrevocably angry nor abject, radical politics can hope to create conditions that will tend to resolve most people's confusion toward the correlated pleasures of pride and sympathy, benevolence and mastery.

But certain desires, the givens of our human nature, and sexual desires not least among them, persist, whether in pride or humiliation. Because they are fundamental, we assign them the same dignity or lack of it we assign to ourselves. Because they are fundamental, we assign to ourselves the same dignity or lack of it we have been taught—in infancy, where such lessons are learned—to assign to our fundamental desires. And because they are fundamental, they must be served somehow, one way or another, in any case. For most people that means secrecy, a wall of pretense. Sexuality safe on one side of the wall, guilty and dark, but not less active on that account. On the other side: the rich find safety for the pleasures of their fraudulently rationalized privilege; the poor find safety for the petty dignity in identifying with the rich, safety for the anonymity by which they are protected against the focused enmity of established power, and also, perhaps, safety from an anxious sense of impotence before the intractable forces of being. For both rich and poor, the same motive, but with objectives specified by differences of condition.

That a radical honoring of sexuality, a radical realism in aesthetics—realism meaning here commitment to the extension of the realities with which art may deal—and radical politics tend historically to go together, that coincidence is a function of no superficial connection between the three movements.

To their audience the radicalism of the radicals inheres in their insistence on the publication of their desires and their insistence on the synthesis of public and private moralities. In publicly honoring their private desires, they assert the moral legitimacy of their happiness and the moral illegitimacy of the society that either does not make human happiness its business or is incompetent to accomplish that happiness. Because sexual joy is everyone's heart's desire, making it the symbolic base of the demand for happiness makes the demand not only individual but by implication equalitarian and therefore necessarily anti-conservative, since social reality makes conservatism always, in fact, a defense of the inequalitarian distribution of honor and well-being. Since everyone knows that sexual joy is everyone's heart's desire, and since most people are heavily invested in dissembling or repressing that knowledge—to protect their sense of themselves from the censure of the morality they've been taught, to protect their own sexuality from sociopsychological prohibitions, and/or to protect the pretense of unsexuality by which they rationalize social privilege—the radicals' prideful publication of their sexuality and the pride in truth-telling inherent in that publication, these together will strike most people not as they are for the radical—a prideful assertion of confidence in truth and the expansive happiness of coherence in private and public moralities; these together will strike most people as ominously full of the terrible dangers of truth and as a menace to the fragments of gratification that only inconsistency protected by willful ignorance can nourish.

The particular style of Melville's radicalism inheres in the particular relation for him of pride, pleasure, and the continuities of human experience that make inequalitarian societies an ugliness and an absurdity. He puts it sometimes in the august rhetoric of "The Grand Armada," sometimes in a kind of bantering plainness, as in the "Loomings" chapter at the very beginning of *Moby Dick*.

Ishmael is describing the rigors of his transition from country school-master, where even "the tallest boys stood in awe" of him, to simple sailor, where in obedience to orders he must jump "like a grasshopper in a May meadow." But, he says,

> What of it, if some old hunks of a sea-captain orders me to get a broom and sweep down the decks? What does that indignity amount to, weighed, I mean, in the scales of the New Testament? . . . Who ain't a slave? Tell me that. Well, then, however the old sea-captains may order me about—however they may thump and punch me about, I have the satisfaction of knowing that it is all right; that everybody else is one way or another served in much the same way—either in a physical or a metaphysical point of view, that is; and so the universal thump is passed round, and all hands should rub each other's shoulder blades, and be content.

The invulnerability of Ishmael's self-respect makes possible the easy humor with which he takes his social abasement. It makes possible the nice double-edged rhetorical device of his proud identification with a point of view so lofty—divine, indeed—that under its eye social gradations appear too small to measure, making us, Ishmael, and captains, and all, quite equally humble. And it all makes so easy a truth that crude, colloquial language and a baldly repetitive syntax will quite do for the occasion, especially as they add suggestion of the ease with lower-class status, hence freedom from the presumptuousness that might go with such prideful metaphysical or social identifications.

Again, the crux seems to be in the mutually supportive relations of pride, power, and pleasure. Prideful self-esteem gives Ishmael the freedom from belief in social gradations, the power to see the mean meaning of such social gradations, the pleasure at once in self-esteem and in the power to make the joke of turning upside down the forces attempting his humiliation, which power itself reinforces the self-esteem that made the power possible. A crucial fact is that the stylistic resolution of the problems the passage deals with is a joking tone, a tone that finds humor, that is, amusement, that is, pleasure, in the meaning of the whole affair. And perhaps most important—for our purposes here, anyway—is that the stylistic resolution comes to its climax in the substantial proposition that the way for all hands to deal with the universal thump is to "rub each other's shoulder blades, and be content." The resolution of our humble and pummeled place in the universe is in the pleasures of affectionate comradery.

That implies, of course, the root impulse of radical politics: radical, since if we *were* turned by mutual misfortune to the pleasures of sympathy and the actions of compassion, if we did make compassion the first principle of social order, the social changes we would be impelled to would be radical indeed. The interesting question here, though, is the relation between self-esteem such as Ishmael's and the radical's response to human travail in the universe. If we esteem ourselves, then we will see no justice in our travail, no dignity in the forces that would demean us. We will see dignity, rather, in the comradery of those who, like ourselves, are victims, too.

But if we are without self-esteem, without an *a priori* sense of the dignity of our desires and therefore a sense of our desert of well-being, the forces administering the universal thump or a local one will seem to us the forces of justice; the community of travail will seem to us the community of dishonor. Our impulse will be not to revile the forces of distress, but to placate them. Our impulse toward those pummeled as we are will not be to make fraternal cause with them, not to rub each other's shoulder blades, but to see dishonor in their travail as in our own, and to do anything we can to dissociate ourselves from them: by reviling the reviled, by imitating and emulating the powerful, lest any peculiarity in our manners, beliefs, desires, professions—whatever—differentiating us from the look of those in established power, will confuse us with the many and prove our indignity, our desert of distress. If, indeed, we can accomplish the power to thump rather than be thumped, that will not only give credibility to the disguise of our indignity; it will give us to hear the ring of justice in the thump we administer, since those who get thumped are proved thereby to share the meanness we know, fear, disguise, but take to be fundamental in ourselves.

The thump is universal. Among the things that distinguish us one from another is the way we respond to it. Most, seeing that the thump though universal is not uniformly severe (as, for example, death, the ultimate impoverishment, though inevitable, can be delayed), seek their salvation in predatory acquisition of such instruments of power, such fragments of seclusive pleasure, as there are; they seek their salvation—perhaps no more than a palliative for apprehension—in avowing allegiance with whatever force proves its power and the attractiveness inherent in its relative safety by giving more blows than it receives. To obscure their dangerous identity with the world's victims, they pursue identification with its conquerors. Melville, however, identifies always with the victims and, especially, with the rebels against those who don't identify with the victims.

I suppose that everybody's anthropology is projective. We assume human nature to be fundamentally what we feel to be fundamental in ourselves. Most are raised to regard themselves as bad by nature, virtuous only under compulsion. Hence most see in the universal thump both proof of, and just reward for, our universal evil; and they spend their lives in anxious imitation of some model of self-denial. With some, however, as with Hawthorne, for example, the universal thump, the inevitable frustration of our wishes, becomes impulse to a universal compassion. Hawthorne's work is more than anything else a lyric to compassion, an evocation of the beauty of compassion, designed to free the capacity for it in his audience, to make it principle and object of our social life. The ideal politics Hawthorne sees as embodying this impulse he has Holgrave call the politics of "the united struggle of mankind." Our capacity for compassion can make of our misfortunes—our need to struggle—the opportunity for our consummate dignity.

And some, like Ishmael, see as fundamental to themselves an immense and immaculate capacity for delight. It is this, I think, that impels Melville to make rebellion against any force denying the right to delight the constant subject of his writing, from *Typee*, his first book, to *Billy Budd*, his last. Indeed, if one's self-esteem is such that happiness is the explicit principle of one's morality, and one's identification with humankind is such that one's species' happiness is a condition of one's own, and if, as it seems, extraordinary privilege has characteristically, though more or less secretly, been the object of persons and systems in established power, then for such as Melville the impulse to rebellion and preoccupation with the possibilities of rebellion are practically inevitable.

But it is also true that Melville describes only rebellions that fail. It is conventional to read Melville as arguing thereby that rebellion is pointless. I suspect such readings are made with a sigh of relief: "Thank heavens. The great writer's wisdom, his illumination of the moral ambiguities and the futilities of rebellion, these show the necessity not of rebellion but of accommodation to established power. Resignation, at the least." In any case—whether or not such readings gratify some readers' perhaps anxious wish to rationalize conservatism—it seems to me clear that Melville's preoccupation with rebellions that fail expresses no rejection of rebellion, no sense of virtue in submission or accommodation. It expresses rather a great rebel's need to know why others' rebellions have failed and to know what he can expect of his own. "Humanity," Melville says in the little story "Norfolk Isle and the Chola Widow," "Humanity, thou strong thing, I worship thee, not in the laurelled victor, but in this vanquished one." Melville says this of Hunilla, a woman who will make no jot of obeisance to mere power, though it take from her all that she loves. In her Melville sees "Pride's height in vain abased to proneness on the rack; nature's pride subduing nature's torture." We are distinguished one from another not by our mortality: that is universal. We are distinguished, rather, by what we live for. The world is such that if one lives for an inclusive benevolence, one will be vanquished. But to have lived thus is to live a life Melville finds worthy to be worshiped. To live thus is hardly to acquiesce to established power. To worship such a life is hardly to honor acquiescence. Our dignity resides not in our victories, but in our cause. Though all whom the Chola Widow loves are killed, though she and they are victims of indifferent power in man and sea, she does not feel herself betrayed by love. She does not turn to see in love the source of her undoing, thence to seek in mere power her safety or her revenge upon love itself. Thus in the Chola Widow, this vanquished one, Melville sees "Pride's height in vain abased to proneness on the rack; nature's pride subduing nature's torture." Love's persistence is its victory. We are torn between the love of love and our antagonism for all those who should have loved us but did not. Indeed, when we cannot draw from the world the love we crave, we despise ourselves as the cause of our misery. The wish for love, the love of it, may be primal; hate may be only secondary, a response to the failure of love. The human infant's utter dependence on parental affection, on the parental motive to feed, warm, support; this certainly suggests the primacy of the need of love, hence the love of it. But we are such, the world is such, that hate will have its cause; it will be brought to life, with its full power forever to generate its kind. Life is so hospitable to hate and humiliation that the very existence of rebellion for the sake of love is love's victory, no less for what it causes than for what it manifests.

Mid-nineteenth-century American life confronted the radical sensibility with the blasting of the millennial expectations by which a hundred years of radical life had been organized. Radicals of Melville's generation could no longer imagine themselves the partisans of the world's essential power and intention. They could not believe themselves to be the heirs of universal meaning. They had to find their own way, and that way likely to be peculiar, evidently, since those radicals who assumed themselves to be models of all nature's intentions turned out to be among the most thwarted by its processes, the most reviled by their societies. The new generation had to see that their dignity, their integrity, lay in loyalty to their own voices, not in loyalty to the universe's voice—for the universe has none. But the young radicals of mid-nineteenth-century America had to define themselves anew not only within and against nature and the universe: they had to define themselves anew both within and against the radical traditions, the traditions of sentimental radical aspiration and expectation, as it happens, in a culture extraordinary in mid-nineteenth-century life for the degree to which it assumed itself destined to be the foremost edge of progress, no matter what it did, and in which, therefore, radical aspirations and expectation were particularly likely to flourish. The young radicals had, for example, to define themselves against the tradition of radical romanticism, which, in its image of the nobility of the primitive, finds focus for its faith in spontaneous primal passion as escape from the degraded and degrading complications of human history.

Hence Melville's *Typee*. Galled beyond endurance by his life as sailor on an American whaleship, by the degradation of "arbitrary and violent authority," "the inhumane neglect of the sick," "the scanty allowance of provisions," the company of "dastardly and mean-spirited wretches, divided among themselves, and only united in enduring without resistance the unmitigated tyranny of the captain"—subjugated thus, the young rebel jumps ship to try the paradisiacal attractions of Polynesian life. At first the ease of a world warm in assent to unself-conscious sensuosity, at first it *is* delight. But primitive life turns out to be no less a tyranny, no less a constraint, than the ship's. The young rebel discovers that for him self-consciousness, individuation, expansive mastery, are pleasures as urgent as any, no less necessary to him than an unashamed sexuality. He discovers that primitive life, with its conventionalized mix of affection and aggression, both shallowly impersonal, its taboos as numerous as they are morally meaningless, like civilization's manners multiplied to constrain practically every minute of life, is no less organized than civilization is by the use of people as things, and that is, after all, the essence of immorality. To escape sophisticated society's use of him as a thing, the young rebel goes back to primitive life. But there he finds people to be not simply proud hedonists: the Typees are cannibals, secretly, furtively, guiltily, but they are cannibals. Which is to say that primitive life is not contrary to the use of people as things: at its core is the ultimate form of that use. Return to primitive life is not resolution of the battle for the sake of human dignity, but abandonment of it, and the young radical must go back to contend for self-consciousness and self-respect and the integrity of his kind, in the civilized world, the only world that knows these ideals at all, even though the familiarity so often breeds contempt.

The young radicals had to define themselves not only against the tradition of radical romanticism and its now obviously fantastic fantasies about the primitive, they had to define themselves also against the mainstream radicalism committed to faith in the moralizing power of entrepreneurial freedom, the tradition archetypified by Benjamin Franklin and embodied in the American Revolution. Hence Melville's story "Benito Cereno." The story has to do with the rebellion of the slaves on a Spanish ship. They have taken over the ship—the *San Dominick*—and demand that it be sailed to Senegal and their freedom. Until the end of the story everything is seen through the eyes of Amasa Delano, captain of an American merchant ship. He is a hearty, prosperous, orderly man, slow to doubt but quick to act when he knows what needs to be done. It is his view of what needs to be done that damns him. He has been accidentally involved with the slave ship and the rebellion on it when in response to her ragged condition he boards her to offer provisions and help in repairs. By extraordinary artifice, the slaves, fearing Delano's intervention against them, make it appear that they are but docile slaves, though they govern the ship. Delano delights in what they make appear to be their mindless animal contentments, their obsequiousness, their pleasure in servitude, their affectionate attendance on their betters. Delano's anxiety over ambiguities in the *San Dominick*'s situation is resolved by the image of the blacks' solicitude and their subservience. When at last, the repairs completed, Delano is leaving for his own ship, Benito Cereno, captain of the *San Dominick*, leaps into Delano's boat to escape his captors. Babo, leader of the slaves' rebellion, leaps after him to kill him. Quickly enough now, Delano realizes the black's intentions, overpowers him, regains his own ship, and, by promising his own men handsome reward in gold, sends them to retake the slave ship.

At the beginning of the story, we see the *San Dominick*'s intricately carved stern-pieces "uppermost and central of which was a dark satyr in a mask, holding his foot on the prostrate neck of a writhing figure, likewise masked." Both the stern-piece and the figurehead are mysterious. The figurehead is wrapped in canvas and under it is roughly scrawled, "Follow your leader." The whole story deals mysteriously with the mystery for Delano: who is leader and who led? Who is who behind the masks of prostrate and conqueror? At the story's climax, in the instant of the mystery's unfolding, we see Delano dash Babo, the blacks' leader, to the bottom of the boat, where with his foot he "ground the prostrate negro." It is Delano, merchant and captain, his liberal entrepreneurial freedom the object and accomplishment of the American Revolution, who is the dark, masked, conquering satyr of the stern-piece. When the Old World contention between master and slave comes clearly to crisis, there is no moment's doubt as to Delano's allegiance. And under the canvas-covered figurehead is the same revelation. The figurehead of the *San Dominick* had been a carving of Christopher Columbus. The rebellious slaves had replaced that figure with the skeleton of the slave trader who had owned them and the ship. It was he who had become the meaning of the New World's discovery. To describe the physical failure of the slaves' rebellion was to describe the moral failure of America's.

And the young radical of mid-nineteenth-century America had to define himself against those whose response to the brutalities of life is to foreswear all purpose, to disengage himself from the brutal and the futile by disengaging himself from everything. Hence "Bartleby." Bartleby is a young man reported to have worked in the Dead Letter Office at Washington, sorting the dead letters for the flames.

> For by the cart-load they are annually burned. Sometimes from out the folded paper the pale clerk takes a ring—the finger it was meant for, perhaps, molders in the grave; a bank note sent in swiftest charity—he whom it would relieve, nor eats nor hungers any more; pardon for those who died despairing; hope for those who died unhoping; good tidings for those who died stifled by unrelieved calamities. On errands of life, these letters speed to death.

Responding to these or other residues of blighted life, to life's absurdly redundant indifference to our best intentions, Bartleby undertakes willfully to expunge intentions from his life. First he gets a job

131

as a copier of legal documents. Not only is what he copies inane in its purposes: what he copies is no purpose of his own. With zealous indifference he must copy every intention, every "will" and every "deed" that is put before him. But even that is not adequately abstracted of life; even that is too close to the necessary doom of positive preference. With austere pathos he must "prefer not to" do even that. Ejected at last from the law office in which he had worked, he goes no farther than the building's corridor: there he sits silently on the banister. He is asked what he is doing: " 'Sitting upon the banister,' he mildly replied." At last for him this moment's act is without connection in time or intention to past or future. At last he is on no "errands of life." His only purpose is to be purposeless. But the society won't have it: Bartleby is taken off to jail as a vagrant. Then for the first time we see Bartleby angry. Perhaps it is in part the social humiliation of the jail, perhaps it's that there his purposelessness is imposed, not chosen. The only choice left to him is the choice not to live at all. He refuses to eat and at last lies down quietly to die. "Ah, Bartleby! Ah, humanity!" This death is pathos, but pathos only. Having foresworn all errands of life, he has merely added another victim to the toll: his rebellion is merely a submission. There is dignity in it: he would not be an agent of malice. His symbolic refusals even engage the sympathy of some left cold by less bizarre remorse. He elicits care, and that is something in a world that does not care much. Indeed, the care he elicits is antithesis to the truths impelling Bartleby to his austere despair. But that confusion Bartleby will not, cannot, see. When he is led off to jail, he, the constable, and a party of some lookers-on must pass "through all the noise, and heat, and joy of the roaring thoroughfares at noon." It is Bartleby's high dignity that he knows to his heart's core the truths of others' hopelessness: only kindness will be mortified by perception of another's pain. But it is not only the pain that is too much for Bartleby: life is too much for him, too. Lonely death is not the all and only truth of life. There is the "noise, and heat, and joy of the roaring thoroughfare at noon." Bartleby passes through it, but he cannot see it. Therefore his kindness that could be antithesis to death becomes instead but one more passive victim. And at last we must turn away from him.

> So true it is, and so terrible, too, that up to a certain point the thought or sight of misery enlists our best affections; but in certain special cases, beyond that point it does not. They err who would assert that invariably this is owing to the inherent selfishness of the human heart. It rather proceeds from a certain hopelessness of remedying excessive and organic ill. To a sensitive being, pity is not seldom pain, and when at last it is perceived that such pity cannot lead to effectual succor, common sense bids the soul be rid of it.

So Bartleby with life. But so too, we with Bartleby. Some errands of life do accomplish life. It is to them that we must turn. Because Bartleby cannot, we must turn away from him.

As had Ishmael to turn from Ahab. The radicals of mid-nineteenth-century America had to define themselves against those whose rebellious enmity to malice is absorbed in the bitter madness of a lust for revenge. In part because the radiance of ideals newly formulated heightens our tendency to misconstrue their power for us as their power for all, and in part because of our traditional incapacity to face as fact the discontinuity between our power and our wishes, and in part because America's freedom from an encumbering past heightened a revolutionary hopefulness, American radicals felt themselves to be the recipients and agents of a benevolent universal will. Ahab's heroism is in his seeing the world's ubiquitous cruelties. His greatness is the formidability of his will. But Ahab is mad; and his madness is in his need to believe that the world is organized by a malign will. His is the sin of pride not in that he dares to oppose God as if they were equals, but in his belief that his pain must be the object of a willful divine malignity. Better enmity than anonymity. Divine enmity is closer to divine love: at least it saves us the dignity of an especial place before nature's eye. If God is not capable of love, at least we are worthy of God's animosity. Better that than the abandonment on the vast sea that drives Pip, the cabin boy, mad. Better that than Ishmael's knowledge of the bottomless white abyss, the world without purpose or order beyond each life's travail to survive.

Ahab's ship, the *Pequod*, is just moving away from another to which it had sailed close to get word of Moby Dick:

> At that moment the wakes were fairly crossed, and instantly, then, in accordance with their singular ways, shoals of small harmless fish, that for some days before had been placidly swimming by our side, darted away with what seemed shuddering fins, and ranged them-selves fore and aft with the stranger's flanks. Though in the course of his continual voyagings Ahab must often before have noticed a similar sight, yet, to any monomaniac man, the veriest trifles capriciously carry meanings.
>
> "Swim away from me, do ye?" murmured Ahab, gazing over into the water.

The antipathetic fallacy. No microcosm is too small, no macro-cosm too large, but Ahab's madness will transform it into symbols that save him, as all religions do, from the sense of humanity's mere self-dependency in the world. From the small harmless fish to Moby Dick, all must be transformed from fact into fantasy.

> "All visible objects, man, [Ahab says in the novel's most quoted pas-sage] are but pasteboard masks. But in each event—in the living act, the undoubted deed—there, some unknown but still reasoning thing puts forth the moldings of its features from behind the unreasoning mask. If man will strike, strike through the mask! How can the pris-oner reach outside except by thrusting through the wall? To me, the white whale is that wall, shoved near to me. Sometimes I think there's naught beyond. But 'tis enough. He tasks me; he heaps me; I see in him outrageous strength, with an inscrutable malice sinewing it. That inscrutable thing is what I hate; and be the white whale agent, or be the white whale principal, I will wreak that hate upon him. Talk not to me of blasphemy, man; I'd strike the sun if it insulted me."

The sun's insult and the whale's, they, too, are masks, but masks of Ahab's devising. To be worthy of such insults is to be very grand indeed. But more than that: if all visible objects are but pasteboard masks, all facts, all acts but symbols, then Ahab's acts, to meet the others, must be symbolic, too. And symbolic acts are easier, simpler than the acts of direct engagement in directly consequential causes and effects. It is not the forces of malice that Ahab hates, but the self-containedness of life, the reality of the real. That is the prison for him, that is the wall through which he must strike. It is existential history that Ahab cannot bear, so he must make life into a symbolic drama. It is simpler, it is easier, if one can believe that to kill malice one has only to kill a white whale.

Pip, left to drown when in fright he jumped from the whale boat, picked up again by accident, wanders about the *Pequod*, crazed by his lonely confrontation with the mindlessness of the universe. Ahab, to protect the boy from a jeering sailor, takes Pip's hand.

> "What's this? here's velvet shark-skin," says Pip, intently gazing at Ahab's hand, and feeling it. "Ah, now, had poor Pip but felt so kind a thing as this, perhaps he had ne'er been lost! This seems to me, sir, as a man-rope; something that weak souls may hold by."

And Ahab's answer:

> "Lo! ye believers in god's all goodness, and in man all ill, lo you! see the omniscient gods oblivious of suffering man; and man, though idiotic, and knowing not what he does, yet full of the sweet things of love and gratitude. Come! I feel prouder leading thee by thy black hand, than though I grasped an Emperor's!"

But the boast is hollow, too formal, seeing symbols again, and not Pip. It would have been a better boast had he said ". . . all hands should rub each other's shoulder blades, and be content."

Ahab thinks he means to be the counterforce to malice and indifference, and he thinks his madness is the terrible price he must pay. But he covets his madness. By it he is saved from immersion in the flood of real, consequential, interdependent human life. By it he preserves the primitive simplicities, the primal drama of his fantasies. Just before the final battle with Moby Dick, Pip meets Ahab again upon the deck, but this time it's Pip that grasps Ahab by the hand, to offer *him* a man-rope. Then Ahab says:

> "Lad, lad, I tell thee thou must not follow Ahab now. The hour is coming when Ahab would not scare thee from him, yet would not have thee by him. There is that in thee, poor lad, which I feel too curing to my malady. Like cures like; and for this hunt, my malady becomes my most desired health."

But Pip will not desert Ahab as he, Pip, had been deserted.

> [Ahab:] "If thou speakest thus to me much more, Ahab's purpose keels up in him. I tell thee no; it cannot be."

> "Oh good master, master, master!"

> "Weep so, and I will murder thee! have a care, for Ahab too is mad."

Ahab's tragedy is that he cannot escape from the fantasied world of primal contests for power, mere power. The rhetoric of enmity to malice is at last a disguise. His rebellion is but a private repetition of an Oedipal sort of ritual. When Ahab stands defiant to let the lightning do its worst, he shouts, "But thou art but my fiery father; my sweet mother, I know not. Oh, cruel! What hast thou done with her?" It is not humanity, not benevolence for which he battles, but it is for omnipotent centrality in all the world. It is that primitive fantasy he will not abandon, though he kill all in playing it out. His madness populates the universe with malign fathers. That he cannot give up. It is easier to fight with fantasied fathers than to accept his father's and Pip's and his own histories and vulnerable humanity and the greater rebellions that such acceptance entails.

The tragedy is that those rebellions do not come to pass without leaders of Ahab's scale in will and power. The tragedy is that Ahab does not lead his men in prideful rebellions for humanity's sake, but only in a bitter and insane crusade of merely symbolic revenge for primitive humiliations. The tragedy is that Ahab is not the leader of rebellion against malice; he becomes instead himself the tyrant impelled by malice, the tyrant against whom sanity and vitality must themselves rebel. Starbuck knows that the only way to save himself, the crew, the ship, is to mutiny. But he cannot bring himself to it. Without Ahab, the men are leaderless, purposeless, a mob of "mongrel renegades, and castaways, and cannibals—morally enfeebled also, by the incompetence of mere unaided virtue of right-mindedness in Starbuck [the first mate], the invulnerable jollity of indifference and recklessness in Stubb [the second mate], and the pervading mediocrity in Flask [the third mate]." * The tragedy is that the crew will go where Ahab leads, but he is mad. The pathos is that without a leader of charismatic power, they go nowhere. They themselves are incapable of the rebellion on which their lives depend.

---

* What about Ishmael? Why doesn't he lead the rebellion against Ahab? He is neither mongrel renegade nor castaway nor cannibal nor merely right-minded nor indifferent nor mere mediocrity. Melville does not seem to have reckoned at all with Ishmael's presence when he accounts for the crew's incompetence for rebellion.

Ishmael has two functions in the novel, both of which preclude his taking a central role in the action. First, he is the observer: it is through his eyes that we see and understand the action. It was precisely to accomplish this kind of "objective" observation that prose-fiction emerged to replace directly exhortational exposition as the major literary form of the mid-nineteenth century. Ishmael is in the novel to observe the action and to contemplate its meaning, not to be the action. Ishmael embodies the omniscient author, not the subject of his knowledge. When Ishmael does stop the movement of the plot's unfolding to contemplate his own thought, it is always in situations of isolated remove from the central events of the novel—at the masthead, becalmed at the center of the whale armada, at the tiller during an eventless night watch. In the many chapters presented directly as drama—speeches, actions, scenes uninterrupted by commentary—Ishmael is never in the drama at all: he is the playwright, not the player.

Moby Dick's structure requires Ishmael to be the novel's moral consciousness without being a moral presence in the events he describes. Melville accommodates that difficulty by making the *Pequod*'s voyage the time and place of Ishmael's education—his Harvard and his Yale, as he says. He is there to seek instruction: preparation for later participations. It makes sense that Ishmael should be the only one to survive the voyage because he was the only one not really of it. He is there not to take part in Ahab's rebellion, but to wrest self-conscious wisdom from it for his own—as ideally students do who pore compassionately over the recorded tragedies of their kind. Hence the justice of the figure of Ishmael's survival not only by disengagement from Ahab's primitive mania, but also of Ishmael buoyed up by the coffin—the death—of even more primitively acquiescent Queequeg.

But of course it is not quite accurate to say that Ishmael alone survives. So does Moby Dick. Pursued as symbol, pursued as matter, pursued 'til he can endure no more, he turns in fury at last to destroy his pursuers.

The young radicals of mid-nineteenth-century America had to define themselves against the tradition of sentimental populism, the tradition that assumed that the people will always put the power of their numbers sooner or later, but in time, to the purposes of reason and life. History—on whaling ships as elsewhere—is made not by the spontaneous emergence of a popular will, but by the coincidence of charismatic power in a leader, the power of numbers in the followers, and the coinciding interests of leaders and followers, without which both potential powers are potential only, a diffused and dissipating anxiety. The complexity of human character—the wildly heterogeneous interests we find in ourselves—establishes the diversity of the crusades we can undertake, the diverse coincidences of leadership and followers for which we are ready, and of which our future will be as full as our past has been. The all-focusing lust for revenge may be monomania in Ahab, but it evokes a resonance in the crew, and the *Pequod* can proceed toward its catastrophe. Had there been another voice, another will of Ahab's power, they could have gone another way. The radical's hope must rest not on the autonomy of the popular will, but on the generating of leaders, and on the social circumstances that generate leaders who can focus the power of the many to be instrument of the most humane among the welter of their interests. It is not least because the *Pequod*'s is a closed and a tiny society that none emerged in it to speak the voice of civilization against the wild impulses to a magical power.

Ahab's rebellion is finally no more than the reiteration of a private, primal, psychological ritual: its public meaning is at last only a disguise. Ahab's rebellion raises psychological questions primarily. The leaderless crew's incapacity for rebellion against demented authority—that raises social questions, questions that impel us to think about the historical conditions on which the moral direction of popular power depends. What are the conditions of rebellion against immoral power and constraint? And more important, when does rebellion become revolution: not only a refusal of submission to immoral power, but assumption of power for the creation of moral community?

This is the subject of *Billy Budd*.

Radicalism is defined by its commitment to the revolutionary—that is, thoroughgoing and fundamental—change in the terms, conditions, objects of social life. Sentimental radicalism is defined by failure to reckon with the diverse, powerfully entrenched resistances to such change; or by failure to know what the revolution cannot accomplish though it succeed; or, knowing the resistance to change and what overcoming it will cost, and knowing how remote from the radical's inclusive aspirations the revolutionary accomplishment will be, by turning, then, pessimistically away as if history's revolutionary extensions of benevolence and reason were therefore nothing. That is to say, radicalism is sentimental in the degree to which it believes malignity, selfishness, unreason, indifference, predatory acquisitiveness to be such superficial human inclinations that no matter how systematically entrenched in social power they are, the most benignly pacific gestures (of prophet or historical process) will spontaneously establish the hegemony of benevolence and reason; or in the degree to which it believes that no matter how long our constraining history of life within systematized enmities, the formal victory of revolutionary forces will liberate us at once to the millennium of unalloyed benignity; or in the degree to which it sees the moral confusion of life as making moral purpose meaningless (simply inverting the alchemy of sentimental optimism, counting the very presence of evil as the obliteration of everything good). Some will not perceive what terrors revolutionary change must undertake; some will not perceive what it cannot accomplish; some who perceive both will be able to see nothing else. Some will deny the weight of the history of fear and malevolence; some will be crushed by the sense of it. Mid-nineteenth-century radicals had to define their own radicalism against these sentimentalities.

Melville begins *Billy Budd* with a two-paragraph preface in which he summarily accepts the meaning and cost of revolutionary change.

> The year 1797, the year of this narrative, belongs to a period which as every thinker now feels, involved a crisis for Christendom not exceeded in its undetermined momentousness at the time by any other era of which there is record. The opening proposition made by the Spirit of that Age, involved rectification of the Old World's hereditary wrongs. In France to some extent this was bloodily effected. But what then? Straightway the Revolution itself became a wrongdoer, one more oppressive than the kings, and initiated that prolonged agony of continual war whose final throe was Waterloo. During those years not the wisest could have foreseen that the outcome of all would be what to some thinkers apparently it has since turned out to be, a political advance along nearly the whole line for Europeans.
>
> Now, as elsewhere hinted, it was something caught from the Revolutionary spirit that at Spithead, emboldened the man-of-war's men to rise against real abuses, long standing ones, and afterwards at the Nore to make inordinate and aggressive demands, successful resistance to which was confirmed only when the ring-leaders were hung for an admonitory spectacle to the anchored fleet. Yet in a way analogous to the operation of the Revolution at large the Great Mutiny, though by Englishmen naturally deemed monstrous at the time, doubtless gave the first latent promptings to most important reforms in the British Navy.

I have quoted the whole of the preface because many Melville readers ignore its relevance to the body of the narrative, and because many who do take the preface seriously seem to me to misread it. It is said that Melville's rejection of revolution is expressed in his pointing to the blood the French Revolution cost, to the new tyranny it installed on the thrones of the tyrants it had displaced. Further, the view that the revolution nevertheless brought "political advance along nearly the whole line for Europeans"—that view is merely ascribed to "some thinkers"; Melville does not assert it himself: to put it in that equivocal way is to deride it. But in the last sentence of the preface, Melville does, explicitly and unequivocally, make his own position clear: that the local mutiny in the British Navy, like the Revolution at large, did, despite all, accomplish progress—"most important reforms"—that it did so is, simply, "doubtless." He asserts his knowledge of what "rectification of the Old World's hereditary wrongs" will cost. He asserts his view that the rectification can in some degree be accomplished. And he asserts his acceptance of the cost; that is, he asserts his positive engagement in the historical processes upon which progress depends.

For Melville, the question is not the possibility of a revolution's moral success. That is doubtless. The question is not the cost of revolution. Do we think the conservation of traditional tyrannies costs our humanity less? Only if the pain of those once privileged is more morally terrible to us than the pain of those on whose suffering the old privilege depended. Will the revolutionary extensions of equality be brutal? Yes. Did we think a history of brutal and brutalizing oppression would breed sweet universal beneficence in the oppressed? The issue for Melville is not the cost of revolution but the history of "hereditary wrongs," the history that makes revolution morally necessary, that establishes the cost of revolutionary change. By 1888–89—when *Billy Budd* was written—Melville found those issues to require no more than flat assertion. The real questions had to do with persons, forces, situations incapable of revolution despite its self-evident moral necessity. It is less the cost of revolution than the impediments to it that the radical sensibility must labor to understand—especially because radicals have tended often to imagine those incapable of revolutionary change to be the bearers of it. It is to uncover such sentimentalities, such failures to perceive the weight of history, that Melville makes *Billy Budd* a story of those who perpetuate or endure the world's hereditary wrongs rather than revolt against them.

The story, in bare outline, is this. Billy Budd, a sailor of extraordinary physical beauty and also extraordinary moral innocence—an Adam before the "questionable apple of knowledge"—is impressed from the merchant ship, *The Rights of Man*, to serve on the great warship, HMS *Indomitable*. Billy himself rather liked the prospect of "martial excitements," and his presence—his beauty, his innocence, his excellence as a sailor—on the *Indomitable* is a delight to almost everyone. The pacific influence of his cheery dutifulness calms the officers made anxious by mutinies, even desertions to the enemy, elsewhere in the fleet. Billy has the look—the strength and beauty—of the sailors' natural leader, the champion of their rights. But he is not such. His primal innocence incapacitates him. His response to another's flogging is only the primal man's self-concern and awe before authoritative force: he vowed he would never do anything to bring such on himself. Billy—sweet, inarticulate, primal innocence, the image of a romantic ideal of moral heroism, the repository of romantic hopefulness for our species' radical possibilities—Billy is incapable of more than dutiful submission, a morally substanceless loyalty to the powerful. But lest the terrors of reality's moral complexity make us nostalgic for the primitive, make us see high virtue in Billy's simplicity, Melville confronts Billy with John Claggart. Claggart, the ship's policeman, is impelled by passions no less primitive than Billy's, no less elemental. But they are opposite. Claggart is as innocent of kindness as Billy is of malice. Claggart appears to be all intellect, all "cool judgment," but his intellect is only the instrument of his heart's depravity, "a depravity according to nature." Lest we think that Claggart's intellect makes him history's man only, somehow less nature's man than Billy is, Melville likens him to the scorpion, "the scorpion for which the Creator alone is responsible. . . ." Claggart's intellect makes him able to take on civilization's manners of cool decorum more easily than Billy can, but his and Billy's antithesis is no less primal for that. And if this society cannot save them somehow from themselves, they will destroy each other. In "an aesthetic way," Claggart saw the charm of Billy's sweet innocence, "the courageous free-and-easy temper of it, and fain would have shared it, but he despaired of it." Because he both envied it and despaired of it, he despised it. To destroy Billy becomes his mania. Claggart manufactures evidence with which to accuse Billy of inciting mutiny. Before Vere, the *Indomitable*'s captain, Claggart presents formal charges. As incapable of rebuttal as he is of mutiny, impotent even to stutter out his innocence, Billy, agonized to protest his loyalty, strikes out at his accuser: the blow—to Claggart's forehead—kills him.

Now Captain Vere is the center of the drama. The administration of justice is his responsibility. But what is justice? Vere is no petty legalist. He is a man of principle, principle submitted to constant and austere philosophical inquiry. His participation in the war against the French Revolution is neither mindless patriotism nor selfish defense of the privileged classes to which by birth he belongs. It proceeds from his conviction that the revolution's ideals of freedom are "incapable of embodiment in lasting institutions." They will breed war and social chaos. " 'With mankind,' he would say, 'Forms, measured forms, are everything; and that is the import couched in the story of Orpheus with his lyre spell-binding the wild denizens of the wood.' " Because most people are in fact only wild animals submitted to formal constraint, societies dedicated to equalitarian freedom and reason will but unleash the beast: they will free the barbaric, not the humane. Humane order is the creature not of freedom, but of authoritarian discipline.

It is precisely the issue of the revolution at large that is raised by Billy's killing Claggart. There is no question of the injustice of Claggart's accusation. Shall Billy therefore be exonerated for the lethal blow? To exonerate Billy would be to honor the right of the lower orders to strike out against their oppressors. To honor that right would be to exonerate not only Billy but the Revolution itself, and that would be to release people from the "forms, measured forms," by which alone, and however morally arbitrary the forms' content, people are kept from the fundamental barbarism of their nature. Committed thus to Billy's death—the law's formally measured retribution for violence against a superior in grade—committed thus to Billy's death as he is to the death of the revolutionary forces, Vere summons his officers to the court-martial proceedings.

But the other officers do not have Vere's austere clarity. Touched by Billy's innocence of character, sensing justice in his response to Claggart's accusation, they would vindicate Billy or at least mitigate the penalty unequivocally called for by the law. They do not see that to vindicate Billy or mitigate the penalty is to condemn the law, and beyond that the society whose will it embodies, and thereby to condemn themselves as agents of that society and that will. The essence of Billy's crime is not the murder. After all, the law requires that Billy be murdered. And the ship is a war ship: its business is to murder. The essence of Billy's crime is that he has killed "a superior in grade." The purpose of the law condemning him is not to prohibit violence but to regulate it for the defense of the military hierarchy and the hierarchical society the military is organized to serve. The officers are caught between their allegiance to their society and their identification with Billy, an identification implying a morality altogether antithetical to the morality embodied in their patriotism. Like most, their wish is to avoid the contradiction, to gloss with local palliatives the fundamental conflict of inclinations, to obscure with a local kindness the meaning of their primary loyalties. But Vere insists that they face the choices at issue. They must "condemn or let go." But if they let go, they must see that in accepting the imperatives of "private conscience," they reject the vow, the loyalty, they swore when they accepted their commissions. In that vow they "ceased to be natural free-agents." Now to assert their free-agency, their right or their duty to obey their own consciences rather than the law—that would make nonsense of their enmity to, their war on, the French Revolution.

But still the officers vacillate. Vere sees that they are incapable of unequivocal choice. He tries a surer argument: if Billy is not hanged, "The people" [the ship's company], knowing the law and the mutinous temper of the time, will interpret the officers' failure to follow the law as cringing before the fear of mutiny. Though Billy intended no mutiny, though, ironically, striking Claggart was his expression of submissive loyalty, an expression made perverse by his primitive inarticulateness, failure to punish him will embolden the crew with a sense of their rebellious power. Then, unless the officers would themselves go over to the forces of revolution, they will have to fear for their very lives. Vere need argue no more. Billy is convicted and sentenced. The next day he is hanged. His death is likened to Christ's. His last words are "God bless Captain Vere." To which the assembled crew with one voice gives "resonant sympathetic echo—'God bless Captain Vere!'" Billy, the handsome sailor, who should have been in all things the people's champion, leads them only into submission. He had not a "moral nature" in "keeping with his physical make." His heart of primal innocence impels him not to moral power but to mindless acquiescence. The still small voice of nature speaks not the language of moral wisdom: only the language of fatalistic obedience. Billy should have been the "Aldebaran"—the red star—of his constellation, his class. But he leads the men only to their self-betrayal. At the moment of his death they sense it.

> The silence at the moment of execution and for a moment or two continuing thereafter . . . was gradually disturbed by a sound not easily to be verbally rendered. Whoever has heard the freshet-wave of a torrent suddenly swelled by pouring showers in tropical mountains, showers not shared by the plain; whoever has heard the first muffled murmur of its sloping advance through precipitous woods, may form some conception of the sound now heard.

The awful potential power of the men's concerted voice is heard first as an inarticulately murmured and "sullen revocation . . . of their involuntary echoing of Billy's benediction." In that revocation the men begin to find the voice without which their power is but the mechanical instrument of their oppressor's will. Billy's death may accomplish what his life could not. Impelled by revulsion from the linked tyrannies made manifest in the execution, the men begin to find the voice of revolution.

> But ere the murmur had time to wax into clamor it was met by a strategic command, the more telling that it came with abrupt unexpectedness.
>
> "Pipe down the starboard watch, Boatswain, and see that they go." . . . Yielding to the mechanism of discipline . . . , the men are dispersed. True martial discipline long continued super-induces in average man a sort of impulse to docility whose operation at the official sound of command much resembles in its promptitude the effect of an instinct.

Having none among them to articulate their purposes, the power of their fraternity is dissipated, fragmented, and integrated again into, and by, the mechanism of their own subjugation. Therein is the story's consummate irony. Vere's pessimism about human nature—his view that people are incapable of moral choice, unworthy of freedom—Vere's pessimism leads him to believe in discipline however arbitrary as the only means to order, and order however immoral as all that we can hope for to save us from the barbarism of our nature. But it is the humane, not the barbaric, that is revolted by Billy's death. The awful irony is that it is the men's history of disciplined docility by which they are undone at the very moment of their surging toward moral purpose, toward proof of their humanity in their assertion of its demands. The irony is that Vere's pessimism creates instruments that do not save man from his barbarism but perpetuate it and destroy its opposite.

The radical sensibility—the love of benevolence and of reason—becomes political when it is wedded to the belief that the willful organization of social life is necessary to the extension of benevolence and reason. Implicit in radical politics is an optimism about human nature, a belief that radical politics can work because people have in them the impulse to benevolence and the impulse to reason—enough at least to make radical change possible and more conducive to human happiness than are the formalized enmities and ignorances the radical opposes, the conservative conserves. What the radicals of the mid-nineteenth century came especially to know was the weight of history impeding radical change, impeding the development of the benevo-lence and reason of which people are capable. For many Americans, raised to believe themselves history-less and thus free of impediment to the most righteous of futures, this knowledge was crushing. No theme in our literature is more ritually reiterated than the theme describ-ing the movement from innocence to experience as a decline and a remorse. Perhaps the most important of Melville's accomplishments for the radical sensibility was his coming to know not only a great deal about human readiness for malevolence and ignorance, the readiness that gives the past its awful weight, and his coming to know that the future will be no less heavy with disparities of human inclination than the past has been, and his coming to know both what the processes of change will cost and what they cannot buy, and still, knowing all this, neither pretending that radical change can come without revo-lutionary change nor turning against the radical sensibility or from it, as if the history of change had bought nothing or as if submissive endurance of an habitual servitude cost humanity's humanity less than revolution does because the servitude is habitual.

It is this that the preface to *Billy Budd* quite flatly asserts. Given the necessity of revolutionary change, the story itself undertakes delinea-tion of those who directly oppose it and those whom only sentimen-tality or ignorance or hypocrisy has imagined to be the bearers of the radical will.

Some Melville treats with no more than a sentence or two of cavalier dismissal. Formal religion is represented by the *Indomitable's* chaplain, "the minister of Christ . . . receiving his stipend from Mars," ". . . the minister of the Prince of Peace serving in the host of the God of war. . . ."

Why then is he there? Because he indirectly subserves the purpose attested by the cannon; because he too lends the sanction of the reli-gion of the meek to that which practically is the abrogation of every-thing but brute force.

At the moment after Billy's execution, when the profound mur-
mur of revulsion and revolution starts like a freshet-wave amongst
the men, Vere commands the *Indomitable*'s band to play a sacred air,
the chaplain to go through the customary morning service: "religious
rites subserving the discipline and purpose of war" are merely one set
among the "forms, measured forms," Vere can bring to bear to return
the men to their docility.

Of commerce as the means by which people will be joined in
pacific and humane productivity, Melville gives only one passage.
The night before Billy's execution, he lies in irons and under guard
between two cannon of the gun deck:

> Over him but scarce illuminating him, two battle-lanterns swing from
> two massive beams of the deck above. Fed with the oil supplied by the
> war-contractors (whose gains, honest or otherwise, are in every land
> an anticipated portion of the harvest of death) with flickering splashes
> of dirty yellow light they pollute the pale moonshine, all but ineffec-
> tually struggling in obstructed flecks thro' the open ports from which
> the championed cannon protrude.

The moral pretensions of the discipline of the business ethic, like
the moral pretensions of the church, are for Melville hypocrisies that
deserve no more than peripheral gestures of contempt.

The story's central subjects are Billy, Claggart, the crew, the officers, and Vere. Melville brings them together in a time of revolution,
a time that makes vivid the terrific and clumsy processes by which
people tediously and uncertainly and in spasms of blood must fight if
we are to give to life a moral coherence above the rest of nature's contentions for merely private survivals. It is in this world that the radical
sensibility must exert its force. It is this fight of which the elements of
the *Indomitable*'s society are incapable. Hence it is against them that
Melville must define his own revolutionary radicalism.

Billy is primal man and as such embodies the romantic fantasy
that return to a primitive innocence will be the means of social regeneration, the means to moral mastery of the immense forces our history

has created. But Billy's innocence knows no virtue beyond loyalty to any power that feeds him: at the court-martial, his stutter calmed by Vere's paternal poise, Billy speaks the highest morality he can conceive: "'I have eaten the king's bread and I am true to the king.'"

But it is not only the moral force of innocence that the romantic anthropology misconstrues. Just as important, it evades the fact that Claggart, like the scorpion, is no less nature's creature than Billy is. The subtleties of Claggart's sophisticated intellect are not impediments to primal benevolence, but instruments of a primal malignity.

In the *Indomitable*'s officers Melville embodies the political anthropology that believes an educated and established administrative class to be the proper bearers of human progress toward civilization. Because such a class is at once above the passions of ignorant selfishness in the masses and the passions of cultivated selfishness in an imperious aristocracy, it will bring a tempering synthesis of reason and kind sympathy to the otherwise chaotic affairs of men. But Melville sees the liberalism of such a class as no responsible synthesis of benevolence and reason: it is merely a gloss of contradictions. The officers are kind enough to wish to palliate their society's most egregious injustices, and they are kind enough (or ineffectual enough) to be content with minor privilege and power. But when Vere presents them with unequivocal reason, when he makes clear that their palliatives are palliatives only, merely obscuring a fundamental brutality, their response is no more than muddled confusion. It is only perception of jeopardy for their own places of minor privilege in the established hierarchy that dispels their confusion and impels them to clear purpose. Middle-class liberalism will moderate the absurdities of inequalitarian society, but when inequalitarian society itself is threatened, liberalism's fundamental loyalties are clear.

As the officers stand to the moral pretenses of liberal middle-class decency, so the crew of the *Indomitable* stands to sentimental radical populism. The hope that our vicious society's anonymously suffering masses will be the bearers of radical social change—that hope is certainly not without logic. The many suffer most and profit least from a system that imposes suffering. It is not silly, therefore, to expect the many to hate not only suffering but also the imposition of it. And it is not silly to expect the many to have effective power for the rectification of the system under which they suffer. With the *Indomitable*'s crew, as with the tyrannized masses everywhere, their very numbers alone mean adequate revolutionary power. And much more important, tyranny itself will have made of the masses something vastly more powerful than mere mass. It is only when the many are systematically unified—transformed from disjointed multitude into coherent organization—it is only then that they become a useful instrument of tyrannical purpose. And it is only when the many are systematically unified that they realize the multitude's power to overthrow the tyrant. The tyranny of an exploitive society is impelled to create the forces by which it can be undone.

To this clear historical logic radical populism adds another, a moral logic, we may call it. Exploitive societies—societies in which the lives of the many are lived for the advantage of the lives of the few, in which the wills of the many are made instrument of the wills of the few— such societies are abhorrent to the radical sensibility in two ways. First is the absurdity of an aristocracy's belief in a differentiating excellence in itself that warrants the subservience of the many. The absurdity of that belief is in its ignorance of the continuity of human nature across the boundaries of class. Such ignorance is an offense to the love of truth, if to nothing else. Second is the utter difference between the aristocracy's and the radical's judgment of what constitutes excellence. The capacity for sympathetic identification is for the radical the very essence of excellence. Hence the aristocracy's belief that excellence warrants privilege—the individuating wealth and power of the few against the homogenizing poverty and subservience of the commonality—that very belief is for the radical sensibility the essence of moral ugliness, the antithesis of excellence. That is to say: even if there were inherent differences of nature corresponding to class boundaries, to regard those differences as warranting exploitive power is to prove not one's excellence but one's baseness.

The moral logic seems to me a clear one. So does the logic by which radical populism describes the historical development of effective revolutionary power in the exploited masses—the historical logic by which tyranny, in organizing the masses for their more useful exploitation, will create the organized power necessary to oppose tyranny. But to these two clear logics radical populism tends to add a third, a sentimental one, it seems to me, a logic impelled by wishes that countermand both perception and reason.

Because wealth and power and the assertive individuality they facilitate have tended to go to the predatory and the exploitive, radical populism tends to associate assertive individuality with predatory, exploitive selfishness. This is, of course, an overly constrictive association. Though much assertive individuality is predatory, exploitive, and selfish, it does not follow that all assertive individuality is such: nor does it follow that anonymity produces benevolence or benevolence anonymity. But these are the inferences radical populism has often allowed itself to make. Presumptuous, exploitive aristocracies make commonness a pejorative term: radical populism does not stop by refusing that absurdity; it tends to make commonness—"the common people"—into the very name of virtue. Exploitive society accepts, accommodates, and depends on the leadership of the vicious: radical populism tends, then, to regard leadership itself as evil, leaderlessness as virtue, and the namelessness of individuals among the masses as itself the necessary and sufficient condition of moral action. Exploitive society has made most individually visible those with unusual luck or talent at exploitation for the sake of private privilege; radical populism has tended, therefore, to see poverty's obscuring of individuality as manifesting not the masses' victimization but their radiant selflessness.

It is this sentimentality that Melville exposes by the docile acquiescence of the *Indomitable*'s leaderless crew. It is not that they are without moral capacity for revulsion at their society's inhumanity; it is not that they are without the humane passion that impels to revolution for the sake of humane relations amongst them. It is that they are without leaders, without someone or some few—for such are never many—whose extraordinary clarity of moral purpose and energy can give focus to the otherwise inarticulate and random pendulations amongst their disparate passions—their moral revulsion, their expansive sympathies, and their anxiety for private safety, which is, after all, the base of the crew's vulnerability to the historied habit of docility. It is this last that establishes the commonality of common people on all sides of social boundaries, on all levels of social hierarchy. It is the regnancy of this motive that finally joins in common brutal cause both officers and crew of the *Indomitable*. The execution of Billy Budd brings to crisis of awful vividness the meaning of the society the *Indomitable* is and serves. It brings to vivid illumination the welter of inarticulate passions, the welter of moral antitheses, by which people can mold and take the mold of their lives. In crises we at last must choose. The welling rumble of revulsion in the crew proves the justice of the radicals' hope for humankind: the inclinations to radical choice are there. Vere's sudden dissipation of that revolutionary energy proves the sentimentality in the populist faith that in crises the radical inclinations will spontaneously and certainly be the ruling ones. The tragedy of the *Indomitable* is that at the moment when crisis impels the crew to choose among the confused diversity of its inclination, only Vere has the power of clarity by which their confusion will be focused to purpose: and the inclination he chooses to illuminate into prominence is the anxiety for private safety, the anxiety by which the crew is fragmented again into machine parts in the mechanical instruments of the tyrannical will. The dignity of the crew is that the execution is for them a moral crisis. Their misfortune is that the resolution of their conflicts of inclination waits on the accident of articulating leadership.

As the *Indomitable*'s crew stands to sentimental populism, Vere stands to "realistic" aristocraticism. It is populism's sentimentality (its tendency to let wishes dictate belief) to imagine that there is no significant difference between moral hero and most people. It is aristocraticism's sentimentality to imagine that between moral hero and most people the difference is absolute and final. Almost everybody has enough of the radical sensibility to feel (at some level) that if such is the case—that if between the good and the many there is no significant continuity of interests and capacities at all—it is an unfortunate case: it would be better if it were otherwise. And if it is legitimate to make love of benevolence and love of truth the rudiments of the radical sensibility, then we may say that almost everyone has enough of the radical sensibility to feel (at some level) that dignity resides in facing unpleasant facts. By its facing the unpleasant "fact" of most people's perfect incapacity for benevolence and reason, "realistic" aristocraticism construes itself—rather than populism—as bearing the full dignity of the radical sensibility: its conservatism, its loyalty to authoritarian hierarchical society, is but recognition of the means that most people's depravity makes necessary if the radical sensibility is to be served.

The confusion in the crew's response to the execution of Billy Budd shows both the error of this political anthropology and the terrible consequences of commitment to its half-truth. The crew's surging enmity to injustice proves the error: their docility before authoritarian force though it command them to murder—that not only proves that populism's truth is but half-truth, too; it means that if the crew lives under leaders that deny their humanity, they will become as their leaders describe them. It is not that Vere's aristocratic pessimism truly understands the reality: it is that Vere's "realism" is a force that creates the reality he imagines himself in austere dignity to understand. Vere imagines "the people" to be beasts that only fear will discipline: so he frightens them with the threat of brutal discipline and makes them thereby into beasts. The theory becomes causal force in its own substantiation.

It is easy, of course, to see the motive impelling sentimental populists to their half-truth. It is easy to see that their error is probably not merely an error, but a willful distortion of perception to gratify their wishes. Indeed, the populists are likely to be proud of their wish for the moral dignity of the populace, and would have no need to dissemble their pleasure in believing it. And it is, of course, just as easy to see the way in which a pessimistic anthropology gratifies the privileged classes, no matter how much they may present themselves as made melancholy by their view of the truth, no matter how much they may imagine themselves dignified by ability to face a melancholy truth. Their pessimistic anthropology is just as sentimental, just as subservient to their wishes, as the populist's optimism, and without the nobility of the populist's wish. But Vere, Melville says, is not to be understood as merely another banal apologist for a banal privatism. And though most pessimistic anthropologies are sentimental, it doesn't follow that all are. Is Vere's error, then, merely an error, a belief honorable for its loyalty to truth, though mistaking truth? Melville gives only one passage—the last passage of which Vere is the subject— to the question of Vere's motives. Shortly after the execution of Billy Budd, the *Indomitable* engages a French ship (the *Atheiste*) in battle, and Vere is fatally wounded.

> He lingered for some days, but the end came. Unhappily he was cut off too early for the *Nile* and *Trafalgar*, the battles in which Vere's prowess as military commander would have come to its full glory. The spirit that spite its philosophic austerity may yet have indulged in the most secret of all passions, ambition, never attained to the fullness of fame.

Vere's execution of Billy Budd, like his war against "the Revolution at large"—these may express loyalty not to hard commands of a somber and unequivocal realism, but loyalty merely to an imperious though submerged passion for fame. Billy's death is necessary if the crew is to be kept docile: the docility of the crew is necessary if they are to remain an efficient instrument of Vere's ambition, if, that is, they are to be Vere's means toward his society's adulation of him—which is, after all, what fame is about. Vere's desire for others' adulation of him may be, then, his commanding motive; it may be simply the wish for fame that dictates his beliefs. If that is the case—and by proposing no other view, Melville gives the story's weight to this one—Vere's pessimistic "realism" is as sentimental as the sentimental populist's idealism or as his officers' equivocating liberalism.

The tragedy of the *Indomitable* is that Vere is the only one in the ship's society capable of knowing the alternatives among which that society must choose. And Vere alone is capable of that concentrated coherence of purpose by which his society will be led to its choice and thereby establish the moral import of its power. Billy in his innocence knows only how to submit to arbitrary, dehumanizing power. Vere in his perverse sophistication knows only how to seek it. The tragedy of the *Indomitable* is that, by the accident of Billy's and Vere's polar incapacities, the crew has no alternative but the consolidation of its worst inclinations.

But it is an isolated tragedy only. Though the *Indomitable*'s society was proved incapable of revolution, elsewhere, Melville says, there were "minds by nature not inferior to [Vere's] own" yet committed to "rectification of the Old World's hereditary wrongs" rather than to their repetition. The historical process of rectification may be brutal, halting, clumsy, and ugly with blood, yet it proceeds. Melville's assent to that process is the inclusive import of his last story. It is his assent to history. The ground of that assent is the perseverance of humankind's revolutionary impulse to the humanizing of relations amongst us.

CHAPTER SIX

Walt Whitman: His Braveries

At the beginning of his Preface to the first edition of *Leaves of Grass* (1855), Whitman says: "The largeness of nature or the nation were monstrous without a corresponding largeness and generosity of the spirit of the citizen." He says this not to express anxiety about the possibilities of moral monstrosity inherent in America's resources of power, but to introduce a eulogy of America's scale and its accomplishments, in which for him the commensurate moral grandeur is so clearly manifest that merely to list some of the names of our places and our deeds is proof enough. He goes on to say that we want only the poet "commensurate with the people," whose job it is simply to say the words of our lives, our wishes, our great free dignity, to consolidate forever the pride we ought to feel in ourselves, what we have inherited, and what we will transmit. If there are those who fear the new order of power—inherent in our freedom, our science, our technology, our diversity as a people—the poet has but to give image to the certain continuity between even our smallest moments of work or pleasure and our sure destiny of magnificent harmony; all the people will see their true selves in those images; their fear will be dispelled; and since fear of ourselves, our powers, one another, our place in the world, is all that stands in the way of knowledge, sympathy, and the moral use of power, the last impediments to the joy of virtue, the virtue of joy, will be removed. It needs only that humanity be fully alive to its dignity for its dignity to be at last fully alive. That vivification is the poet's work, the work Whitman announces himself here as having taken up. In the Preface's last sentence, he proposes, too, the criterion by which his success in that work will be known: "The proof of a poet is that his country absorbs him as affectionately as he has absorbed it."

Twenty-first-century readers of Whitman are likely to find these effusions of confidence in nature, the nation, the spirit of the citizen, the sure sympathy between great poet and people—we are likely to find all this hard to take. Whitman's confidence is likely to engender less a joyous sense of power than, say, a melancholy reminder of a time in which it was easier to be so naïve. We know too well the monstrosities of which the citizen and the nation are capable, the hideous uses to which the mastered resources of nature have been put. To Whitman the journey east and west meant an enriched harmony of wedded diversities. To us of the twenty-first century, it can well mean global devastation. And the proof of a poet's greatness will be the people's absorption of him? We'll absorb him, all right. Let him die first, then moulder awhile; then pretty soon we'll resurrect him for evisceration by graduate students and ritual transubstantiation into genteel innocuousness by schoolteachers.

Whitman's best poems are likely now to seem to us to be "Out of the Cradle Endlessly Rocking" or "I Saw in Louisiana a Live-Oak Growing"; the poems that know the expansive pleasures of love and community not in excitement for their immediacy or their immanence, but in the pain for their inaccessible remoteness.

> I saw in Louisiana a live-oak growing,
> All alone stood it and the moss hung down from the
> branches,
> Without any companion it grew there uttering joyous
> Leaves of dark green,
> And its look, rude, unbending, lusty,
> Made me think of myself,
> But I wonder'd how it could utter
> Joyous leaves standing alone there
> Without its friend near, for I knew I could not. . . .

It is in such if any of Whitman's lines that we are likely to see truths of *our* condition vivified. It is not the dignity of measureless mastery that we hope to know at first hand; only the dignity of quiet acceptance of our solitude, our loneliness, our exhaustion. Whitman is likely to be most moving to us now when he sees himself and us not in epic processions of "Progress," but in the little rows of debris left by the tide.

> I too but signify at the utmost a little wash'd-up drift,
> A few sands and dead leaves to gather,
> Gather, and merge myself as part of the sands and drift.

> O baffled, balk'd, bent to the very earth,
> Opress'd with myself that I have dared to open my mouth,
> Aware now that amid all that blab whose echoes recoil
>   upon me I have not once had the least idea who or
>   what I am. . . .

If Whitman's voice builds to high passion without breaking our identification with him, it is likely to be when the passion he sings of is not love, but love lost. We are less likely to believe "the barbaric yawp" shouting consummations than the cries like those of the he-bird in "Out of the Cradle Endlessly Rocking," his mate perhaps dead, perhaps lost. If she is only lost, he must sing so she can find him. If she is dead, he must sing the agony that cannot be contained. He is the "singer solitary," singing "uselessly, uselessly all the night" "the cries of unsatisfied love." Ever after, like the thrush in "When Lilacs Last in the Dooryard Bloom'd," he is "The hermit withdrawn to himself, avoiding the settlements," singing by himself the

> Song of the bleeding throat,
> Death's outlet song of life,
>   (for well dear brother I know,
> If thou wast not granted to sing
>   Thou wouldst surely die.)

We have had since Whitman several periods in which the excited expectation of joy emerges again, among the young, at least, but it seems that under those periodic renaissances of hopefulness the constant has been the maturing accommodation to the inevitability of despair. We have come to know best what Whitman knows of the hermit thrush: if we are to be sustained at all, it will not be realized love that sustains us, but only the persistence of our longing for love. Such is life's enmity to love that even our longing must seek refuge to survive. Art—the thrush's solitary song—is love's monastery, refuge as dreams are for life's profoundest wishes, the wishes that life cannot fulfill: "Till human voices wake us, and we drown."

Yet it seems that if a twenty-first-century audience finds the power of truth in Whitman's poems that evoke the anguish of love forlorn, that audience must reconsider its view that there is no truth in Whitman's poems of confidence. The same view of human nature is fundamental to both kinds of his work. If people are anguished in the world because it frustrates an essential need to find and give sympathy, affection, and love, then people are closer to being what Whitman said they are than an unmitigated despondency accounts for. If we are mortified by the vicissitudes of sympathy and the need for sympathy, then the anthropology at the base of Whitman's confidence in the 1855 Preface is not as sentimental as it is likely at first to appear to us to be. Whitman was confident about people's use of power because he assumed our love of sympathy would sooner or later make power an instrument of sympathy. He was confident about the people's use of a great poet because for Whitman the essence of great poetry is sympathy extended by knowledge and made vivid.

If there is truth in the poetry of despair for sympathy betrayed, then there must be some truth in the poetry that says sympathy is a force to be reckoned with in our species' affairs. We must temper both our rejection of the poetry of exuberant community and our acceptance of the poetry of lonely anguish by recognizing the denominator common to both.

By 1876, Whitman had made many poems of both kinds, had despaired of their reconciliation, had felt reality mocking him for his early "arrogant" poems—"with mock-congratulatory signs and bows,/ With peals of distant ironical laughter at every word . . ."—and then had come to see the underlying logic giving continuity to all his work. In the Preface to "Two Rivulets," new material to be added for the 1876 edition of *Leaves of Grass*, Whitman says:

> While I am about it, I would make a full confession. I also sent Leaves of Grass to arouse and set flowing in men's and women's hearts, young and old, (my present and future readers,) endless streams of living, pulsating love and friendship, directly from them to myself, now and ever. To this terrible, irrepressible yearning, (surely more or less down underneath in most human souls,) . . . I have given in that book, undisguisedly, declaredly, the openest expression.

What changes in the twenty years since his starting out as a poet is not Whitman's conviction about the "terrible, irrepressible yearning," but his understanding of how deep down underneath in most human souls it is. He had always known, of course, that our capacity for sympathy and our need for it can cower in fear of failure behind bastions of defense or aggression. See "Song of the Open Road" (1856).

> Behold . . . ,
> Through the laughter, dancing, dining, supping, of people,
> Inside of dresses and ornaments, inside of those wash'd and
>   trimm'd faces
> Behold a secret silent loathing and despair.
>
> No husband, no wife, no friend, trusted to hear the
>   confession,
> . . . death under the breast-bones, hell under the skull-bones.

Or "Song of Myself" (1855).

> Here and there with dimes on the eyes walking,
> To feed the greed of the belly the brains liberally
>   spooning,
> Tickets buying, taking, selling, but in to the feast never
>   once going.

> Many sweating, ploughing, thrashing, and then the chaff for
> payment receiving,
> A few idly owning, and they the wheat continually claiming.

But in the early poems Whitman believed that our yearning for sympathy rather than for conquest or submission had only to be summoned loudly and clearly enough for it to tear all impediments away at once and forever. Our virtues are but dormant. The poet is only he who has waked early. He need only call us out to the full light of the new day.

> Whoever you are, come forth! or man or woman come forth!
> You must not stay sleeping and dallying there in the house. . . .

> Out of the dark confinement! out from behind the screen!

So he calls. And calls. And calls. Until at last he sees himself as he is reflected, not in the eyes of an emboldened nation of brothers and sisters and lovers, but in the solitary thrush crying uselessly all the night, or in the "chaff, straw, splinters of wood, weeds and sea-gluten,/ Scum, scales from the shining rocks, leaves of salt-lettuce, left by the tide"; until he is "baffled, balk'd, bent to the very earth . . ."; and until he brings himself to know, as he does in "Passage to India," that if the human inclination to sympathy is to be empowered, it will be by historical processes longer, longer and more complicated by far, than at first he had imagined. By 1871, when "Passage to India" was added to *Leaves of Grass*, Whitman knew that the enterprises of civilization had no guarantee of imminent success, that the moral dignity without which the largeness of nature or the nation were monstrous had no guarantee of spontaneous unfolding, that the poet who would speak to all men and women and for them had no guarantee that anybody would listen to him. He knew that the work of civilization—of knowing and accomplishing both individuality and community despite the menace of the unknown and our diversities, of knowing and accomplishing coherence of inclination despite the diversity of our inclinations—is for most, at most times, a mad hazard to the security of ignorance, impulsiveness, and hostility to the different and the daring. He knew that nurturing extravagant aspiration to harmonies not yet made may be no more than to nurture failure abysmal in proportion to the height of aspiration; for thus failure is proportioned. And he knew that if, given these menaces, we settle for safety, for ignorance, for the opportunism of greed and fear, it will be to have died with the possibility of life, of dignity, of expansive happiness simply untested.

It is the sense of all this that gives the force to the last lines of "Passage to India," despite the two-hundred-fifty lines of grandiloquent rhetoric very like his early poems, in which Whitman has been announcing the Suez Canal and the railroads and the trans-Atlantic cable as both symbol and instrument for the final joining of what fear, space, impotence, and ignorance have kept awfully asunder.

> Passage to more than India!
> . . .
> Cut the hawsers. . . .
> . . .
> For we are bound where mariner has not dared to go,
> And we will risk the ship, ourselves and all.

Whitman's poems had always known the delicious swagger of benevolent power, the delight in the confident gesture of affection confidently offered. What he came to know is the dreadful humiliation when the swagger is derided, when the gesture of offered affection is scorned. He came to know, that is to say, the dreadful risk the open delight in potency and the open love of affection entail. Those are, after all, the vicissitudes of the radical sensibility itself, the risk from which most of us recoil and cower, though it mean abandonment of our heart's desire. The force of the last lines of "Passage to India" is that in them commitment to delight survives perception of the risk.

And again, if we can identify with the voice at the end of "Passage to India"—the voice vibrant with the thrill of grand enterprises fraternally dared, with the melancholy of the enterprise's known uncertainty (of old wrecks remembered)—if we can identify with that voice, then we must reconsider, at least to qualify, our rejection of the poem's earlier announcements of the moral import of modern technology.

The risk at issue in "Passage to India" is the risk of the species' modern technological power. Power is always a risk. When we have it, we must choose amongst our purposes, endangering the easier confusion of inclinations that impotence protects. Power is a risk because with it we confront our enemies, and they may have more of it. It is a risk because it may fall into the hands of those who will use it nefariously. Hence the long history of radical moralities that see pastoral isolation or asceticism or some other form of chosen impotence as the only avenue to virtue. Hence, given the fact that it is the development of economic power to which America has above all else devoted itself, the irrelevance of escapist moralities to the real moral issues of American life.

Whitman's great contribution to the specific content of the radical sensibility in America is his acceptance of the risk of modern economic technology, his sense of the moral possibilities inherent in it, and his sense that if modern economic technology cannot be made the instrument of the radical sensibility, that if its power cannot be put to the purposes of benevolence, if it cannot empower at once the work of both individuation and community, then we will indeed have lost the ship, ourselves, and all.

When we dissent from Whitman's lyrics of certainty that technological progress is the force destined to unite all humankind in fraternal harmony, we must see that it is only the certainty—not the aspiration from which we must dissent. And if we accept Whitman's acceptance of the *risk* of technological power, we must see that if there were not some justice in the view of human nature underlying the earlier certainty, the risk would not be worth taking. One who takes it would not be heroic, but only blusteringly foolish. Exactly as our anguish in a world hostile to love proves that we do after all have the love of love in us, and that there is, after all, more justice than both radical and conservative misanthrope will assume in Whitman's poems predicated on believing so.

People love love and they love power. The problem is their integration, their synthesis. Earlier generations of American radicals had tended either to believe, as Jonathan Edwards did, that the problem would be resolved by some sudden supernatural installation of love in the seat of absolute power (if not that, then unmitigated catastrophe); or to assume, as Benjamin Franklin did, that the natural laws of commerce would harness the love of power all unwittingly to the purposes of benevolence; or to assume, as Ralph Waldo Emerson did, that the evil consequences of the love of power could be transcended if people would only get away to pastoral nature where the love of love, being nature's essence, splendidly throbs and will call forth the love of love in people themselves. It is in the style of this last, the style of Emersonian romanticism, that Whitman found his beginnings. But from the first moment it was a beginning with an extraordinary difference.

At least since the American Revolution (of which freedom for the development of American manufacture was a primary object), the central work of American history has been the creation of an industrial society. Industrial society means, among other things, the planned integration on a large scale of highly specialized work (what Marx called the socialization of labor). The planned integration on a large scale of highly specialized work means, among other things, enormous productivity, enormous power. But American society vested authority to plan the integrated and specialized work in the hands of the privatist entrepreneur (that is, whoever happens to have or control the capital to initiate the work). The sanctioned object of that authority is the maximizing of private profit. This means that the entrepreneur's interest is at once to maximize productive power and to minimize the effective will of the workers, the degree to which productive power will be turned toward their interests, their objectives. Privatist industrialization meant most of all that in the contention between the interests of privatist capital and socialized labor, the privatist entrepreneurs would have extraordinary power in pursuing their interests as against the laborers'. In the degree to which laborers shared the privatist morality, capital's power would be practically unchecked. That meant that while privatist industrialism created the masses' unprecedented power, it could create also their unprecedented humiliation, both as individuals and as a class.

The rise of industrialism and the rise of Emersonian romanticism are coeval. The connections between the two movements are complex. One is struck by the number and sometimes the perversity of the connections. Obviously Emersonian romanticism is in part a reaction to industrialism. Industrialism made industrial workers anonymous and replaceable parts in a vast machine: it told them they were nothing. Emerson told them they were everything. Industrialism told workers their private inclinations were an irrelevance to moral order. Emerson told them their private inclinations were the essence and source of moral order. The city and industrialism created each other and their mutual stench and filth. Together they are for the poor, at least, the place of anonymity without privacy, contact without recognition, touching without meeting, making without having, want amidst plenty, impotence surrounded by power, desires perpetually excited and perpetually thwarted, constant competition and constant losing. Perpetual humiliation; pride's last ditch a sullen anger and somebody else worse off still. The industrial city told the workers that they were failures. Emerson told them to go to the country, where—if they had the city-made tools to sustain them—their powers are unrivaled and the world will seem made for their delight. The perversity of the privatist industrial city is that by the planned integration of highly specialized work—by the socializing of work—it has made the species unprecedentedly powerful: by the privatizing of the objectives of work it has fragmented the species, impoverished, humiliated, and anguished the individual. The perversity of Emersonian romanticism is that for the sake of the moral unification of the species in pride and benevolent potency, the sense of which possibility must have been made psychologically vivid by the species' power manifest in socialized labor's conquest of nature, it proposed pastoral retreat, the fragmentation of work, the dignification of individuals by their isolation. "Trust yourself," Emerson said, but only, he turned out to mean, when you're alone.

What Whitman accomplished was the emotional synthesis of Emerson's sense of human dignity—the legitimacy of human passions—and the terms and scale and power industrial society gives to human community. Emerson's fundamental intuition—the intuition organizing all his work—is that malevolence and willful ignorance are not primal inclinations but reactive ones. We are malevolent toward people and the truth in the degree to which we feel neither beloved nor at home in the world. Emerson's whole work is to make people feel beloved and at home. "The misery of man appears like childish petulance, when we explore the steady and prodigal provision that has been made for his support and delight on this green ball which floats him through the heavens." The family—where at first we are provided for—is the microcosm in which our sense of ourselves, hence our stance toward all else, is established. Most families have managed that badly. Emerson's job is to stand *in loco parentis* and, speaking for the universe, to let us know that the familial denigration by which we were humiliated was a mistake. He will embolden us doubly by his own confidence in the universe—his proof that one can belong—and his conviction that such belonging is also our own just desert.

Stephen Crane has a poem called "Once I Saw Mountains Angry":

> Once I saw mountains angry,
> And ranged in battle-front.
> Against them stood a little man;
> Aye, he was no bigger than my finger.
> I laughed, and spoke to one near me,
> "Will he prevail?"
> "Surely," replied this other;
> "His grandfathers beat them many times."
> Then did I see much virtue in grandfathers—
> At least, for the little man
> Who stood against the mountains.

This *is* the virtue of grandfathers. By their successes and their confidence in us, their heirs, we know our possibilities. To be for us such a grandfather and father and teacher, making us beloved and at home in the world, is the strategy of Emerson's work. It is that strategy that Whitman took whole from Emerson. "Song of Myself" ends:

> I bequeath myself to the dirt to grow from the
>   Grass I love,
> If you want me again look for me under your boot-soles.
>
> You will hardly know who I am or what I mean,
> But I shall be good health to you nevertheless,
> And filter and fiber your blood.
>
> Failing to fetch me at first keep encouraged,
> Missing me one place search another,
> I stop somewhere waiting for you.

And "Crossing Brooklyn Ferry":

> It avails not, time nor place—distance avails not,
> I am with you, you men and women of a generation, or
>   ever so many generations hence,
> Just as you feel when you look on the river and sky,

> so I felt,
> Just as any one of you is one of a living crowd, I was
>   one of a crowd,
> Just as you are refreshed by the gladness of the river
>   and the bright flow, I was refresh'd,
> Just as you stand and lean on the rail, yet hurry with
>   the swift current, I stood yet was hurried,
> Just as you look on the numberless masts and ships and
>   the thick stemm'd pipes of steamboats, I look'd.

And "Song of the Open Road":

> Allons! the road is before us!
> It is safe—I have tried it—my own feet have tried it
>   well—be not detain'd!
> . . .
> Camerado, I give you my hand!
> I give you my love more precious than money,
> I give you myself before preaching or law;
> Will you give me yourself? will you come travel with me?
> Shall we stick by each other as long as we live?

But, though Whitman takes this stance from, or shares it with, Emerson, there is a crucial difference. Or two, rather. First, of course, is Whitman's introduction to American literature of the insistent honoring of sexuality: for its centrality as a human impulse, for its delights, for its symbolic importance as the most intense fusion of potency, pleasure, love, and the wedding of diversities, and (by generation) continuity across time. That is, of course, Whitman's most famous innovation. Some twentieth-century movements have made it the exclusive principle of their radicalism, believing that if individuals could but concentrate to free their sexuality from constraint, all impediments to freedom, creativity, and beauty would be dispelled at once (thus has Emersonian sentimentality about the social effects of self-reliance been appropriated by the twentieth century: a minor irony given the fact that it was the centrality of sex as subject in Whitman's poems that made Emerson nervous about them).

But it is not only here that Whitman enlarges upon Emerson's battle against the mountains of established social hierarchy, the mountains that humiliate us with stinted sustenance and preachment of our need for submission to constraining decorum. Emerson saw people debased by communal enterprise and communal power used only to make private opulence. He could not see that it is neither the opulence nor the power inherent in communal enterprise but the privatism that is nefarious. So he preached self-reliance and pastoral retreat. Whitman's great accomplishment for the radical sensibility in mid-nineteenth-century America was to see that communal enterprise and opulence did not have to be the instruments of privatism and debasement. They could in fact be the instruments and expression of unprecedented concerted creativity, pleasure, and pride. Whitman first, and practically alone of the radical writers of his generation, saw not degradation but effusions of creative power in the factory, the mill, in "stevedores unloading ships by the wharves," in "the fires from the foundry chimneys burning high and glaringly into the night," in "swift streaking engines," "the steam-whistle, the solid roll of the train of approaching cars," in the "trip-hammers crash . . . , the press whirling its cylinders," in the "word of the modern, the word En-Masse."

> This is the city and I am one of the citizens,
> Whatever interests the rest interests me, politics, wars,
> markets, newspapers, schools,
> The mayor and councils, banks, tariffs, steamships,
> factories, stocks, stores, real estate and personal estate.

These are the works that organized American life. What Whitman did was to assimilate into the radical sensibility the sense that such works could be made the instruments of humane purpose. Indeed, if they were not, it would be by persistent contradiction of their inherent structure. Their function is willy-nilly to bring people together, continually discovering to them their communal power, the only power by which our species could conquer at last nature's resistance to the primal wish for ease, freedom, mastery, community, love—the wish not only for wealth but for commonwealth, and commonwealth not only as expedient for accomplishing private wealth, but as necessary for the fundamental delight of shared purpose, shared work, and shared success.

Of the writers of his generation with whom we've dealt here, Whitman alone felt that the terms and scale and power of social life established by the industrial revolution were sources of his dignity rather than his denigration as a human being. Perhaps that is because he alone of the major writers of his generation was the child of a working-class family. Whitman's father was a carpenter, and an unsuccessful one to boot. He worked mostly in Brooklyn, then a fairly sparsely settled suburb of Manhattan. The city-factory's speed and scale of productivity must have seemed marvelous compared to the slow, antique, and comparatively lonely work of the carpenter.

And there would have to have been a very great difference between the working class's and the gentry's response to the density and diversity of the city's population, jobs, entertainments. Compared to the working class, the educated gentry has always had a great deal of what is now called "cultural enrichment" available to it. In such terms, the city made no radical difference to the gentry. But to the working class, the city was a boon: compared to the relative monotony of poor suburban or rural life, an extraordinary amplification of stimuli, excitement, opportunity to learn and to do. Melville had said that the whaleship was his Harvard and his Yale. But his wresting of an education from experiences altogether peculiar for one of his natal class was made necessary by a demotion, a constraint rather than an amplification of opportunities: Melville's father's financial failure, the family's descent from wealth to genteel poverty, deprived him of the real Harvard or

Yale, the education to which he had, as it were, been born. We may call Whitman's Harvard and Yale his work as apprentice printer, then journeyman, then writer and editor for the newspapers of Brooklyn and Manhattan. But for one of Whitman's class, this was in no sense a demotion or constraint of opportunity. Work on the big-city papers meant for Whitman involvement in rushing and large-scaled commerce and politics, sophisticated science, art, entertainment, a life marvelously rich compared to the tedium of ignorance, routine, and monotonous sameness, of physical and psychic exhaustion, in which his father had lived the life of a failing suburban carpenter.

What I am suggesting is that Whitman's class experience may be at issue in the central figure of his work: the figure of the instruments of socially concerted power that defined his time's particularity pressing us to unfold new freedoms.

Genteel literature's antipathy to the machine and the city is hardly unrelated to the fact that in pre-industrial American society the established gentry already had leisure and luxury in both things and culture to grace it. Indeed, for the established gentry the industrial revolution could mean deterioration rather than improvement of the products and services and the quality of life they'd always been able to buy. They needed neither more nor better than the artists, artisans, farmers, laborers, and servants had been able to supply. And the industrial revolution certainly meant an awful attack on the ease, orderliness, and grace of the country life the gentry had known and mastered. But, for the working class, the artisans, farmers, laborers, servants, themselves, the industrial revolution was likely to mean more and better of everything. For the gentry the industrial city offered nothing necessary, certainly nothing the cities of Europe could not make up without at the same time undoing the provincial ease and comeliness of American country life. But, for the working class, the city was in every sense a way upward and outward. Whitman's boyhood trips to Manhattan must have been vivid with a sense of the city's excitement.

In any case, Whitman's first edition of *Leaves of Grass* is. Whether or not it was the working-class experience that made it possible, in 1855 Whitman presents himself as the poet not least of whose accomplishments is the feeling—and the exhortation to those who might otherwise see themselves as history's victims—that modern industrial power is but the emanation of our species' own internal potency, not the imposition from without, but another instrument in, the progress of civilization.

In the early poems, however, this view, despite its newness for the radical sensibility, is given no particular emphasis. Whitman undertakes to find in everything he sees some justification for confidence. In the catalogue poems, as they've been called, every item suggests its opposite, and Whitman's job is to show that opposites can be, should be, counterparts of harmonious diversity, not antitheses in brutal, myopic, bitter, exclusive contention: city-country, men-women, old-young, art-science, labor-ease, land-sea, past-future, solitude-community, and so on and on—all are synthesized with equal emphasis to make inclusive image of humanity's radiant organismic identity. It is part of the strategy impelled by the sense that it is fear that keeps us from humaneness. If Whitman can, in exuberant abandon, touch anything and all things, touch each and its opposite, and still find only delight or the promise of it, coherence and its enrichment, then there's nothing to be afraid of, and we may at last look at ourselves and one another with the affection that confidence alone can dare. Whitman will parent our pride with his own. It is a strategy that Whitman takes up from Emerson and develops from the point at which Emerson left it. If our fundamental desires—what we really want—are good, then the problem is to embolden us to get what we want. Emerson undertakes to accomplish that work by persuading us that all Nature conspires in love for us, making everything for our delight. Whitman's first accomplishment is the amplification of this Emersonian view with the sense that the city and the machine and the history that made them are no less natural to us, no less an extension of our inherent powers, no less the tool and place of our delight, than is the farmer's field or his plow or the country sky at night.

But Whitman had not only to extend Emerson's view of Nature and the natural; he had to break with it. He had to break with its certainty and its dependence on an externalized, a supernatural will as the source both of certainty and moral legitimacy. By 1871, the break (as far as Whitman could make it) was made. In "Passage to India" Whitman has catalogued the voyages of discovery, the expeditions, the inventions, the art, the science, the religions, all the work impelled by "mortal dreams" and mocked by life. Then:

> Ah who shall soothe these feverish children?
> Who justify these restless explorations?
> Who speak the secret of impassive earth?
> Who bind it to us? what is this separate Nature so
>   unnatural?
> What is this earth to our affections? (unloving earth,
>   without a throb to answer ours,
> Cold earth, the place of graves.)

These questions are not, as by themselves they might seem, the rhetorical questions of despair. Whitman answers them with confidence that

> All these hearts as of fretted children shall be sooth'd,
> All affection shall be fully responded to, the secret
>   shall be told,
> All these separations and gaps shall be taken up and hook'd
>   and link'd together.
> The whole earth, this cold, impassive, voiceless earth,
>   shall be completely justified. . . .

The certainty persists, but Whitman knows now that it is not Nature's will but people's on which the radical sensibility depends. And by the end of the poem, that certainty, too, is overcome.

He knows that it is human work on which the empowering and the humane focusing of the human will depend; and he knows that the empowered will may not, after all, be humane. He knows that our history of remorse and humiliation makes power a horrendous risk. We may never learn to see one another except within the vicious circle of the fear that engenders enmity, the enmity that engenders fear. But we die in any case. That *is* certain. At least let the work of the life we live have objects equal to the scale of our anguish.

Among the relevancies here is that as Whitman accomplishes the break with Emersonian certainty and faith in an external, ahistorical source of moral power, his concentration on modern economic technology becomes more and more emphatic. What had been in the early poems but one in an effusively lyrical catalogue of undifferentiated means to progress has become in "Passage to India" the central subject, the crucial issue. The poem's argument (its hortatory style warrants our calling it that) is simply this: fundamental in human history is the ideal of the universal fraternity of humankind at home in a world made bountiful by human mastery. For most of history, the force of the ideal for human beings has been manifest in its persistence despite life's frustration of it. Frightened for survival, we have had to see one another as enemies; yet our religions' fantasies of harmony ("Towers of fables immortal fashion'd from mortal dreams") and our anxiety (we are "feverish," "fretted children") amidst the enmities of the actual, these prove the strength of the radical ideal in our nature. And it has not persisted in wishes only. For its sake, too, we have sought mastery over nature. And we could succeed. The tools, themselves at once the product and instrument of cooperative creativity, that can make nature bountiful and all peoples known to one another, are in our hands at last. The radical dream can become reality. At last we can create the world in which ignorance and fear for survival need no longer have the force to keep us from the benevolence and potency we crave.

It might as well be said here that if "Passage to India" is fundamentally nonsense, then radical politics since then is also fundamentally nonsense. For the distinguishing conviction of radical politics since the middle of the nineteenth century has been this double one: that the human capacity for benevolence and humane creativity will be empowered in the degree to which we are free of the need to compete for sustenance; and that the astonishing productivity of modern industrial power, if unleashed from its use for privatist exploitation, can be the unprecedentedly effective means to that freedom.

Whether this conviction is nonsense or not, we cannot yet know. No fully developed economic technology has as yet been turned boldly from the purpose of private wealth to the purposes of commonwealth. Might it be? Well,

> Cut the hawsers. . . .
> . . .
> For we are bound where mariner has not dared to go,
> And we will risk the ship, ourselves and all.

For me, Whitman's bravery is beautiful—and shows again that "there can be great use in grandfathers."

CHAPTER SEVEN

Politics' Vicissitudes

I

Because I am about to change again the form of my argument, I want to talk for a moment about the reason for such changes. The specific content of the radical sensibility in America has changed fundamentally in the course of its history, those changes make historical periods, each of those periods seems to me relevant in a different way to the radical sensibility today, and those differences require—or at least warrant—different modes of exposition. Thought in the period that includes Edwards, Franklin, and Emerson was by its consistent millennialism fundamentally sentimental. The especial use now of reviewing that period is delineation of the persistently attractive sentimentalities so that we may have a better chance of overcoming them. Poe, Hawthorne, Melville, and Whitman seem to me to have been able to devote their talents of mind much more to the examination of reality than, as with earlier writers, to the support of simplifying faiths. Their work is important for the realities they illuminate rather than for the devices of self-protective thought they exemplify. The use in reviewing their work is recovery of the truths they tell us of. Edwards, Franklin, and Emerson are more useful to me now for the evasive attitudes they typify than for the particulars they describe, so I have written about them in terms of categorizing generalizations intended to clarify the typical. In my view, Poe, Hawthorne, Melville, and Whitman established for the radical sensibility the terms by which it could understand its real place in the world. In writing about them I have tried to follow their lead rather than to stand back to get a second guess at their motives.

For the last hundred years the radical sensibility's work has been for the most part directly political rather than theoretical. The rigors of that work obliged it to foreswear open-ended inquiry and to reduce to bare minimum the terms by which it would understand its circumstances and portray its goals. Often, however, that reduction simplified both too far and too rigidly. What may have been begun as a political activism's necessary shorthand became instead an impediment to understanding or even a defense against it. All too often radicals have spent their major energies in factional contention among themselves in which each faction defends the particular reductionist dogma it has resorted to as a stay against confusion. And often the reductionisms settled on are but modernized forms of those classically formulated by Edwards, Franklin, and Emerson. That is why the review I am about to undertake of radical politics of the last hundred years is restricted to roughly generalized terms: I mean to focus most the typical errors of theory that, it seems, the Left needs continually to remind itself to avoid. It is the other side of the same need that warrants our paying close attention to Poe, Hawthorne, Melville, and Whitman.

Before the middle of the nineteenth century the primary work of the radical sensibility in America was to codify its aspirations and to vivify them not only against those who sought harmony by constraint of the universe of moral identification but also in despite of the puniness of the radicals' power to create the situation in which radical ideals would be nourished by freedom from want and fear rather than stunted by competition for survival. Edwards' concentration on the meaning of benevolence as the principle of psychic and social integrality, Franklin's concentration on the consequences of poverty, and Emerson's concentration on the love of creative energy implied by our anxiety when we live only as engines of commerce: these were their positive contributions to the maturation of the radical sensibility. But to codify when we do not have adequate instruments of enactment does not seem enough. The farther away our goal, the more likely we are to have fantasies of its being around the corner. Dreams of glory come long before glorious accomplishments. The idea precedes and is simpler than the realization. That is necessary: that is the actuality that expansively integrative, innovative creativity (the will to make new and wider orders of harmony) must face. And we are very bad at facing it. The remoter the conception of an ideal from the time of the maturation of the powers that could realize it, the more likely we are to be transcendentalists. The narrower the reach of our skills, the more likely we are to imagine for them a universal efficacy or to imagine even that goodness needs no skills (e.g., "the meek shall inherit the earth"). The difficulty and the loneliness of the first steps of a new adventure toward civilization, toward the new connections that had not before to be clearly held in mind, toward the newly wide horizons to be actively lived in, heighten memories of the ease of a narrow barbaric impulsiveness, and that frightens us into exaggerated descriptions of the delights of the New World and of the ease of getting there.* So we deny the difficulty and the loneliness, the little scale of what we can do that is but a jot against the vast scale of what must be done, the variety of wills opposing or indifferent to ours, the uncertainty of everything. So as not to reckon with the consequentiality of what people do that's bad, Edwards proves that it's all bad, and names what's good the work only of God; Franklin proves that the laws of economics will save us from ourselves despite ourselves; and Emerson proves that private enterprises of love and honest poetry are the lever that will move the world. The language of these reductionisms has changed, but the motives persist, and many still try to make the world feel manageable

---

* And we have reason to be afraid. It is from the foremost edge of intellectual and natural modernity that Germany plunged into Nazism. Interesting too that it was the Jews Marx, Freud, and Einstein that epitomized Germany's intellectual progress, and that it was the attempt to exterminate the Jews that epitomized Nazi Germany's barbarism. Perhaps it seemed that elimination of the Jews could be the final solution to the galling demands of civilized benevolence and knowledge.

by these three devices of evasion—by believing people universally evil and thereby legitimizing disengagement from this world (a belief that can serve a secret affinity for the status quo as well as it can serve a passive waiting for supernatural deliverance); or by believing that nothing but economic systems and circumstances have causal force and thereby ignoring the brutalities and banalities that so readily live by the morality of the jungle and that economic well-being may not undo; or by believing that the expression of the individual's passions will illuminate the fraternal identity of the species and redeem us all forever from the moral oppression of societies and customs.*

That Poe, Hawthorne, Melville, and Whitman were in a fundamental way free of these reductionisms suggests that their time was propitious for wisdom. Let me repeat here something of my earlier argument about the causes for that good fortune.

Those causes have essentially to do, I think, with the radical increase in the scale of power wielded by society. Before the middle of the nineteenth century—before the industrial revolution and its concomitants, the greatly increased density and interdependent connectedness of population—people had to be especially aware of their weakness. They had to see the great disparity between the conditions of social life they sought and the instruments of social power they had. Seeing Nature as vast and of a piece and powerful, our species as small and divided and weak, people sought power where it appeared really to be—outside themselves—and hoped that that external power would do for them what they could not do for themselves: bring them together and make them at once strong and good by consolidating their purposes. Edwards postulates a god, Franklin a natural law of supply and demand, and Emerson an over-soul. Seeing the weakness of benevolence in its battle against malice and

---

* I am assuming for the moment that readers will make their own lists of present movements that carry these old orientations.

indifference, they constructed faiths that people's battles are not to be taken seriously: according to Edwards that is so because everybody is fundamentally malevolent, hence nobody's victory can have moral meaning; according to Franklin that is so because nature uses our greed as a goad to productivity; according to Emerson that is so because everybody's really fine and our battles are simply a mistake. The fundamental difference in the work of Poe, Hawthorne, Melville, and Whitman is that instead of looking above people for some force that would bring them together, they looked into them to see first what motives have kept them apart; second, to see what inquiry into the natural history of motives might suggest that we could do about it; and third, to see what means of battle would give benevolence and knowledge a better chance in the continuing struggle against malevolence and ignorance. My guess is that that relocation of interest—from the outward to the inward, from the anti-historical to the historical, from the need to believe in some unconditional redemption to the need to examine the conditions of moral change, from faith in a force that will govern the human will despite itself to faith that the moral will can empower itself by understanding itself, its situation, and its enemies—that relocation of interest is a function of the general feeling of potency excited by the particular potencies manifest in the industrial revolution and its concomitants of change in the conditions of social life.

This view is not contradicted by the fact that the continued increase in industrialism's power to integrate labor and make it productive has sent many back to pre-industrial pessimisms and millennialisms. It is easier to respond with reason to the moral failures of the first flush of power than to the moral failures of the tenth. It is easier from the eminence of a new mastery to look with reason's eye at the long processes of progress than it is to keep believing in an old mastery's moral potential when looking back at the long series of its corruptions.

In any case, whether for these or other reasons, Poe, Hawthorne, Melville, and Whitman had available to them ways of thinking about life that, when taken together, make for the radical sensibility a fundamental orientation that honors the actual no less than the ideal and adds thereby to the vulnerable beauty of radical intentions the enduring weight of radical understanding.

Because it is according to this understanding that I mean to review the last hundred years of the radical sensibility's experience in America, I had better try to say what I take to be the crux of it. It includes especially Poe's sense of the rarity and oddness of moral excellence against the dark, vengeful inclinations to destroy (ourselves and others) by which societies no less than individuals may be impelled; Hawthorne's sense of the ways in which we inherit with our society the patterns of contention that teach us to hate the best among us and within us; Melville's sense of joyful revolutionary pride that will not betray dignity's dangerous demands for pleasure and community by escape to the safety of subservience or to a merely symbolic rebellion or to a willful ignorance that rationalizes a cynical pursuit of privilege such as Vere's no less than it rationalizes Bartleby's passive resignation; Whitman's sense of modern technological power the moral wielding of which could make us proud, the fruits of which could make us free for the pleasures of community, free for the beautiful self-aggrandizement that comes with the use of our energies with, rather than against, our kind. Together these could make for the radical sensibility the basis of a socialism mindful of the particularity no less than of the dignity of its aspirations, mindful of the historical good luck that formed it no less than of the historical complexity that makes its future uncertain (mindful, that is, of the conditionality of its own creation no less than of the conditions that nourish its enemies), mindful of its great connections in the past and surely in the future no less than of the cul-de-sacs of thin sentimentality that frustration of its desires will lead it to take; mindful that unless it masters the modern scale of social power, and despite the risk of brutality all power entails, its dreams will be only pipe dreams and our best possibilities will drown in the blood spilt by avarice (avarice not any more for the stuff of survival or luxury—of such stuff there can now be enough—but avarice for the dignity that insecurity assigns to dominance).

To know the importance of these concerns we have only to think of the contemporary movements that don't know them at all. Take, for example, the movements that think that if the beauty of love were but brilliantly enough announced, everybody would throw off at once all the awful ways of enmity. Or those that will know so little the cost of history that they imagine all the world's most oppressed people to be the bearers of its highest virtues. Or those that will know so little the diversity of people's readiness for benevolence and knowledge that society's characteristic reviling or imprisoning or destroying of some of the best of the species is either ignored by them or shocks them into a torpor of disillusioned bitterness or sends them to prove that the reviled cannot have been so good after all. Or those so frightened by the misuse of modern technology and the power inherent in the concerted labor of large-scaled social institutions that retreat to sweet pastoral impotencies is the only progress they can imagine. Or those that can manage disengagement from the established inhumanities only by intoxication.

All these sentimental confidences—in the proletariat's or peasantry's thoroughgoing moral excellence, in a universal language of love, in pastoral simplicity, in the superficiality of human evil and the essentiality only of goodness—are ways of denying two things: they all deny the depth and firmness of the differences of interest and inclination that organize people's lives, their affinities, their enmities; they all deny the weight of history, the depth and firmness of the patterns of group-relating that societies inherit, impose, and transmit—the patterns by which particular interests and inclinations are focused and empowered.

The work of Poe, Hawthorne, Melville, and Whitman was to illuminate the truths that would be uncovered by freedom from the need to deny our diversity as a species, the complexity of our characters, and the weight of our history. The primary work of the radical sensibility since the middle of the nineteenth century has been to try to accomplish political power. That work is quite different from (indeed, it tends often to be unpropitious for) the pursuit of wider understandings. More than a relatively rudimentary and fixed understanding may in fact get in the way of the necessarily repetitive work that pursuit of political power requires. Nobody has energy for everything and we must apportion the energy we have. Often, however, political work seems to require of us not only that we settle for established understandings and deny intellectual inquiry our primary energy: often the sustaining of political energy seems to require of us that we invest in such misunderstandings as will keep off an enervating sense both of the remoteness of our objects and the incompleteness of their effects. We have not only to believe that we will get what we're after soon: we have also to believe that when we get it, we will have gotten pretty nearly everything that counts. The energy for thorough devotion to a job seems to require at some level something of a fanatical sense that one's work is not only necessary and good, but also primary—in the sense that from its accomplishment all other goods must surely follow. If it is good that we do our work with all our hearts, then this fantasy ought not to be carelessly derided, for it seems necessary to persistence and also to the discovery of how far in consequences the work in fact will go (it's the attempt to prove a theory universal that discovers the theory's limits). The real fanatics are those who do not and will not also know that their fantasies are fantasies, useful (in one of the psyche's corners, as it were) because they legitimize concentration until the work is done or proved impossible; harmful (and then often deeply so) when they forbid recognition of the necessity of other works and find intolerable the perception of the speciality rather than the universality of their own work's consequentiality.

Because nobody has energy for everything, we need at the time of the thorough application of the energy we have, to forget its limitations and the partiality of the understanding it applies. If that is intolerable to us, we choose passivity—which is simply leaving responsibility to somebody else. We do that, I suspect, either because we don't really care how the things at issue come out; or because our motives are confused and we don't know what we want most; or because we can't give up the child's wish for an omnipotent parent somehow to manage it all for us.

If in the last hundred or so years of the radical sensibility's pursuit of political power it has tended to settle for settled understandings and an exaggerated view of its work's consequentiality, it is not necessarily demeaned thereby. No more than the surgeon with a patient on the table is demeaned when he does not use the occasion for innovative inquiry, and, in his zeal to apply what he already knows and can do, he forgets the social, psychological, and biochemical vicissitudes he will send his only surgically-mended patient out to face. Which is not to say that he need not think on these things afterward. If he does not, his surgery will become primitive and his zeal fanatic and foolish, of which an eventual bitterness and humiliation is likely to be the price when energy flags and he must confront at last his work's failure to accomplish what he expected of it.

Much of the Left's narrowing of theory and its tending to see its own as the complete and only work has been no more than the necessary cost of concentration, self-consciously tempered and rectified when there was room for that. But many were not so ready for reason. For many, the narrowings and exaggerations were not temporary devices of concentration but articles of faith, the only condition of energy rather than a temporary support of it, and reality's inevitable blasting of these dogmas left their devotees exhausted and with no foundation to sustain their radicalism itself, let alone their political energy.

The political work of the radical sensibility is now mostly in the hands of the young, of the New Left. They too will settle for the reductionisms and presumptions that seem to be the cost of focused energy. Hopefully, they will do so more self-consciously than the Old Left did. They must if they are to avoid the disillusionment in which by the 1950s the Old Left found itself wandering.

II

Since the beginning of the nineteenth century, the central work of American society has been the making of the industrial power now accomplished, the industrial power by which—despite the privatist motives of its creation—the whole society could live as until now only a fraction of society could live: at once economically rich and free of the need to devote their primary creative energies to economic work. Theoretically, the socialist possibilities of industrial power and the socialist structure of industrial labor could have been pursued and created by socialist intentions, putting to consistent socialist use the power that had been made, and avoiding thereby the ugly condition of American society today: lives of brutal poverty lived amidst unused plenty; work of brutalizing drudgery, without vocation, though the machines have been made that could free everyone to seek vocation; socialized labor used to create and wield the technology of destruction in defense of privatist society, privatist morality. Socialist intentions could from the first have made moral sense of the socialist means we have for a century and a half been creating and using. But they did not. The reasons are no doubt many. Three seem to me of particular force. First, nineteenth-century America inherited an understanding of formally established social institutions as defenders of traditional aristocratic privilege. Second, the scale of America was immensely larger than any concerted intention and plan could reach. Third, and not least, I think, the history of life without enough for everybody made it impossible for most to see others except as contenders for inadequate supply, made it impossible for most to conceive of universal plenty as a rational object or to see the opportunities of plenty even when they had been accomplished. The memory of poverty tends to make us all anxious: it will organize our perception of wealth even when we're rich.

Since the beginning of the nineteenth century, America has been making unprecedentedly powerful instruments of wealth and using them according to the canons of poverty. For the first half of the nineteenth century, American radicals tended to respond to what was for them the misuse of the new instruments of wealth by proposing that we give them up altogether. Since the middle of the nineteenth century, the work of political radicals has been to turn the created instruments of wealth to the purposes of humane community. Concentration on the need for that work, on its cruciality, was Whitman's contribution to the specific content of the radical sensibility in his generation. So doing, he laid the groundwork for the particular political focus of the profound wisdom the radical writers of his generation had accomplished for our culture, free of the sentimentalities—Edwards' sentimental inutilitarianism, Franklin's sentimental utilitarianism, Emerson's sentimental romanticism—by which earlier generations had tried to avoid perception of human complexity, the natural and historical contingencies, determinants, and impediments of the radical will, its chances of success.

My argument is this: Poe's sense that amongst us excellence is more likely than a banal stupidity is to look grotesque, and his sense of the dark and brutal psychic forces by which individuals and societies may be impelled to catastrophe; Hawthorne's sense of the weight of history under which the best in us struggles and dies, and his sense of the social forms by which the meanest in us is most nourished;

Melville's sense of the revolutionary power that benevolence must accomplish, and his sense of the myriad merely symbolic gestures of revolution we seek as surrogates to save us from perception of reality's myriad contingencies; Whitman's sense of the deliciousness, after all, of generative power and his sense of the city, of politics, of industry, of art as forms of generative power no less natural to us than sex is, and his sense that inherent in modern economic power is the possibility of liberation from the fear that impels us to live in spasms of enmity and humiliation; all these together focusing the radical sensibility's fundamental loathing of the arbitrary divisions by class or race or culture or gender by which our species seeks privilege and by fantasy or hypocrisy defends itself against the knowledge of our fraternity—all these together made the foundation of an ideology by which the radical sensibility could now oppose mainstream privatism not merely by reviling it or running from its accomplishments.

III

If Poe and Hawthorne and Melville and Whitman wrought from the benevolentist point of view literary images that implied human complexity, that implied an individualism consonant with communalism, a naturalism neither sentimentally optimistic nor pessimistic, an instrumentalism beyond mere market values, the socialists were the first to construct the theory of a political-economic system appropriate to these images. The socialists were the first political theorists among radical benevolentists to realize that the alternative to privatist industrialism was not, could not be, and because of industrialism's instrumental power, ought not to be either pastoral retreat or some final pessimism or Christian exhortation for the industrialist's self-control. The socialists were the first to look for more than the appeal to the industrialist to temper with mercy and charity the power to enforce and acquire. The socialists said, simply, that the society should take over the industrial power and turn it directly and unequivocally to the work and advantage of the commonwealth. They were the first to propose a social program appropriate to contemporary economic possibilities and institutions and consonant with—more than that, motivated primarily by—preeminent commitment to benevolence as the organizing principle of social life.

The privatist substantive argument was this: universal (or at least national) well-being would be the necessary though indirect product of the liberation of individual acquisitiveness; if each has, all have. And since the way each gets is, they believe, necessarily ruled by the law of supply and demand (the privatist's analogue to the romantic's faith in a beneficent nature, in natural law identical with moral law*), the demands of all will be met, all will be served and well. That is, the goals of universal benevolence will somehow be accomplished by liberating its antithesis, private acquisitiveness, privatist competition for private well-being. Adam Smith's economics are the corollary of Newton's physics, a mechanistic universe ordered by, obeying the dictates of, an overarching moral will, God's will. The privatist ethic is in this way consonant with a triadic Christian tradition of which parts of the Protestant revolt partook: the good of all is a primary goal; we are, as a species, essentially depraved—that is, the good of all is a matter of indifference to most; an omnipotent God orders all things; hence despite human depravity, all that is, is ordered toward the good. The business ethic's radical divergence from the Christian tradition is this: salvation for the business ethic is not an eternity of other-worldly bliss, but a lifetime of this-worldly money success.

That is, of course, a radical divergence and implies many others. Among them is the Christian hope to moralize human action by constraining the human will as against the business ethic's wish not to

---

* Of course some privatists agreed explicitly that universal well-being was in no sense their goal anyway. Rich are rich, poor are poor: that's the way it is and that's the way it ought to be.

constrain the will but to empower it by wealth. Christian hopefulness depends on divine regulation of our character and the eventual transformation of that character itself. The privatist business ethic's hopefulness depends on God's or nature's regulation not of our character, but of the effects of our expressing our character freely. The selfish pursuit of wealth is not the sign of our damnation but the instrument of God's or nature's benevolent management of human affairs. Success in the pursuit of wealth depends, or is supposed to depend, on making or doing something people need, hence is itself benevolence in effect though not in intention. To tamper with human willfulness, the willfulness that damned us out of Eden, is a Christian necessity; but it is a privatist sin, since to do so is to tamper with the very medium of progress in the natural order. And of course there is wealth on both sides of willfulness, as it were. Willfulness gets wealth if it can, and willfulness is empowered by wealth once it has it. Willfulness naturally seeks wealth; wealth facilitates willfulness. That is why a Christian anthropology implies the traditional Christian denigration of wealth—"It is as easy for a rich man to enter the gates of heaven as for a camel to go through the eye of a needle." But the privatist ethic sponsors individual willfulness to use it for the sake of wealth, and it sponsors wealth for the sake of the willfulness it facilitates. Though Christian theory is often inconsistent with Christian practice, the theory, in any case, seems consistent within itself. Privatist practice certainly does seem consistent with privatist theory—no one would accuse our society of stinting its active devotion to private profit—but privatist theory seems fundamentally confused, or equivocal, or, at least, ambivalent.

Wealth certainly does create freedom—or certain kinds of it anyway. To want that freedom is to assume that it will be well used. Very few, I think, would defend freedom as an absolute value, no matter what would be done with it. Defense, then, of the freedom wealth facilitates must rest on the assumption that we are good enough, morally dependable enough, motivated enough by benevolence, and intelligent enough to act effectively for the sake of benevolence, to make of that freedom a moral opportunity. Wealth, then, is a value because people are good enough to use it morally. That seems a necessary assumption for the defense of privatism for the wealth it creates and the individualized way it wants wealth spent. But the defense of privatist freedom for the competitive pursuit of wealth, a system in which only competition—competition for the buyer's dollar—forces people to give their work moral social direction, a system in which only fear of poverty and love of private money profit, force people to do any work at all—that defense would seem to rest on the assumption that people are not good enough, are not motivated enough by benevolence or intelligent enough to act effectively for the sake of benevolence to work for anything but their own private gain, to plan for anything but their own competitive advantage, to think at all in inclusive, cooperative, long-range social terms without ruining the natural balance on which alone their well-being depends, and without which there could be no hope at all. That is to say, the argument for the free private use of wealth depends on an optimistic anthropology; the argument for the free privatist pursuit of wealth depends on a pessimistic anthropology. This is a fundamental confusion in the privatist worldview.

This confusion is compounded in the contradictory anthropologies of the American mainstream's politics and its economics. Our democratic politics rest on the assumption of the majority's generally dependable reason and virtue. Our privatist economics rests on the assumption of the concerted majority's moral and intellectual incompetence and laziness. To be sure, consistency is not an overriding moral criterion. A vicious premise is better contradicted than carried to its logical conclusion: and indeed our argument for what we're doing may be irrelevant to what in fact we do. Self-consciousness rarely includes more than a glancing sense of our realities. And the privatists could almost always say quite accurately that for whatever reasons and despite whatever mistakes of logic and perception and despite whatever remoteness from a theoretical efficiency, their system produced more wealth than did any other.

The fundamental socialist response was that even if the privatist plan *did* work, even if liberated private acquisitiveness did produce unprecedented wealth and unprecedented distribution of wealth, it was no less remote from a decent idea and ideal of human nature, social organization, and civilization. For the socialist the primary evil was not poverty, but privatism itself; the primary goal was not economic well-being, but socialism itself, the ideal, the beauty, of community, cooperation, sympathy, benevolence. This was not anti-individualism, but anti-privatism. The socialists were the heirs of the Renaissance, and their inheritance was belief in the integrity of the individual, the legitimacy of the individual. Their view was simply that the logic and the beauty of individuality is toward benevolence, toward sympathetic cooperation amongst individuals: that the integrity of the individual is not and cannot be independent of the integrity of the community of individuals; that a society of mutually indifferent rich people is hardly less ugly, is perhaps uglier, than a society of mutually indifferent poor people. Communitism in this sense was their response to the business ethic's privatism. To the privatist faith in a beneficent natural law that frailly human institutional planning would only impede (the faith implicit in the commitment to this moment's profits), the socialists proclaimed in opposition their faith in the powers of human rationality, faith in human reason as the most dependable among the natural forces for the progress of civilization; faith, that is, in human power to live consciously in an extended social and historical continuity. Opposing the business ethic's faith in economic action as the primary and inclusive function of dignity and virtue, the first and final instrument of salvation, the socialists proclaimed their belief that economic well-being is to be seen as liberation to more direct involvement in the world of more particularly human problems, where benevolence and mastery need not exhaust themselves in meeting problems of survival. The socialists argue most against the economic suffering in a privatist business society not because economic well-being was their final concern, but because economic suffering was the most flagrant manifestation of privatism's power to inflict pain and to keep people from the world of knowledge and benevolence and extended order. Their breakthrough, however, was not here: their breakthrough was the recognition that society need not retreat before industrialism, but could appropriate it, master it, make it an instrument of liberation from problems of survival, a subject of communal mastery, and an expression of communal integration. By this breakthrough it escaped the now obviously necessary failure of earlier reform movements to meet the strength of privatist expansiveness.

One of the cycles that history shows is the movement between reliance on the individual and reliance on the institution; between self-consciousness by individuation and self-identification by communal place; between particularly intense feeling for the individual and for the communal sanctities. The changes in concentration not only respond to each other, but depend on each other. Those born to familial chaos learn no individual dignity, but only suddenly diffused urges for primitive balm, or, if the chaos included a taste of affection, vengeance on those who gave a little affection but not enough. We are enraged by the loss of pleasures we once had. Past luxuries of pleasure become the imperatives of our dreams, our ideals.

It takes concert to form institutions and concentration on the bases of concern to perpetuate them. Creation of explicit institutional hierarchies of privilege and power begins with selection of those who have in extraordinary degree the qualities that define the communal identity, the basis of citizenship and fraternity. Sooner or later the privilege and power are used not to perpetuate and defend the communal integrity, its character and aspirations, but only as an opportunity for individual imperiousness and private luxury. Privilege becomes no longer a reward for whatever the community defines as excellence, but a booty to be wrested from the community's subservience: power becomes not the responsibility of excellence, but an instrument for the defense of privilege. The institution no longer expresses and consolidates communal identity, but represses demands and petitioners, and fragments society into merely the haves and the have-nots. Individuals must turn again to themselves to discover anew and define anew who they are and what they want. Even some among the haves chafe under the sense of the arbitrariness of their division from the have-nots, the commonality. New images of identity are formed, individuals discover anew concert under them, and join together to express them, to perpetuate them, and to wrest from the old arbitrary aristocracy the institutional power of social purpose, the social instruments of fraternity. New hierarchies are established, and sooner or later the cycle is repeated. And so it goes. But it does seem that the cycle moves up. At each stage, the level of opposition is higher, the goals sought go deeper and wider. The problems now are not of families and tribes, rituals and hunting grounds; the problems now are of international government and liberation of the individual not only to surer survival, but to mastery of the full apparatus of civilization. The history of the extension of knowledge has delivered to self-consciousness a wider and wider grasp of the ground and the disparity of our motives, the stuff of our identities. The elaboration of power, the expansion of the boundaries in which social and individual wills have force, this has exposed to consciousness the human continuities underlying disparities of race, culture, class, gender, and time. Hence the cycles of institutional change and renovation, of renewed necessities of introspection and consolidation—those cycles move in general up to include more and more of the species' possibilities as objects of social integration; institutional betrayals of social ideals are betrayals of higher levels of aspiration.

Before the socialists, radical dissents from privatist-industrialism were sent skulking to the tenets of despair or to the anxiety of irrelevant panacea or to the puny consolation of patchwork succor and reform, dismissed by the power in the grand gesture with which the entrepreneur could indicate his accomplishments, the forces he had mastered to his will, the work and the hope for expansive mastery and well-being and organization in which he could engage the society. Given the appeal of economic well-being, the entrepreneur of privatist industrialism could say robustly that his system worked. The socialists were the first to see that they did not have to foreswear the entrepreneur's accomplishments of power to express their belief that privatism was no less ugly for being successful, and that they did not have to accept the ugliness of its use as weapon of competition to continue the development of its expansive, integrative instrumental power.

It is important enough to repeat that the socialists began as the heirs of the traditional Judeo-Greco-Christian devotion to the communal, the cooperative, to the moral preeminence of concert as against privatism. They were heirs of the Renaissance in their belief in individualism, but the individualism that can only be liberated by the integration, not disintegration, of the community—the perennial discovery that one's legitimate particularity suggests the legitimate particularity of others, who by sympathy, concert, or at least tolerance can make community. They were heirs of the Enlightenment in their love of the beauty of rational order and in their belief that rationality is the species' greatest power, that only by integrative, informed planning are people likely to raise their affairs above the trepidation and moral disorder of nature in which the purpose of each is pursued piecemeal and apart. And they alone among the radical reformers were the willing heirs of the industrial revolution. Their novelty and their recognized danger to the status quo of mainstream privatism was in their attempt to create a political movement that would consolidate the whole inheritance and with it challenge the privatist entrepreneur as he had not before been challenged. They were not, as they have often become, simply a movement to make industrialism a more efficient producer of "goods," a pleasanter place to work, and a system of even more extensive distribution. They were a movement to unite benevolence and power, a movement for which individual or social wealth was less a goal than a device, an important one to be sure, but only the device for freeing people from the necessary moral barbarisms of poverty and its corollaries; freeing people to the society in which cooperation—in economic action as only one among many other cooperations—expresses the human pleasure of community. The idea of human nature implicit here—and hardly to be overemphasized—is that privatism would discontent not only the losers in privatist competition, but even most of the winners as well. The species is such that cooperation is not for us merely an expedient; it is a way to express a fundamental desire for and pleasure in sympathy. To be sure, people like to win, to stand above, on top of. In part that may be paying back for a potential companion's failure of sympathy. But surely people get a fundamental pleasure from success defined as superiority and conquest, and surely antipathy and indifference are characteristically human. Yet when society facilitates no central cooperative actions, human nature chafes not only at the social consequences of such a lack, but even at the very lack itself, the desires left unexpressed, and we prove the complexity of our natures. It is this complexity that gives the essentially human tension to human life. A crucial problem for society is to sponsor and facilitate those modes of action that resolve the tension in favor of sympathy and benevolence. It seems that much of most people's competitiveness expresses not so much a desire to give pain as to support pride. People may become competitively benevolent as readily as they become competitively malevolent. The question seems often to be, which side is the self-esteem that depends on esteem from others, which side is one's pride buttered on. A moral society's business is less to suppress malevolence than it is to engage competitiveness in socially productive and desirable competitions, in which victory expresses both excellence *and* benevolence. Those whom we call philanthropists may act less often from love of people than from love of esteem, but they are not necessarily less socially useful for that, nor less a sign of human readiness to be engaged in the work of the commonwealth. Resistance to benevolent social change is perhaps most of all resistance to the loss of status in identification with those most esteemed under the status quo. Hence the reliance on establishing the personal rather than the ideological unattractiveness of radical reformers, putting them outside the status system of the status quo. If radicals are to depend on anything but brute force, they must elicit ideological agreement from those within the society they mean to reform, and their proposals must seem consonant with their audience's view of the virtuous possibilities of their own natures. The socialists' program was based not only or even primarily on the economic logic of concert as against privatist competition, but also on the psychology that asserted the fundamental human need of concert as against moral isolation. Hence they would say that the failures of privatism would not only be economic inefficiency but psychological inefficiency; it would produce not only the poverty characterized by slums but the affectional poverty, the moral discontent of people left to patch up with fragments of guilt and benevolence that should have been the integrative principle of their social lives. Not the only principle, to be sure, but the integrative principle—without which the love of mastery will divide people not only from one another but within themselves.*

---

* Societies remain static by learning to tolerate or ignore more or less self-contradiction. The radicals are those who find the self-contradiction intolerable, take one or another side of it, and propose to establish unity in its name. The true profit-is-all entrepreneur is really, in that sense, a radical reformer who, in the classic conflict between the business ethic and the Judeo-Christian ethic, proposes unity and consistency in the name of business and the profit motive. The socialists, raised, as nearly all people are, to believe in kindliness, sharing, sympathy, and cooperation, are often those who find intolerable, and refuse to make the switch to, what is called the real adult world of "survival of the fittest"; those who refuse to confine what they were taught in childhood to call virtue, to the private life of family and friends and class, leaving those outside the pale to watch out for themselves. If in our society children act fairly consistently within the Judeo-Christian ethic, they are said to be good children. If they continue so through adolescence and speak out for a political-economic system consonant with that ethic, they have been said to

In America it is not so well remembered now that socialists used to be called idealists, soft-headed optimists who, by their trust in the possibilities of and for human benevolence and reason, proved themselves incapable of dealing with the brute actualities of human nature and social organization. They were also seen, of course, as the worst kind of rabble rousers, especially if they did not have upper-class backgrounds to scotch accusations of a merely selfish desire to re-divide the wealth in their own favor. But it is only since the rise of Soviet power to compete with the United States on its own terms that the native socialists have been seen only as dark-browed pessimists, clandestine and power-hungry misanthropes, the agents only of a diabolical alien tradition. Though idealism was used as a term of disdain, it was descriptively just. The privatists were, in the sense described earlier, pessimists. They say that human reason is too puny a faculty to be entrusted with more than the immediate and the local; hence the virtue of enforced fragmentary

---

have the political measles—an expression at once denoting their deviation from the mainstream's norm and connoting the hope that the contradiction of the status quo will go away and, like the measles, not come back again. If they continue so to act into adulthood, they are said to be the worst kind of menace to society. And they are such a menace to the status quo just in so far as the social morality they preach can call up in the society at large the image of virtue taught almost all of us in childhood, hence angering us with the exposure of our own self-contradiction. The idealism taught us in childhood does not go away. Rather, we are taught to apply it only locally, and to learn different moralities for relations between classes, genders, parties, sections, nations, races, and so on.

The question is, how forceful can the appeal of the socialists' more unified morality be? Is there at least the residue of early lessons in virtue for the socialist to call on? And is there that in most people which would make socialist success more personally satisfying to them? Certainly the status quo's appeal to our desire for public esteem is generally, nowadays, very great, greater than the socialist's appeal to consistency even when the privatist public esteem is got only vicariously by identification with the actual winners in social competition. Nevertheless, the case for the psychological relevance of socialism seems supported when the public defenders of the status quo depend on suppressing all sympathetic presentation of socialist *ideology*, and keeping before the public an image of the socialist as simply *personally* unattractive. And of course the socialist concedes the appropriateness to human nature of privatist aspirations when so much of socialist propaganda depends only on bizarre images of grotesque capitalist gluttony. But the question is *not* whose image of villainy is likely to have more propagandistic effect, but whose image of the good, the socialists' or the privatists', is more appropriate to human possibilities, is more likely successfully to integrate the complexity of human desires.

competition. The socialists were optimists and idealists. According to their anthropology, people are such that community and benevolence are for them not only necessary expedients for confronting impediments to the individual will; they are themselves fundamental desires of their nature; their happiness resides in them as well as from them, and is not possible altogether without them. And they believed in the necessity and the possibility of reason as the power of the human will; the more that is made the province of its authority the better. And they were idealists in their belief that happiness resides not only in the embrace of luxury and beauty and order, but just as fundamentally in the making of it. The mainstream has for a long time been confused about the meaning of work. On the one hand we have what is called the Puritan doctrine of at least the moral value of work, the rightness if not the pleasure of it. But on the other hand, a rudimentary assumption of the privatist-money society is that work is an unfortunate necessity (in Judeo-Christian terms, the curse of Adam's fall), that we have to be forced to do it, and that the object of work is to be liberated from it. Hence the confusion when the enforced leisure of retirement turns out to be a burden. A rudimentary socialist belief is in the joy of the work; the creation itself, when it is a consistent expression at once of the communal and the individual and the powerful. The pleasure of recreation is an important part—as the word ought to suggest— the reinvigoration of the power to create. Work is a penance only when, as in the privatist society, it expresses no more than a defense against private poverty. Happiness resides in it when it expresses our fullest aspiration for extended continuity.

With this view, with this triadic intention—to integrate the communal and the individual (to make social notion express concert and benevolence rather than the merely private), to deal consciously with an extended spacio-temporal continuity (to integrate this moment with an extended past and an extended future), and to liberate people to the full creativity of their wills—with this synthesis of the Greco-Judeo-Christian, the Renaissance, and the industrial society, the American socialists set out to reform their world.

CHAPTER EIGHT

Reductions and Disillusions:
Some Hard Times for the Left

I

Just as privatism became a reduction and rigidification of the radical propositions by which it was born, so too the socialist movement underwent reduction and rigidification. Whether by the human tendency to oversimplification, whereby the corners of an idea's complexity are ground away to make a dogma for a time apparently able to roll over anything; whether by the particular exigencies of the American situation, wherein the American's preoccupation with economic action forced itself on the socialist's desire to speak to the mainstream; by these and/or other causes, socialist ideology (triadic at least) was reduced—and quickly—from the complex and integrative to the simple and exclusive. Socialism in America became hardly more than a plan for "the more just distribution of the fruits of labor," and for greater economic efficiency and productivity. Poverty, which had been only privatism's most flagrantly cruel consequence (of which awareness was heightened by the wealth that privatist industrialism had created), became practically the socialists' sole concern, the elimination of poverty their only appeal. Taking at random from professional socialist literature Daniel De Leon's still reprinted "Socialist Reconstruction of Society" (1905), the only privatist evil he attacks is poverty, and the only but apparently all-embracing socialist virtue that he proposes is that under socialism laborers will get back (rather, never relinquish) the full "goods and services" value of what they produce.

No doubt there was for the socialists more than the elimination of poverty implicit in or symbolized by their rudimentarily economist program. The desire to eliminate poverty itself expressed an idea of sympathy that was alien to privatist actuality if not to privatist theory. But the trouble lies not simply in a symbol of either too vague or so close to a literal situation as to be mistaken for it alone (as when Upton Sinclair's *The Jungle* was taken to be no more than an exposé of Chicago stockyard conditions). The trouble was that in the exigencies of social action, the socialist had come not only to meet the privatist industrialist on his own ground, but to meet him on no other, to have forgotten to insist that the privatist-industrialist's ground was not enough ground for humanity to stand on. The socialists' fundamental concern had been sucked up and lost in dealing with particular disorders: the cause was forgotten in dealing with effect. And the trouble perhaps more importantly was in the degree to which the socialist came late or early to share the privatist faith in a reduced instrumentalism. Like the privatist, liberated from medieval asceticism (though, to be sure, going beyond the privatist faith that secured luxury was the goal of progress), the socialist had come to believe that economic security was, for the laboring class at least, all that was needed for the beginning of the millennium. We have discussed the socialist faith, a faith held, indeed, as a fundamental postulate of American democracy, that benevolence and reason are essential in human nature. This became a faith that history has shown people to be less than perfectly benevolent and reasonable not because of some qualities equally essential though contrary, but because of impediments in their situation rather than in their nature. Hence all that was necessary to the millennium was to remove the impediments, and benevolent reason would flower perfected. Certainly poverty—and indeed it is certain—certainly poverty and the consequent contractions of impoverished life, the primal necessity of survival at any cost, even if the cost is another's survival, are nearly insurmountable impediments to the flowering of what tendency to virtue there is in human nature. The socialist sentimentality, only a variation, to be sure, of the sentimentality characteristic of a great deal of philosophical anthropology since the Renaissance, was that once people were liberated from poverty, they would be liberated at once to unimpeded progress in the perfected society.

In this sentimental anthropology, in romantic populism, lay the American socialists' essential weakness, waiting to be exposed and in the exposure to shrivel a great deal of radical reform energy.

In part in order to speak directly to the mainstream, the socialists had reduced their program to merely a more efficient economic system: the privatists' apparent success left the socialists with practically nothing to say to the mainstream. And because the socialists had come to believe in humankind as essentially virtuous and reasonable and only superficially vicious and unreasonable, the superficial to be wiped away by mass wealth; because, then, privatism's unprecedented distribution of wealth produced no apparent moral regeneration and hence seemed to disprove the socialists' romantic faith in human nature and economic well-being, many socialists had nothing but alas to say to themselves. All the ground was cut from under them and the privatists could appear to command the field as all their own.

II

The massive exposure of socialist reductionism took sixty years to be completed. From 1893 until World War I the American situation forced no reappraisal of socialist theory. Unlike earlier economic crises, the depression of 1893 went on and on. It was harder than ever for Americans to accept their sufferings in the way that the sufferings of earlier depressions had been understood as no more than the necessary rigors of healthy purgation of the weak and inefficient, the parasites in America's economic system. Great reform energy was generated. For a time—for the next twenty years—it seemed that the most reduced socialist position was proved sound enough. Privatism could not even work on its own terms. It produced not mass wealth but robber-baron wealth and mass poverty. The term robber baron is interesting. It carried the terrible feeling that America had *not* escaped feudalism. America found itself not a society of equal and manly competitors, but a society of ignoble serfs preyed upon by a gluttonous feudal nobility. Despite the *fin-de-siècle* despair, reformers were everywhere, and twice Eugene Debs, running on an explicitly socialist ticket, got more than a million votes. This (and the 1930s) is the great time for old socialists to remember. The easiest argument was right enough. Privatism was in every sense a failure. And the greatest socialist wish, the moral voice of the masses, seemed about to be heard as never before. If the strongest part of the labor movement was AFL privatist "plain-and-simple" craft unionism, that was the work and the wish not of the great working class, but of the few small-time robber barons of labor, Samuel Gompers and the other traitors currying favor with Wall Street royalty.

The rise of the socialists continued until the beginning of the First World War. They had very nearly become an effective part of the mainstream. But the war itself, as so often before, took the energy that might otherwise have been political, and the pacifism of many socialists, their refusal to take part in a "capitalist war," made them seem a menace to national integrity. What mainstream appeal the socialists had left was demolished by the postwar opulence and the political repressions of the 1920s, the Palmer Raids and so on, of which the Sacco-Vanzetti case was the terrible dramatic climax.

But though they had ten years without a public voice, though 1920s luxury again restored privatism to the public confidence and seemed again to be fulfilling privatism's promises, and though the ugliness and inanity of 1920s luxury turned many from any hope for national morality or culture, the socialists had many places other than a reexamination of their economism and their populism to turn to. Some kept their populism intact by blaming all social failures on a few powerful individuals. Charles Beard, for example, in his *Rise of American Civilization* (1927) suggested that President Wilson got

America into the war and turned back the rise of industrial democracy single-handedly and only to protect his own political power (Beard later explained America's part in World War II in the same way, with FDR the villain). Returning to the old hope that isolation from the dead weight of a history of European corruption was the only way to make America a "city on a hill," a beacon of progress through democracy, industry, and education, Beard preached American disentanglement from the Old World and its sins.

But this was a retrenchment in panic. The main source of socialist life was not isolationism, but a new internationalism, turning not to America alone, but to Soviet Russia and the great socialist experiment. We will take up in a moment the consequence of this new allegiance. For the present it need only be said that the socialists survived the 1920s by the faith in the possibilities of the future that Russia gave them. Lincoln Steffens was only one of many to see Russia and report that the future worked. Bill Haywood, a founder of the International Workers of the World (IWW), exiled himself to Russia for his last years when staying in America would have meant jail. John Reed, a socialist hero, a villain to the mainstream, died in Russia, and his tomb there became a shrine.

The Depression of 1929 recreated the situation of 1893. Again the socialists had domestic relevance and domestic life. The extent of the depression proved again privatism's internal failure; the landslide elections of the New Deal seemed to exonerate the masses, socialist intellectuals were called to Washington to take part in government, socialist novels and plays were popular as never before. Real reforms were made. Yet in 1938 there was more unemployment than in 1933. It became clear that the New Deal had accepted from the socialists only piecemeal, more or less peripheral, ameliorations, and that thereby privatism had been saved rather than transcended. And then World War II. The united front against Fascism and Nazism made all other issues academic. As with the Civil War, as with World War

I, periods of great reform energy were funneled into a single crusade in which the clarity of life and death struggles set complexities aside. And the war ended the Depression and created the boom times of the late 1940s and 1950s.

The 1950s, of course, were importantly similar to the 1920s; both the wealth and the political repressions were repeated. In the 1910s the depression returned the argument to the Left without making clear the need for reexamination of theory or doctrine or dogma. A new depression would again have destroyed the privatist hegemony. But the privatist economy sustained by the military budget kept off depression, and large-scale socialist energy for any broad domestic program seemed quite dispelled as it was not in the 1920s. The radicals of the 1920s—however the irrelevance of mass wealth to mass morality should have threatened their theories, or however political repressions did in fact threaten their lives—still the radicals of the 1920s were not so undermined in spirit as were the American radicals of the 1950s. In the 1920s, Americans could look away from American moral catastrophe to concentrate all hope on socialism in Russia. And again, of course, the ground of their hope was eventually to crumble under them. The horrors of Stalinist tyranny and Soviet international power-politics were most shockingly what the Russian experiment proved out, and most American radicals of the 1950s were left, as they thought, without illusions and without hope. That so many radicals turned to some kind of professional anti-communism expresses the intensity of their old illusions, the shock of their disillusionment, and the desire, having found community and solace nowhere else, to find it at last in the very mainstream they had so shunned. Anti-communism became a *carte blanche* to the mainstream's bosom, and many once radical seemed to look there for some final, at least minimal, repose, the repose, perhaps, of a final self-denied and self-denying bitterness. We can say that in a way the radicals of the 1950s reaped the consequences of old naïvetés, naïve hopes, sentimental faiths. First, the socialists found themselves salesmen of wealth to a people who already had wealth. Hence the socialists' numbing sense of their irrelevance to American life. Secondly, by popular indifference or antipathy to all radical moralists, and by the tawdriness of that which engaged the popular imagination, the depraved uses to which the populace gave its attention and its wealth, many socialists felt their populism, the avenue to their socialism, finally disproved. Evolution in America had come to seem as vain a hope as revolution in Russia.

Now, to be disillusioned with American populism because mass wealth produced no mass virtue was in any case too quick a generalization. It seems downright silly to assume that opulence got by privatism will turn the masses away from or lift them above privatism. It very rarely did so for the old profiteers from the status quo, and it only exposed the naïve basis of radical American populism when it didn't do so for the masses. Surely the Left was never very much surprised when the rich defended the status quo. The pleasures of wealth point as logically if not as humanely to gluttony and defense of wealth as they do to sharing the liberation for other affairs. Privatism and the individualism that suggests the integrity and desirable community of all individuals; these two have nothing essential to do with each other. Privatism is the morality that defines economic people as competitors, judges them by their power to buy or their power to menace. Privatist wealth, however broadly distributed, proved nothing final about the effects of wealth and nothing final about human nature except that we're not likely to let go of what seems a good thing, even for something that may be a good deal better. In a competitive business society, wealth is necessarily insecure. When defense of wealth is a constant, it ought not to be surprising that people are not finally freed to concerns other than wealth, or that they regard their economic neighbors as dangerously covetous enemies. It is a truism that we covet most that which we don't have or that which we are in pressing danger of losing. The effect of wealth gained and secured as one of the consequences when communitism is an essential motive: this has yet to be substantially tested or proved. If socialists were disillusioned when under privatism the American masses' relative opulence produced no noticeable moral elevation—that is, if the socialists were disillusioned by the moral quality of postwar American life—then the socialists had forgotten their fundamental assumption: that the mode of economic action that acquires wealth influences crucially the moral quality in the uses of wealth.

The essential error in socialist populism is *not* the assumption that necessary preoccupation with competition for survival is likely to heighten people's anti-sociality. Nor is it the assumption that people have in them that which makes benevolence, communitism, and the wedding of benevolence and mastery an integral appeal. Emerson's proposition—that when the morally heroic discover the truth of their own hearts they discover at least an element, however weeded over, of their brotherhood with most people (Emerson would have to say *the* brotherhood of *all* men)—this is an essential proposition in all populism and is indeed supported by the continual emergence in history of people acclaimed heroes for their assertion of extended benevolence and mastery. Perhaps the essential error in socialist populism is in its simple melodramatic dualism. The socialists almost came to assume that poverty proved personal virtue in the poor as well as social vice in the society that tolerated poverty.

Socialist literature is often caricatured for its own melodramatic caricature of the greedy capitalist smashing the kindly proletarian. Derision of this archetype of radical propaganda is justified. One is not *necessarily* morally different from one's fellows if by chance or design one succeeds within the social pattern one's society prescribes. When we ask the entrepreneur to temper his mastery with charity, we ask him to do as a personal act of will what the society as a whole cannot do, and to undo what the society as a whole has done. (What Captain Vere in Melville's *Billy Budd* does is precisely to refuse to let society evade self-knowledge and responsibility by allowing a local humane melioration of a generally vicious social order to obscure the general viciousness. Vere's ambiguous heroism is in taking on himself the social sin, in standing unambiguously, unequivocally, and making the society stand on its primary loyalties, thereby to be utterly exposed.) So when we ask for private benevolence to patch up the victims of public policy, we ask the privatist to let the society hide its first principles by obscuring the consequence of its public policy. The socialist hope for social progress must be based on the assumption that the social order can be a primary influence on the moral quality of individual action. This applies to individual action of the rich as well as the poor, under privatism as under socialism. The socialists contradicted this assumption when they painted the privatists as individually and autonomously culpable for social vice. Perhaps the motive of the contradiction was that thereby they could support their sentimental populism with the obverse of the privatist's personal guilt, with the hope that poverty in a privatist society was an act of autonomous individual will, a moral choice, a virtuous refusal to play by privatist rules. When most of American labor history, for instance, proved only a will to re-divide the spoils and no will to make competition for spoils less the center of social life, many socialists had to pay with disillusionment the cost of their own sentimentality. But they paid more than was called for. The proposition that the social order can be a primary influence on the moral quality of individual action, and that the complexity of human character has within it that which a social order based on benevolence and community as well as mastery could heighten into prominence—this the moral failures of labor movements and political movements had not at all disproved.

And as the social order influences individual action, so human nature influences and is in greater or lesser degree expressed by a particular social order. Privatism is no less a function of human nature than a contracted social life is a function of privatism. Many socialists had simply come back to an Edwardsian anthropology for the rich (they are purely evil), an Emersonian anthropology for the poor (their pure virtue is but under the surface and to come out), and a Franklinian economism as a theory of progress (the standard of living is the only issue of serious moral import).

And the American radicals' disillusionment with the Russian experiment was again too simple. I have said that the modern socialist revolution—a Western movement—came as a child and heir of the Renaissance, that it did not repudiate Renaissance individualism, but instead proposed that individualism could best be expressed in some form of integrated cooperative community; that socialism carried also modern Western rationalistic temporalism—mastery by rational integration (comprehension) of the extended present, its past, and its long future; and that it repudiated asceticism in favor of instrumentalism, in particular proposing to inherit, by force if necessary, modern industrialism. It could hardly be more significant that Russia, and more so China, were not Western Renaissance cultures. They had no central tradition of individualism. They did not *rediscover* community: they had never left belief in its moral preeminence. To be sure, the church-state in its corruption had failed in its assigned role of the benevolent direction and integration of particular affairs, but that generated rebellion against the particular form of centralized control, not rejection of centralized control or the justice of individual immersion in the communal good. Russian or Chinese indifference to the killing of the state's enemies or to suppression of individual freedom or comfort offends and contradicts essential Western devotions, but it is perfectly consonant with uninterruptedly traditional Eastern communitism. And severe restraint or suppression of present desires for immediate pleasures may contradict what I have called the Western discovery of, and commitment to, the immediate, but it is quite consonant with traditional Eastern denigration of the present in favor of some remote past or some otherworldly future. What

the East imported of modern Western social and economic theory
was not all the Western socialists wanted to export. Or perhaps the
East did import the whole theory, including the assumption that, only
or most expeditiously, by establishing fast the instrumental power of
industrialism, could room be made for the individual, and time for
the present be created. But though you may instantly import a theory,
you cannot instantly import a tradition. In any case, the Eastern rebellions were not, in a sense, communist revolutions. Anti-individualist
communitism they already had altogether. The extremes of Stalinist
tyranny were explained in Russia as the consequence of the Stalinist
cult of personality, the cult of individual power. The Eastern revolutions were industrial, created within the framework of the old worldview rather than, as in the West, part of a total switch of centers. The
industrial and political revolutions of the East have not—despite the
relative absence of individualistic freedom—failed to be what the East
wanted them to be. Hence the often proved naïveté in Western expectations of massive popular unrest, disenchantment with the regime,
counterrevolution just waiting to be touched off. The Westerners and
the few Westernized hoping for the realization of what the revolutions
would have meant to them—they are the disenchanted. But their
enchantment was naïve and inappropriate in the degree to which they
assumed that traditional authoritarian, anti-individualist communitism could be eliminated by fiat and without the long and laborious
creation of a new social sensibility.*

---

* Many were alienated from the Russian Revolution when the Kerensky government fell. But
it was as unlikely that the Kerensky government could have survived and imposed its Western
liberalism on the alien Russian culture, as unlikely as the survival of the Weimar Republic or as
unlikely as it proved impossible for Jefferson to impose his pastoral individualism on a federal-
izing American society. Schumpeter has pointed out that the British socialist government failed
of its intentions because it was installed before the full development of monopolistic corporatism;
the socialists had no alternative but to administer (and soften the edges of) corporate privatism.
There was as little political as there was economic tradition and development for the kind of centralized authority the socialists needed if they were to create socialism. The Mensheviks' westernized liberalism was just in the reverse way inappropriate to Russian political reality. The British

When the separation of East and West was breached, the Easterner saw most prominently the power of Western industrialism, the wealth it could create, indeed the exploitation it could enforce. It saw the tools of industrialism fully developed. It did not propose—and could hardly have been expected to—some slow, gentle, easing transformation of its primitive economy. It proposed to remake the economy at once, to create industrialism at once, to meet the West on its own terms at once. The East had the political institutions to dictate such a transformation; it had the traditional poverty both to lighten a sense of the rigors of economic transformation and to heighten a sense of what was to be gained; and it had the traditional communitism to give psychological approval to the whole undertaking.

At the moment that the Russian Revolution or later the Chinese Revolution undertook to create industrialism, it should have been

---

socialists had no adequately centralized economy to take over and their traditional liberalism forbade creating such an economy by force. The Mensheviks had no domestic tradition of political liberalism to administer, and their liberalism forbade taking over the traditional authority. They were simply outside the pale of Russian political experience. The Bolsheviks were not: hence they could create the economic institutions.

As has often been said, perhaps Marx's prediction that only fully developed capitalism would produce communism was as much wishful thinking as analysis. Marx was committed centrally to faith in the civilizing power of industrialism, and he must have not only believed, but hoped that it could be appropriated at one fell swoop in its full power and, once appropriated to communal purposes, exported as a fact rather than as theory to the non-industrialized world. But Western privatism tempered itself from within with piecemeal reforms and has avoided any thoroughgoing political-economic change. Marx thought that political systems were irrelevancies as initiators of change, that economic power had to be appropriated if one were to create and establish what he hoped would be the politics of communal will. But the East had the political institutions of centralized control. It turned out to be easier to appropriate the political institutions and with their authority to create almost from scratch the economic institutions, the machinery of industrialism.

In proposing the "withering away of the state" Marx avoided, it seems to me, recognition of both human complexity and human heterogeneity. In postulating the most advanced capitalist economies as necessarily the first to create communism, he mistook a circle for a line. That is, he assumed that politics, an expression or manifestation of ideologizing human will, is only the manifestation of, and is altogether created by, economic condition. It turned out that politics— theorizing human will—could set out to create an economic condition. To be sure, economic condition essentially affected the course the will took, what it wanted to do, and the way that it did it. But the relation is circular, or better, integral, not linear in the sense that politics merely comes directly out of economics.

predictable that the economic transformation would come at the terrible cost of the repression of the individual. There was no substantial Eastern tradition to oppose the oppression, and the sight of Western wealth and power and the traditional danger of Western intervention made the drive for industrialization terribly intense and defensive and ruthless. At that point the West had (and still has, as the economic transformation spreads) a great, a wonderfully great opportunity. With its enormous power, ironically the enormous surplus power that otherwise plagues Western economic stability, Western industrialism could have facilitated the creation of modern Eastern industrialism. It could thereby have decreased at least the length of the terror by which the East would create industrialism on its own. But the logic of Western privatism did not go that way. The logic of privatism was toward hostility, aggression, isolation, sabotage, and counterrevolution. And the logic of much Western socialism had come to be a kind of Emersonian hope that a revolution could undo in the moment a sociopolitical psychology, a long history in the making, and a Franklinian hope that economic well-being was all the revolution need accomplish. Surely these hopes had to fail. And when they did, most American socialists were left alienated and impotent, reduced to a kind of Edwardsian pessimism. They left the world to the polarities of East and West and the hostilities that kept the world at the edge of some final disaster. Somehow it is less the disaster that appalls than the opportunity missed and again missed to make our unprecedented power an unprecedented instrument for the liberation and humanizing of humankind, the humanizing of the human condition. The East has great things to learn from the West. It has to learn the integrity of the individual. And the West has great things to learn from the East. It has to learn the integrity of the community. Together they could make a synthesis devoutly to be wished, a synthesis that in the making would demean neither thesis.

III

To summarize. The socialists came in the 1950s to be without important influence in America not only by the effective power of mainstream antipathy to them, but also by the history of events that exposed the sentimentality in their own position and left them, thereby, with really very little to say or do. Most of those who were above resorting to the semblance of program in professional anti-communism had little to do but snipe—with the special irony of those who know they are talking mostly to themselves—at the particular and local absurdities, self-contradictions, and cruelties of the privatist system. Socialists are born into a world where selfishness, privatism, moral isolation, are the socially sanctioned motives of economic action, sanctioned as if somehow the rhetoric of devotion could make it other than a rudimentary evil. Privatism is sanctioned by the belief that people are such that their essential motives are all privatist,* but that liberating their privatist desires contributes to the commonwealth by the fortunate dictates of natural law. For example, the law of supply and demand or the law of cyclic depressions that weed out inefficient producers, and so on. The medieval belief in people's essential depravity, paid for in a day of final judgment, was replaced by belief in people's essential depravity made useful by a God who also saw to matters of day-to-day efficiency. When the religious sanction became unfashionable, Darwinian evolution was appropriated to support belief that only unimpeded competitiveness would ensure the just dominion of the fittest. The socialists (also synthesizing many traditions, but especially the anthropology of romanticism, the rationalism of the Enlightenment, and the instrumentalism of the Renaissance)

---

* This anthropology is often supported by a confusion between the words *selfish* and *private*. We are said to act always in the pursuit of pleasure—minimum pain may be the maximum pleasure possible—hence we are essentially selfish. So be it. But it does not follow from that, that we do not get an essential pleasure from giving pleasure, an essential pain from seeing another's pain.

said that people also want community; that we are, in one tendency of our nature, fundamentally socialist; that is, sympathetic identification with one's fellows—of which cooperation is the expression in action—is fundamentally necessary to our happiness.*

So, the socialists said that in important degree people crave cooperation for its own sake and for the sake of the work it would get done. And they carried intensely the feeling that this side of our nature is our most attractive one. And they said that a social system could be devised that would maximize our tendency to benevolence and the direct contribution to communal affairs. And they proposed that the long-range planning of human affairs, given the most extensive rational examination of the human situation, was again one of the most beautiful of our possibilities. And they said that the first order of business was to eradicate poverty so that people could be free from the brutalizing struggle for mere survival. And to do this, they said, and at the same time to engage the species' best motives, the community must take over the ownership and the administration of the means of production and distribution, the whole instrumental power

---

* For proof, we can assume that a privatist morality for the family would be unbearable. On a larger scale, no one doubts the pleasure of socialist morality within, say, an army fighting a war the soldiers agree to be just. International socialism is simply the logical extension to one's full social context of what one knows to be true of local relations.

To be sure, a family without privacy for its members would also be troubling, as armies without respect for individuals are unbearable for many, if not most. But privacy and privatism are not the same thing. Celibacy is not often the desirable alternative to a family life too restrictive, and the hermit's cave is not generally the desirable alternative to the army. Voluntary association is the synthesizing alternative to both suppression and isolation. What one looks to make or find is some environment that synthesizes both one's desire for privacy and one's desire for community. Importantly, it is a synthesis, not a compromise. Compromise implies some mutual loss for mutual advantage. But for most people either privacy or community alone would be intolerable. The positive value of each depends absolutely on the presence of the other. In a privatist system people find all sorts of ways to express the communal impulse. The trouble is that these ways tend to be peripheral to the main business of the society, more or less trivial as social action. They are unsatisfactory in the degree to which the communal impulse is merely a peripheral, secondary one. The degree to which people are freed from the vocation of making money seems often in this country to be proportional to the degree of the centrality of communal works. Socialism's great contribution would be the fusion of the vocational and the communal.

of industrialism. The introduction of this last idea and its integration with the traditional canons of benevolentist morality, that was the socialist breakthrough. But in the course of the American life of socialist thought, the movement, perhaps dominated by traditional American economism, became more and more narrowly a movement for greater economic efficiency alone, assuming that economic security alone would automatically liberate us all to a fuller civilization. But American privatism produced unprecedented mass opulence, so that the reduced socialist position had nothing to say to the culture as a whole. The opulence produced no liberation to civilization, so the socialists had for themselves nothing but a sense of humanity's failure. When Eastern communism did not undo traditional Eastern tyranny over the individual, the American socialists were left alienated, so they felt, from all they had ever believed, and with no place to turn. The hardest thing is commitment to the complex and uncertain; so we construct certainty: but we pay for the respite from doubt when reality blasts our dogmas.

The failures of socialist theory most to be stressed are these: sentimental anthropology and its corollaries, sentimental populism, economism, and sentimental expectations for the revolutions in pre-industrial societies. Theoretically at least, everything may be seen to follow from the anthropology. Given the failure of faith in an absolutely powerful and moral God and, hence, a world homogeneous, morally unified, in which apparent difference, tension, and complexity were merely grafted on a fundamental moral coherence, people turned their faith toward people. But the new humanism was only half a break. It dropped the old otherworldliness, but it kept the old absolutism, only this time it was absolute human homogeneity and virtue at the center, surrounded with only superficially engrafted difference, tension, vice, and irrationality. And when we imagine that we can accomplish universal harmony, we tend also to imagine that some single agency will be the means by which we accomplish it. See the late eighteenth-century radicals' faith in political equality. See the early nineteenth-century romantics' faith in spontaneous passion. The craving for untrammeled moral order survives the destruction of each of its temples. The crumbling of one millennial faith leaves its energy to surge up again for the next generation's rebuilding. The nineteenth-century utilitarian view, built on the other half of the romantic's half-truth, illustrates the repeated pattern. According to the utilitarian, a morality is a system descriptive of the way to maximum happiness. Clearly cooperation is most efficient for any long-run mutual satisfaction. Postulating a fundamental compatibility amongst all human purposes—this followed immediately from belief in essential human homogeneity—and postulating rationality as a fundamental human characteristic, it followed that removing the impediments to human reason would establish at once universal cooperation and compatibility. The Marxian view seems simply to be that economic struggles and inequalities are the original and all-generating impediments to human rationality, hence the source of all moral disorder. By eliminating poverty, we eliminate economic struggle, and, hence, all fundamental impediments to human cooperation and compatibility.

Belief in the "withering away of the state," the death of politics is but an extension of the same logic and the ever-desired belief that people are fundamentally alike, equal not only in the deservingness prescribed by benevolence, but equal or identical in their natures, hence their desires, hence their compatibility. Any thoroughgoing benevolence has a very hard time in this world. The benevolent must sooner or later confront the difficulty of wishing well to antithetical and mutually destructive wills. This is the fundamental dilemma of benevolentist philosophy. It craves a world of universal compatibility and it finds a world full of essential incompatibilities, the lion and the lamb, the visionary and the timid, the mediate and the immediate, the indifferent and the loving, and so on and on. The fact of the dilemma turns people to find some way out, some way less rigorous than commitment despite recognition of perpetual conflict and hope of raising the level of antitheses. It turns people, if not to a god and the mystery of overriding unity, then to faith in the inessentiality of apparent incompatibility and more or less easy uncovering of identity. The heart of tragedy is, perhaps, in the absolutely necessary failure of the universalizing will to find the world as it desires it, the absolute necessity of confronting strong but mutually exclusive desires. The alternative to the experience of tragedy is more or less sentimental evasion. Marx constructed the anthropology that predicts the end of politics.

Politics are now expressions of the present form of nation-states, and certainly political forms will change radically when, as they should and probably will, the present forms of national division wither away or are somehow undone. But looking toward a millennium without politics seems to me to include a sentimental view of what politics is. In their revulsion from privatism's dignifying of competitiveness and immersion of people in their enmities, the socialists have concentrated on the species' pleasure in, and capacity for, concert, cooperation, reasoned agreement. That concentration—to which they were pushed by the privatists' preoccupation with selfishness, unreason, and malevolence—has led them to misconstrue history's widening horizons of accord as an infinitely extendable unanimity. Since politics has always been forms of competition for social authority, socialists have often tended to see politics in the future, at least, as an inessential human activity, made necessary in the past only by an encumbering history from which social morality will liberate us.

Belief in politics as a fundamental activity of human societies follows from the assumption of essential complexity, heterogeneity, and tension within the individual and in the species. Politics is the choice and administration of policy, of goals and means, and it is the choice and administration of one policy amongst many possible policies. Politics is also the choice of a system of government and of particular governors. One's politics is also a system for choosing a system. Most generally, it is a system for patterning the expression of the communal will toward whatever are taken to be communal affairs. A political system means systematized competition for the choice and direction of the policy of government, and presupposes continual differences amongst us. Belief in political liberty follows from belief in legitimate differences. Liberty and politics and government go together as a way in which the different may coexist, attempt rapprochement, and establish as extensive a community of choice as human difference allows possible. Belief in righteous dictatorship to be followed by the end of politics implies that the dictatorship will eliminate all illegitimate differences, that all differences that make for political differences are illegitimate, and since politics is a way of establishing one choice over another, politics will die as differences must, since under the dictatorship all of us will have arrived at our essential unanimity.

Ideally politics is simply a way of carrying on discussion of certain kinds of issues, and ideally government is simply the institutions of communal action, action it is the business of political discussion to clarify and choose. But actually government has been, more often than not, institutions of repression and the protection of privilege, politics has been the more or less brutal competition for mastery of institutions of repression and privilege. At the very best of actual possibilities, politics is discussions that are closed arbitrarily; that end not with arrival at universal agreement, but at some arbitrarily appointed time and with the choice by vote. The voted choice may well be simply wrong or it may well be right for the successful voters only, utterly antithetical to the interests of the voters who lost. Fear of politics has led people to faith that in the long run (so easily appropriated to all fantasies) all but ideal politics will be unnecessary. But credence for that fantasy presupposes that no discussions for choosing communal action need end before universal agreement, and that universal agreement is possible on all important communal issues.

But if, as it seems to me, people's capacity for socially concerted reasoning and agreement on extensively integrated plans is radically limited (though radically less limited than privatism believes) by gross discontinuities at once in people's horizons of perception and in their social willfulness, their desires for social prominence and authority; if, that is, people are so unlike in what they see, how much they see, how far they see, and how much they want to do, then there are at least two major dangers in the socialist anticipation of a millennium of unanimity, a society without the need for systemized competition for political authority. The first danger is, as I've said perhaps too often, the socialists' own disillusionment when the populace ignores or reviles its defenders, is indifferent or antipathetic to opportunities for even its own obvious advantage, and, indeed, undertakes the wars of ignorant enmity with the passions of crusaders.

The second danger—in the long run more important, since every generation will renew disgust with misery for which there is no necessity but our species' own moral failure; even as each generation repeats disillusionment when its young dreams fail—the second danger is that societies constructed without preparation for radical discontinuities in people's tolerance for the unusual, in people's lust for power, and in people's talent for leadership; societies that do not prepare for and legitimize competition for leadership will simply isolate the innovator and make the pursuit of power covert, clandestine, and irresponsible because unexposed to public criticism and defense.

For socialists as for America as a whole, equality is the essential moral commitment, no less psychologically intense for being foggily defined, actively and guiltily subverted. Honor for, and benevolence toward, the integrity of individual desires is the principle on which America became the first nation founded on a principle. But we came to ascribe to Nature or God the same principle of equality we so wanted and demanded from ourselves. "All men are created equal" is the essential ambiguity of American social and political thought.

Perhaps the essential misfortune of being is in the disparity of human talents. The terrible disparity amongst people's desires comes in part from the disparity in how much they see, how deeply and how far they see. The tawdriness of human history is in the disparity of power and wealth that people get and with which they can command others. In enmity to this kind of inequality, America, trusting ever in the justness of Nature, refused to believe in an innate inequality of wisdom. Hence the principle of equalitarian politics.

But Americans believe also in the justness of business competition and its consequent inequalities of wealth. Both are believed to proceed from and be morally warranted by inequality of talent, proved if all contenders are given an equal start. American mainstream thought has one anthropology and a consequent morality for politics, and another anthropology and morality for economics. Belief in equality and essential human virtue and wisdom is the basis of our politics, our democracy. Belief in inequality and essential human selfishness is the basis of our economics, our privatism. This is the crucial contradiction or equivocation in American thought. But there are truths on both sides of the contradiction, and democratic socialism is an attempt to synthesize them into a whole truth. Democracy is a socialist idea. It is the politics of cooperation; its ideal is people discovering common purpose and choosing to act together. It is the politics of concerted human will, not as an expedient, but as an essential moral beauty. Right choice by coercion is less attractive than right choice by self-conscious willful agreement. Democracy is the politics by which the greatest number are enlisted to make the will of the community. It is the politics of the faith that people are in adequate degree attracted by the idea of community, capable of taking useful part in it, and get a fundamental satisfaction from it. Socialism is no more than the extension of this anthropology and this moral idea to economics and to all communal affairs. Inclusion of more and more people in the mind of the community, as willful choosers rather than only as more or less willing subjects, has been a primary direction of social history.

Democracy in politics was the synthesis of medieval communitism and Renaissance individualism. Democracy proposes community by concert rather than by coercion. Socialism is a function of the tendency to greater inclusion. Whether or not socialism is inevitable (I cannot see that atomic annihilation is impossible), it is evidently propelled by its consonance with major traditions. Its synthesis of politics and economics is easy as a conceptual problem. Its most difficult synthesis will be of its moral aspiration and the recognition of human complexity, heterogeneity, and the weight of tradition and historically implanted character that every moment carries.

Privatism in economics recognizes disparity in talent and is a system for distinguishing those who have more of it. It also recognizes the dangers of public authority. It began as antithesis to arbitrary privilege, arbitrary authority, and arbitrary reward, and as antithesis to competition by brute physical power. Privatism's rational clarity was its integration of act and reward and the instrument for supporting choice. Money acquired was the proof of talent and the reward to it and an instrument of its will all at once. But it turned out that wealth came often to be as accidental as blood; and worse, that the talents privatism rewarded and thereby elicited were as often as not the meanest of which people are capable; and that the authority that privatism invested in the talented—that is to say, the economically powerful—was very rarely directed toward the society's advantage and the extension of the people's moral life.

Socialism must find a better way of both distinguishing excellence and assigning its proper authority, of protecting freedom without simply making a vacuum to be filled by money's power to command, and of enlisting human competitiveness directly in the positive business of social life.

For most of our history, monarchy has been the solution to the problem of leadership: inheritance or the sword has been the way to the throne, the index of competence to lead. But government by the few, arbitrarily chosen for blood or simply for military prowess, has almost always turned out to be government for the advantage of the few, neither wise not just, merely more or less corrupt, nasty, self-defensive, and repressive of the masses' capabilities. Rebelling against kings and aristocracies, discovering the moral irrelevance of distinctions by family or class, and progressively uncovering the degree to which all human qualities are socially and historically conditioned, we have in our political history moved more and more toward democracy, toward making common humanity the denominator of political legitimacy, the ultimate repository of political power. Since aristocracy came to mean not excellence, but arbitrary distinction and privilege, the tendency has been to identify citizenship and political authority not by extraordinary particularities, but by the abstracter qualities that identify the species, and in that sense unite it. Fear of arbitrary privilege and perception of the conditionality of differences has led us to assume some underlying universal identity that ought to be enfranchised and installed in power. And having discovered that people are not so bad as medieval culture said they are, the tendency has been to go altogether the other way, and believe people a great deal better than they are; to believe as fact one's wish that the species be better, more reasonable and more kindly, than many of the individuals one knows. In the past, power has tended to go to those particular and extraordinary mostly for their avarice. We have looked, then, to the abstracter qualities that define us as a species for the source of political hope. Nature perpetuates life by numbers rather than individuals; the species is secure though the individual's life may be desperately precarious. Perhaps, then, morality will be safe with numbers if not with individuals.

And I think most would agree that the democracies have in general made more livable societies than the aristocracies could. I think most would agree that democratic life has humanized the species. But one of the constant criticisms of our democratic societies is that they fail adequately to sponsor excellence. Certainly, though they have undermined the autonomy of brutish privilege, they have not made the wisest their leaders. The democracies may tolerate excellence more easily than aristocratic societies tended to, but if they have molested it less, they do not willfully profit more from what the excellent would teach, nor follow more closely where the excellent would lead.

In part this failure may be due to the traditional democratic failure to reckon with diversity of talent, of ability to lead, of wish to lead and wish to follow as facts of social life.

Perhaps the most difficult transition for our culture in general and equally for the socialists in it is to a new idea of the meaning of excellence and to some clear theory of choices properly private, those properly public and communal, and those properly to be assigned to specialists, to those distinguished by a demonstrated excellence. Such specialization is always operative in fact, but when it is left to chance rather than principled choice, the chances are good that the effective specialization will be less desirable than principled choice would make it. Democracy, whether privatist or socialist, has tended too easily to assume the proper universal authority of the majority of the general populace. Too often this has meant simply the abdication of authority to whatever individual or group would forcefully go about getting it, appropriating whatever instruments of coercion were at hand.

For the socialist, democracy is not an expedient. It is an essential, integral expression of the very socialism of the socialist, preeminent dedication to community, concert, the fullest civilization of which the people are capable. But the dangers of socialism's democracy are those common to any democracy; they appear to be that the mass becomes itself coercive, if not of the majority then of minorities, that it will allow a tyrannous authority to its officials, that the risk of the new and the expansive, being always frightening to those contented with present success, will be beyond the mass. Eastern socialism has often proved out these dangers. Western liberalism may reduce them, but socialists' traditional romantic populism may impede rationalized distribution of choices just as it weakened the socialist movement itself by hoping for too much from the populace.

Where socialist commitment to democratic morality is coupled to the traditional romantic populism—the belief that humanity in the mass is not merely amenable to civilization but by nature universally craves it, demands it because it is the essence of its aspirations, and will inevitably create it out of the chaos of its crises—where the wish for universal wisdom and virtue is transformed to faith in it, the socialists bred their past disillusionments and their disillusionments to come. Shock at the moral failures of the populace—when labor unions abandon anything and anybody to get some increase in pay, when the American labor movement itself became no more than plain-and-simple privatism, internally competitive just as corporations are, when the eyes and ears of the masses can hardly ever be turned from the banalities of mass culture (now almost always a pejorative phrase)—when this shock disillusions the socialists, it is in part because their expectations were too high. It also indicates the failure of internal consistency in socialist theory.

Socialists have always assumed that poverty degrades people, at least keeps them from what they could be. That, in large part, is what is wrong with poverty. It has equally been assumed that wealth got in an immoral system tends to degrade people by perpetuating in them the will to maintain the system that produces their wealth. It degrades them further by the psychological tension in repressing the perception of immorality. But socialist disgust and disillusionment when privatist boom times produce unprecedented lower-class opulence but no lower-class benevolence demonstrated that the socialists had come to the self-contradictory belief that the proletariat would not really have been degraded by poverty, and that when even in the workings of the privatist system proletarians would make it to the economic level of at least the lower-middle class, they would not be governed by the sociopsychological rules that had governed their predecessors. The socialist tradition in America apparently had come to hope that the mass would be *a priori* virtuous and wise, *independent* of the social situation in which its wealth was created, untrammeled by its old poverty or its new opulence or the pattern of social relations in which it had lived. Had the socialists not come so to hope, had they not lost sight of the original socialist anthropology insisting more than on anything else that the particular integration and moral direction of the human will was in large part a consequence of the pattern of human relations a society sponsors, they could not have been so disillusioned by the tawdriness of popular will in the 1920s and the 1950s. Secondly, they could not have hoped that the depressed classes of "backward" cultures, though having had no history of political responsibility, though illiterate and hence without even a literary experience of the theory and practice of participation in government, that these depressed masses could be enfranchised by one fell swoop of revolution and made instantly capable of humanitarian democracy as few people, however educated and experienced, had been. That many socialists had come so to hope would seem to be demonstrated by their extensive disillusionment when the revolutionary governments in backward cultures continued old political repressions, though presumably to dictate new social directions. Such socialists seem to have become transcendentalists like Edwards and Emerson, substituting political revolutions in the backward cultures for Edwards' sudden incursion of grace, and opulence in America for Emerson's liberation to unity with the over-soul. And they had become quite Franklinian in hoping that economic struggle and repression and poverty were the only impediments to virtue, and that economic well-being brought with it at once the full capabilities of the highest civilization.

Certainly sympathy for the proletariat does not need to mean utter identification with it, whereby the proletariat's moral failures—as certain as the moral failures of any group—must necessarily be followed by the abandonment of the whole socialist position. Radical reform movements are made necessary by the fact of human imperfection. Surely it is absurd, then, that faith in a radical reform movement should depend on belief in human perfection.

It is necessary for socialists, as for American culture as a whole, to reappraise the significance of economic well-being. The socialists must first make clear the meaning of their socialism. Opulence by greater efficiency in production and equalitarianism in distribution is neither their first nor their last goal. Their first goal is the ideal of benevolence, of sympathy and cooperation, the ideal that makes social action, the life of the community, a communal enterprise. The ideal is the essential beauty of community integrated not by fortuitous consonance of piecemeal purposes, but by fundamental pleasure in the community. Socialism is first of all the proposition that there are great things that people would rather do together, and that economic action can be among them. Our essential socialist characteristic is clear in the pleasure we know when others ask us to join in their communal affairs. Our essential anti-socialist characteristic is clear in the pleasure we get from the feeling of power when another is excluded, however arbitrarily, in the hunger we know for honor, or ease, or power that makes others appear to us only as enemies or impediments or irrelevancies to our wills.

Privatism as an economic system dignifies and enhances the anti-social, believing that nature will see to it that the best people win, and that in their victory will be everyone's advantage. Whether the best have won or not, certainly in privatism's creation of industrialism there has been at least potential advantage to all. But socialism says that we have not thereby won very much. The best in us has not won. Privatism makes social life a contest in which the anti-social is given every advantage. Socialism is a political-economic system for giving the advantage to people's socialist character, for liberating the social-ist pleasures, and for making general well-being and the extension of mastery not a fortuitous consequence of selfishness but an inte-gral consequence of benevolence. If the danger of socialism is the loss of liberty, traditional American libertarianism makes socialism here most likely to be free of those dangers. Democratic socialism wield-ing the great instrumental power of our industrial machinery could be America's great contribution to the world. The present source of socialist influence comes from the East. There it carries the weight of traditional Eastern indifference to, and even suspicion of, individual liberty. The great American possibility is that the weight of its tra-ditional individualism would liberate socialism from the danger of community integrated by repression at the same time that socialism liberates individuals from the contracted life of corporate privatism and the anxieties and the tawdry contentments and the repressions of privatist self-defense. It seems clear that no autonomous benevolence in nature or in people will suddenly turn all things right. The question is, can we create the situation in which propensities for benevolence and mastery are expressed in more than feelings of guilt, moments of aspiration, fragments of melioration. Can people's best desires be made an integral part of the daily business of communal action, of communal enterprise? It is my thesis that the old socialist faith that they can has been discredited only in the degree that socialism came for the sake of simplicity to contradict the fundamental postu-late of its anthropology—that given the complexity and heterogene-ity and hence the diverse possibilities of human nature, the character of individual action is profoundly dependent on the social situation and its history: it is there that people's morality—the pattern of their choices—is elicited.

That is, of course, an easy and obvious truth. The difficulty comes in working out its political implications. The fact is that though everyone's choices are a function of their opportunities, the same range of opportunities elicits radically divergent patterns of choice from different people. The same range of opportunities has diverse attractions in it and creates diverse allegiances. What leaps out to some is a chance at a victim, to others a chance at civilization, to others—most, perhaps—the need to find in someone or something the look of authority, a prescriber of choices, a brew of power in whose shadow one may find the repose of certainty and belonging.

That is why it seems unreasonable to assume that economic well-being, however equally distributed and however cooperatively accomplished, will eliminate deeply consequential contentions from human affairs. We don't know what future innovations the ones we now demand will liberate us to imagine. But there has been a great deal of experience that teaches us to suspect that the more thoroughgoing and expansive the innovators' intentions, the more silly or repulsive will they seem to most who administer the established way. Politically oriented people have good reason to sense most vividly the fact that politics have been more or less complexly disguised, but are essentially simple economic contentions, competitions for economic power in situations of economic scarcity. But radicals have been less reasonable when they assume that the end of economic scarcity will mean the end of political contention. Scarcity as we have known it will be overcome, but a kind of scarcity is of the very nature of reality. Every act fills its time and space to the exclusion of all the other acts. You cannot build two buildings on the same site at the same time. And the more matter, the more life, an act organizes, the more contention among diverse intentions there will be for the right to organize it. General economic well-being will not only make more and more room for individual and local autonomies: it will make (and depend on) wider and wider integrations of work and creation. If power to plan and execute these integrations is not made the subject of overt political contention, it will not thereby be made more "the people's" power, but less so: it will go to those who are best at getting such power privately and covertly. Socialists, it would seem, should be the last to argue that such talents are likely to institute the best intentions, the innovations that most extend the humane. We must make a politics that guarantees the innovators a chance openly to seek their constituencies: not less to counteract power's tendency to corrupt by making us want to keep it no matter what its moral content, than to counteract weakness's equal tendency to corrupt by teaching us subservience to whatever established power happens to command.

It does not betray the radical sensibility's commitment to humane dignity to know that its future will be as tense as its past has been. It does not dignify the radical sensibility to pretend that old half-truths have no truth in them because they were used to justify injustice. It may be a submerged but frightening suspicion that conservative pessimisms are really right that leads radicals first to believe that the future must be perfectly discontinuous with the past if we are to believe in it at all, and second, to become hopeless pessimists ourselves when the new world turns out to be as complicated a process as the old world had been. Radicals do better when they know that modern socialism is not a sudden leap above history, but an attempt to consolidate the best that's in history.

Modern socialism is, after all, a logical historical consequence of Western privatist industrialism: its greatest child, I would say, however frightening the child is to the parent insulted and threatened by the child's assertiveness and engagement in a new future—playing out again the drama of the parent who feels accused and abandoned by the child's wish for particularity. Many parents want to make more than a contribution to the future, they want to make its perfected finale. A parental fantasy is to create for one's children a perfect world. As religion expresses our inability to tolerate imperfection in the universe, so anxious, defensive, and accusing parental conservatism expresses our inability to tolerate our own imperfection and the slight significance of our life's work. And so, no doubt, the child's absorption in a sense of the parents' failure, ignorance of the parents' virtue, the failure of compassion for the parents' ordeals express the child's inability to tolerate imperfection in the parent, express the blasted wish that the parent *had* made the world one and whole and perfect. And perhaps there is also in the parents' failures a foreshadowing image for the children of their own failures, the ominous insight of how little they too may accomplish. The desire for unmolested, for finished, unity often makes conservatives of parents and radicals of their children, and often will make conservatives of the children too, in their turn.

It seems that the ironies and ambiguities and complexities that experience teaches can turn the Icarian aspirations of the young into the surly, defensive, moral timidities of age. Rarely can we know at once the truths of both. I think, though, that it is not necessarily sentimental to say that it need not always be so. Melville wrote *Billy Budd* when he was seventy years old, and the writing box in which the manuscript was found had this legend written under the lid: "Be true to the dreams of thy youth."

CHAPTER NINE

The Exuberant Radicalism of the 1960s

This book took too long to write. My sense of its most pressing object—of the people I want most to talk with and what I want most to say—changed as the social situation changed and I have had from time to time to stand back to decide about that again. My underlying commitments have been the same, but I have had to refocus my sense of the terms of their immediate relevance. Right now what I think most about is the factionalism of the Left. I know that factionalism can be useful: it can press us to refine and sharpen and extend our understandings. A soft, loose amity can sponsor a merely sloppy benignity. But factionalism can also be fratricidal, and on the Left it often has been. The main reason for that is, I think, that radicals are always few, preponderant power is almost always their enemy's, and so, needing some more manageable contests, radicals fight among themselves. The radical's situation is rarely emotionally luxurious, and living always without luxury is depressing: perhaps to argue method with those who share one's fundamental commitments feels like luxury compared to the nasty work of arguing with those who think the status quo fine. But it is a bitter, surrogate luxury, one that radicals cannot well afford, dissipating against themselves, as it does, energy scarce in the society to begin with.

Factionalism is one of the ways in which radicals deal with frustration. We react differently—less well, as a rule—to frustrations that surprise us than to frustrations we expect. One of the things I want this book most to say to the New Left is that we must try not to add to the frustrations inevitably imposed by capitalism's power, the frustrations that come only from our own sentimental expectations. The point of the history I've delineated here is that we should be surprised by neither.

When in the early 1960s the New Left began, it was remarkably free of factionalism. The sense was that what joins radicals is so much richer than what divides them that it deserves to be particularly vivid in their sense of one another. What surprised young radicals through much of the sixties was not frustration but success—the speed and relative ease with which their movement spread. What surprised everybody was that the young radicals were mostly children of the affluent, though convention has it that class position dictates political allegiance and being raised to upper-class privileges ought to make one's politics the defense of privilege. The extent of the exceptions to that rule raises some interesting questions about the sources of political orientation, questions into which I want a little later to look. For the moment my point is that an exuberant sense of success and well-being permeated the first years of the New Left, and factionalism was therefore slight then. That exuberance had, I think, several sources. For one, the first focus of New Left action was civil rights for blacks. In part because America is now an imperialist nation and imperialist nations keep their own under-classes loyal by distributing some of the loot of empire among them, few had an interest in keeping the American blacks peculiarly deprived, and the managerial classes, at least, saw that the pursuit of international empire would be better served by mollifying than fully opposing domestic radical agitation for the sake of the blacks—because of all this the civil rights activists were quick to get rectifying laws, promises, and rhetorical support from the liberal mainstream. For the radicals to get so fast such large-sounding concessions felt like power.

The mushrooming of their movement amongst students felt like still more power. The 1950s sense that radicals are few, far between, hidden, and morose, was replaced by the sense that there is one restive under almost every student's skin, eager to come out shouting and grandly to get busted at the first confrontation with the hypocritical repressiveness of established academic, government, or corporate authority. And because the student radicals could not be accused of seeking merely their own economic advantage—many already had that and were clearly rather jeopardizing than advancing or protecting it—they had not only the feeling of power inherent in the sense of the unquestionable moral dignity of one's own devotions (a sense that sacrifice has always been felt to prove), they had also in the wonderful surprise at their own altruism, and in the exhilaration of militancy for its sake, the grounds for a newly optimistic political anthropology that made them feel more powerful still. We have always understood that if anything will produce revolutionary intentions, it is the loss of accustomed economic advantages: the spread of affluence after World War II had therefore no little part in the Old Left's depression of spirit. When it turned out that children of the affluent were among the most likely to become radical—that in this unexpected way capitalism was producing the partisans of its overthrow—when the very grounds of pessimism turned out to be the grounds of optimism, the relief was enormous, quadruply delightful, contributing still more fuel to the expectation of an imminent revolutionary transformation of American society.

And this was not all that induced such expectations and the expansiveness of radical energy that came with them. Perhaps the most important was the success of the Cuban and the Vietnamese revolutionaries. If these two tiny powers could survive the colossus' might, then clearly the colossus was not so mighty. To be sure, had there not been counter-colossi, Russia and China, in the background, America would probably not have hung back from the total obliteration of the Vietnamese or Cuban revolutionary forces. These Davids' success against Goliath depended on their having their own Goliaths behind them. But that doesn't change the look of the contest or the extraordinary news in the fact that small revolutionary movements can survive against imperialism's concerted power. Imperialism is not new. What is new is the small colonized powers' ability to survive in revolution against it. And nothing will embolden radical inclinations and heighten solidarity amongst those who have them so much as the discovery that established authority is after all vulnerable and displaceable. Then people discover how constrained life was under it and how much nobler life will be when those in league with the future will at last have displaced the declining fathers of the old way and the old rule. Inclinations that had been denigrated and inhibited by fear of an omnipotent-looking authority's displeasure with them become gorgeous when it's discovered that authority's displeasure is losing its teeth.

The revelation that the capitalist fathers' international power was mutable and waning, heightened and was in turn heightened by what the children of the affluent would know at home. "There is something," Hawthorne said, "so massive, stable, and almost irresistibly imposing in the exterior presentment of established rank and great possessions, that their very existence seems to give them a right to exist; at least, so excellent a counterfeit of right, that few poor and humble men have moral force enough to question it, even in their secret minds." Even those few outside the pale of wealth who do have the moral force to question and to oppose wealth's authority do so with the somber sense of the unequal battle they've taken on and of the dreadful retributions for them if they lose. But the children of the rich are not only likely to be safe from the worst retributions: they also know from everyday experience that their parents are not the paragons their rank and great possessions cow the world into believing them to be. Of course, when all the world defers to the parents and their class and either hurries to do their will or is crushed, these children tend to be deeply unsure about the meaning of what they know—the meaning of the "exterior presentment" they know to be a fraud. Children in such circumstances tend to feel either that they must be wrong about their parents or that their parents are aberrant of their class, peculiarly undeserving of its privileges of power and luxury. Both feelings turn against the children—making *them* feel peculiar and alone—making *them* bear the weight of the accusation properly the parents' and their class. With what liberative force will the children grasp, then, the world's proof that their parents' social power is as porous as their private virtue? How expansive for the children will be the discovery that the parents' tumble from authority and the desert of it first joins the parents to their class (thus saves the children from the sense that it's only their parents that are frauds), then joins the child to all those who suffer humiliation at authority's hands.

My guess is that the New Left was so full of a sense of humor, of fun, of sport (a sense that quite differentiated it from the Old Left and made the Old Left nervous) in part because they were the children of the established authorities they opposed and knew close up how hollow their parents' social dignity really is. People in great public offices are ominously imposing in a way they are not when seen at home. The joke many on the New Left knew and were delighted to publish was in the old secret of the outrageous discontinuity between authority's magnificent public demeanor and the scruffy tensions of its privacy. Puncturing a balloon of pretension and presumption is more fun and easier when you know it's only a balloon, having yourself seen it inflated.

And as is usually the case, the parents contributed not only indirectly but also directly to their children's radicalization.* I suspect

---

* When parental hypocrisy or some other form of ambivalence about fundamental values gives children reason not to admire their parents—reason to wish not to see in their parents the model of their own future—children want, then, to feel that there is no binding connection between themselves and their parents at all. When one's past does not make the future look promising, one wants to have no past. (Mark Twain's fantasy that his parents were not his parents but strangers entrusted with some aristocrat's orphan—that was a conventional fantasy bred out of a conventional wish, both much involved, I think, in Huck Finn's "lighting out for the territory" and away from all society's drags on his "freedom." He wanted to be where there was no history.) Since history is always the record of binding connections, an unattractive history engenders antihistoricism. When one knows too frighteningly well where one's errors and a tendency to them come from, one will be prepared for the sake of liberation from them to deny the fact that one's truths have a history, too. The Marxian insight sentimental radicals most consistently ignore is bourgeois society's creation of the situation, the energy, the instruments, and the ideas for a real rather than a merely fantasized socialism. It would be easier to be hopeful if history were morally straighter, less ironical and convoluted, and quicker. But it isn't, so fine wishes and frail hopes look to escape the past and its intertwined ways and its slowness.

that the permissive child-raising that became fashionable after World War II has had a lot to do, quite as its enemies say it has, with the increasing rebelliousness of American adolescents. I don't know why permissive child-raising became so fashionable. Perhaps the spread of affluence after the war spread self-respect among those who got it (privatism has always devoted itself to heightening our tendency to feel economic condition to be the index of personal worth), and their increasing self-respect led them to respect their children more than earlier generations respected theirs. In any case, respect for the child's nature is clearly the fundamental principle of permissiveness, and equally clearly permissiveness became the fashionable mode of child-rearing among the affluent classes. Dr. Spock's book on child care argues committedly for the first, and by becoming one of the best bestsellers of all time is an index to the second.

If children are taught that they are nice, hence that their desires are, the gratification of their desires will come to seem to them the principle of justice. The trouble that makes for the children comes when they confront the fact that their desires are many and not necessarily compatible and that justice is not so easily come by as they may once have thought: as they grow they must more and more choose between antithetical interests, not so much more easily chosen among for being their own. But that is (or can be, anyway) a civilizing trouble. The trouble for the parents comes when it turns out that they will have empowered in their children both a general self-respecting assertiveness and particular desires the parents themselves do not admire. That also is likely to be a civilizing problem, tending increasingly to displace old, authoritarian timidities, but more fraught with contention and remorse than is the problem of the individual's confrontation with his or her own complexity. Sex is the most vivid stuff of these problems. In our culture the development of respect for sex has taken a long, long time. Very few have accomplished it altogether. The liberals who became parents after World War II had got so far as to regard infant and child sexuality—that is to say, essentially pre-social sexuality—as probably good and proper. Though such hesitancy as the parents felt about even the pre-adolescent sexuality of their children must have gotten stronger as the children got older and closer to social sexuality, and though the hesitancy no doubt got communicated to the children and may be involved in their later pursuit of somewhat impersonal sexual relations (impersonal sexual relations are closer to the pre-adolescent auto-sexuality the parents less hesitantly condoned); still the liberal permissive child-raising styles that became fashionable for the affluent classes in the 1940s were striking for their view that pleasures—and sexual pleasures not least among them—are nicer than pains, hence people are more justly gratified than thwarted. When children took this view into their adolescence and their relations with one another, the parents were often shocked and furious, as if it had not occurred to them that open and prideful and equalitarian adolescent sexual relations were simply an implication of respect for infantile sexuality. It had more than occurred to the children: it had been bred into them. When you begin by teaching people that their desires are good, you make them proud. If, then, you suddenly take it all back and tell them that their fundamental desires are not nice, the pride you've already engendered will make them respond to the reversal, your fury, your threat of rejection, and the assertion of your authority with their rejection, their fury, and their rebellion— especially when your own sexual activity makes your denigration of theirs look absurdly hypocritical.* And it is also likely to teach them to feel common cause with all who suffer under the logic of unequal inhibition. Again, I don't think that it is class guilt that makes the children of the affluent become radicals in alliance with the economic interests of the poor as much as it is an expansively prideful sense of

---

* Just as it is depression—a sudden deprivation of accustomed rewards—not continuous poverty, that makes a people demand economic reform.

fraternal identification with the deprived, all of whom together will have the power to overthrow the authority that in its different ways deprives them all. To prideful victims, victimization itself can come to seem to be the badge of virtue. There is an accurate—if morally perverse—justice in the trial that found Dr. Spock a key conspirator in the movement to support both the Vietnamese revolutionaries and the Americans who refused the draft to fight against them.

My point is that all these concomitants of the rise of the New Left in its early years—the initial successes of the civil rights movement; the optimisms and the sense of easy potency that came with the inherited affluence of many of the young radicals; the undoing of the old fear of broadened bourgeois success as capitalism's stay against radicalization; the elation that came with the revolutionary nations' victories against American imperialism, charging the air with energies liberated by capitalism's presaged decline; the success of the sexual revolution, so readily consummated by individuals, generational in its breadth, and lending its rhythm of expectation to the revolutionary politics with which it was connected—all this gave to the New Left in its early years an expansive, exuberant confidence, and such confidence inclines us to amity rather than to factionalist dispute and exclusivism.

But these optimisms and successes bred not only confidence and amity. They bred also the expectation of the imminent revolutionary transformation of all of American society. The tempo of the radicals' particular successes was felt to promise general political success at the same tempo. People astonished and delighted by the speed and ease and pleasure of their own radicalization couldn't help assuming the same speed and ease and pleasure and the same political direction for practically everybody. Certainly for those so much more oppressed than college students are by privatist society and thereby with so much more to gain from socialism.

That is to say, America's radicals had again (in circumstances extraordinarily conducive to it, to be sure) succumbed to millennialism: the expectation of the sudden and total beatification of the world. And again the expectation was wrong. It turned out that though the future may belong to socialism, in America preponderant power is still capitalism's. And by the late 1960s frustration of their expectations and their desires—and the assassinations of their leaders—again turned many on the Left to vent their angry energy on one another: again factionalist dispute became a preoccupation. Instead of regarding a wide diversity of activisms and activistic styles and activist objects—as the New Left did in the early 1960s—as a way to make sense of the radical sensibility's wide diversity of social contexts, of psychological orientations, of talents, of degrees of seriousness, of capacities for continuous political concentration, and of its very pre-revolutionary situation, the New Left came by the late 1960s to regard such diversities as failures to be corrected by internal contention. Again capitalism's power to endure and to impose its cruelties on the world surprised the radical sensibility and made it strident or melancholy. The spasm of revivified, concerted anger generated in the spring of 1970 by the invasion of Cambodia and the government's killings at Kent State and Jackson State had spent itself by the fall. The New Left entered then a period perhaps of contraction, at least of reconsideration. Everybody of every age seemed suddenly to have gotten older.

It is pretty clear that the New Left's prospects are not what for a long time the young radicals thought or felt them to be. And it is also pretty clear that the New Left is at best imperfectly free of the Old Left's sentimental optimisms that set it up for the ennui and rancorousness and the spiteful factionalism of the disillusioned.

So I want to say again that though the radical sensibility's prospects are not millennial, it does not follow that the prospects are only bitter. My sense is they are as good as, perhaps better than, they have ever been. We know two things that we didn't know before, and they both promise much. We know that though America has rather petit-bourgeoisified than proletarianized its under-classes, it has proletarianized

the under-nations, and they have become revolutionary as Marx pre-
dicted the proletarian would. A general pessimism based on America's
failure to produce a revolutionary working class (like an optimism
hanging fragilely and anxiously on the belief that we will produce one)
seems to me simply too nation-bound. Despite America—and also
because of it—the pre-industrial nations are going their own revolutionary way. That America does not now and may never want to
have a future commensurate with its humane possibilities does not
mean that the world will have no future or only a desperate one. It is
no more crucial to the species' progress that its finest understandings
and intentions be spoken in English than it was that they be spoken
in Greek or Latin.

And secondly, we know that privatist affluence tends to produce
some radicalism among its own heirs. Marx and most radicals since
thought it would do so only when the affluent felt themselves in danger of being forced by the most powerful competitors down into the
ranks of the proletariat. But it has turned out for many that radicalism
is not only a reaction to private economic danger. Something *inherent* in its commitments to the extension of benevolence and humane
mastery appeals to us, and the freedom that relatively secure affluence gives us lets us feel that appeal and the pleasure of self-respect in
identifications across the national and racial and gender lines of class
interest. Thought is reactive: our predecessors' errors focus our atten-
tions and narrow them for the work of contradiction. The patient sentimentality of the romantics and the rationalists who expected virtue's
radiance or its logic alone to draw history forward—these sent Marx
to look for something meaner and more dependable as the motive of
progress. He found much. I'm sure we are not yet finished filling out
the implications of his discoveries. But we can also say to Marx that if
class interests alone explain one's politics, how are we to understand
him? It is not only the juxtaposition of the means to wealth and our
own poverty or fear of it that radicalizes us. There is something in us

that makes equalitarian well-being and work of which the object is humane mastery the condition of our self-respect. That even secure bourgeois affluence can excite some of us to that possibility surely substantiates our socialism.

But all that is again too general to mean much for my argument against radical factionalism and the sense of impotence that leads to factionalism.

It seems clear that the rise of radicalism in America can at the very least inhibit America's military imperialism. To do that is to reduce the major inhibition of the revolutionary transformation of the pre-industrial societies. And to do that is to make a major contribution to the empowering of the radical sensibility in the world.

CHAPTER TEN

Technology and Democracy

I

Part of the absurdity of human history is that the enormous powers our species has made to extend its dominion over nature, to enfranchise its will in the world, may at any moment be used to destroy the species, to wipe out the history of its development. A primal moral idiocy has the use of tools it has taken a whole species' history to make. It is absurd because of the extravagant polarity of the possibilities. The idiocy would be pathetic only were it not for the fact that no less characteristic of our development is the progressive extension of knowledge, power, and human community. It takes a long civilizing history to generate revulsion toward the use of power for the sake of ignorant enmities. It is important to stress that the absurdity necessarily implies both the great progress and the banal impulses toward catastrophe. If the sense of absurdity is not merely to alienate us from the work of civilization, it is important that we understand the concomitants of the progress that makes our time so dramatically heightening of human complexity. Because our literature of the absurd is nowadays so good at delineating the idiocy and the madness and the trivial greed that organize so much of our use of the power we have, we must try also the difficult business of delineating rather than implying through the forms of our disgust the ideas of virtue we hold to, and their lines in the network of history.

It seems to me that progress toward civilization may be subdivided into work of three kinds: economic work, of which the object is acquiring sustenance; intellectual work, of which the object is understanding; and political work, of which the object is establishing social purpose and directing social action.

Economics. We, like other animals, give a major part of our time to getting sustenance. Our economic history is extraordinary in that we have gotten radically better and better at economic work. The progressive extension of our power to make our environment yield sustenance has meant a progressively extensive shift from preoccupation with survival to preoccupation with luxury, a progressive reduction in the time needed for economic action, and, as work has gotten more and more specialized and its products shared, there has been a progressive multiplication of the kinds of work that get sustenance. All together, this has meant an increasing extension of choice as to how one will spend one's time. Our history as economic animal is a history of the decrease in the degree to which nature has imposed the duration and form of economic work. Within the possibilities of automation, restrictions upon choice of economic work or freedom from the need of it will now be imposed primarily by society, by a society's ability to choose the freedom automation makes possible. The freedom available traditionally to a hereditary aristocracy, to those born free of the need to work for sustenance, now could be available to all the members of any highly industrialized society, if the society would choose it. Ever since we have had a social history, we—our society—have been able in increasingly ample degree to choose the relation between work and sustenance. The contemporary climax in human economic history is that now societies may choose to sever altogether the dependence of sustenance on economic work.

Intellectual work. If by self-consciousness we mean consciousness of the diverse inclinations that motivate our actions, the heterogeneous determinants of the will, the complexity of desires for whose sake we undertake action and that we must somehow integrate and choose among so that we can undertake action; if, that is to say, by self-consciousness we mean understanding of the relation between action and the complex of impulses that makes will, then human progress toward self-consciousness has been very great. Our history can almost be said to be progress—fluctuating, to be sure—toward confrontation of our own complexity and the historical, hence malleable, ground of our will, and toward the recognition that morality is the hierarchical patterning of our own desires. The primitive moral sensibility is expressed in the idea of the taboo, the dissociation of moral significance and inclination. The infant and child live by taboos and learn rules of behavior out of necessary deference to the morally arbitrary power of the parents. Virtue for children is that which is felt to please parents, who are the initial source of the child's security or jeopardy. Virtue for primitive people is that which is felt to please the arbitrary power of personified nature, the source of their security or jeopardy—personified so as to be psychologically comprehensible. Some children—perhaps those whom parental love gives a sense of self-respect and of security—learn to trust their own inclinations, since those inclinations are part of the person the parents admire, and such children thereby learn to become somewhat easily aware of more inclinations than merely the inclination to please parents.

Our history of progressively successful adaptation to nature and of nature suggests to us that nature must after all like us very much, hence we are likable, hence our own inclinations must count for something in the world, just as children's inclinations count with the parents who love them. Hence the progressive inquiry into the heterogeneity of inclinations, in part simply to see how they might be satisfied, which of them or which pattern of them we finally want parental nature to attend to. Self-knowledge is a function of self-differentiation and self-respect, neither of which is engendered in a situation of constant jeopardy and fear. They are engendered amidst the luxury of security, the habitual expectation that we will be gratified. The history of our progress toward security in nature is the history of our progress toward self-knowledge. Taboos are systems of arbitrary, impersonal compliance. Religion is the halfway house, the mixture of compliance and assertion of the personal inclination that will fix the parental obligation to provide security. Taboo makes no moral distinction between the powers to be placated—it proposes to placate them all. Religion asserts the moral qualities—the human standards—that the god must represent if people are to remain under obligation. Naturalistic morality, a contemporary of the modern mastery of nature, comes at last to assert that a morality is no more and no less than the systemizing of one's own wishes, and depends altogether on one's own power for its success in the world. Security makes us willful enough to comprehend our jeopardy. Benign parentage facilitates the willfulness, the sense of independence, that makes it possible, paradoxically it may seem, for us to face the degree to which we may be alone.

We look out as we look in, when we have been raised not to fear what we will see. Empiricism bespeaks confidence that experience will support rather than humiliate us. It seems no accident that the breakthrough in self-consciousness initiated by Freud should have come just after the Romantic period (the period characterized by widespread faith in the wisdom of the heart, the rectitude of spontaneous inclination, a corollary of the Romantics' belief that nature loves them), and that the Romantic period should have followed the industrial revolution.

The history of our progress in ability to establish ourselves in nature, with more and more time to give to the niceties of our own desires, is also the history of the progress in, and ability to see, the modes of natural relation. The knowledge of one's own particularity is knowledge of one's difference from others, which means perception of the ways in which others are particular, too. Discriminatingly to consult one's own desires means discriminatingly to investigate the modes of force amidst which and upon which one's own desires must be acted for. Hence the course of knowledge includes increasing perception of antitheses and compatibilities amongst our own desires, increasing perception of difference and continuity amongst us, and increasing perception of the particular forms of the willfulness of other elements of nature. Projection is a primary mode of human perception. As our own heterogeneity becomes known to us, the heterogeneity of the world can be known too. That we perceive by projection means not only that we project our character, but also that we project our wishes onto the universe. Thought is part of the instrumental apparatus for acting upon the environment, and just so far as reality remains remote from our wishes, just so far does thought—given our very limited ability to endure frustration—make up the difference by fantasy. The progress of our instrumental power is parallel to the progressive decrease in the need for magic, the need for thought to displace the source of power. Our wishes need fewer supernatural powers to support hopefulness; we imagine fewer of them into the universe; as we grow confident of our ability to manage natural forces, we look more and more closely at them, until we discover that all life is but the ways in which the forms of matter exert themselves upon one another, each organism resisting and pushing to establish the particular pattern of its own survival. We are extraordinary in nature for the diversity of environments in which we can survive, the diversity of conditional patterns compatible with our contentment. Ours is the extraordinary problem that we must *choose* amongst relatively diverse modes of behavior. Our history is extraordinary in that it makes a greater and greater amplitude of choices available, a wider and wider province of choice in which each must live, a wider and wider world in which choices have effect. Within that history is the progressive culling out from human thought of belief in supernatural—in extrinsic—sources, supporters, or dependencies of the will. The will has its own natural history. Progress in the knowledge of that history is a part of progress in the will's potency. The growing amplitude of the will's domain supports the pride that makes self-knowledge possible because attractive. But the will's domain is only the promontory from which the will sees, from which it stands looking, an insatiable imperialist, at farther and farther horizons. The will sees always farther than the will commands;

hence pride alone learns humility (unvaried impotence learns only humiliation), and perhaps it is only pride that learns sympathy for all those who like itself yearn and fail in nature's massive mixing of wills.

Politics. The subject of politics is those institutions for directing communal life. The overall history of politics shows a progressive increase in the size of the political unit—from the cave to the tribe, and so on—a progressive inclusiveness of the people as equal participants in the political will, and a progressive extension of the range of actions made subject to the political will. The great thrust in the politics of the last two centuries has been the radical extension of suffrage to people whose wills had not before been thought to have any political legitimacy. Part of the history of the will's domain has been a growing equalitarianism—the view that anyone's will ought to have as much social force as any other's—and a growing cooperatism—the view that people acting in chosen concert are more effective and more admirable than people acting alone or under coercion. Governments have been less and less thought of as devices for repressing inclinations to evil, more and more thought of as the instrument for the expression of human concert, itself a good and at the same time the best way toward the social good. The species' progress suggests the individual's worth. As the extent of the will's domain grows larger, action must be more and more the cooperation of masses; as individuals discover the potency of their kind, they discover their own dignity. Politics is the formal pronouncement of what in the day-to-day life of economic action the will discovers it can do. Tribal fathers and kings are work-a-day political corollaries of the gods our wishes create to care for us in the cosmos. Democracy is the political corollary of the masses' discovery that they can take care of themselves. Wealth's value—indeed wealth's meaning—is defined by degree of freedom of choice. Wealth has to do with ownership, and to own something is to have it subject to one's will, to have the power to direct its use. As societies have by an increasing scale of socially integrated economic action gotten richer and richer, the populace has had available to it an unprecedented freedom, and they have come not only to respect their own wills but to respect also cooperative action in which their wills are expressed most potently. The history of the species' increasing economic potency includes the history of each one's increasing ability to own oneself and, in concert with the masses of which one is a part, to own one's society, to own, so to speak, the political institutions that define the society's proper objectives and regulate the institutional instruments for getting there. The history of politics has been in general, that is to say, a movement toward democracy.

Democracy is a complex idea. It can be taken to express the species' self-respect. It can express the moral ideal of cooperation and sympathy. It can express the individual's fear of the dangers of prominence and the desire for the easing safety of immersion in anonymity—the wish to be not a person but a particle of the people. It can express faith in a general wisdom, or faith, merely, that the disorderly and ineffectual populace is less dangerous in authority than individual power is likely to be.

Whatever the possible meanings of the idea of democracy, the major force in the history of its progressive engagement of human commitment has been in common people's discovery that they *can* have the kind of freedom, the effective willfulness, that only aristocracies had before, and in moralists' feeling that all people ought to have it because individuals trying to survive is the essence of life in nature, because the choice of concert is beautiful as it manifests the progressively discovered continuity of human nature under the superficial differences of class or race or gender or culture.

The history of the techniques of work includes the progressive socialization and progressive specialization of labor. Specialization enhances and is enhanced by individualism—the belief that an individual's particular talents are socially legitimate and useful, and that therefore the society ought to provide wide freedom for their individualized development. Socialization of labor—that is, the extensively organized and planned cooperative work of large numbers of workers that has been more and more characteristic of every kind of labor, from the farm to the factory to the university—enhances and is enhanced by the ideal of popular sovereignty, the ideal that nothing that affects the people's life should remain independent of the people's concerted will, that political work as much as economic work should be the subject of extensively organized and planned cooperations.

In progress from the familial cave to the intercontinental coalition as the key boundary of political geography, society has progressed radically in its ability to facilitate both individual differentiation and cooperative public power. An essential complexity—at times it seems the essential irony—of human social life is that each depends on the other and each can be the cardinal danger to the other. Democracy's virtue is in its attempt at synthesis, its attempt to be at once the politics of differentiation and of public cooperation, its attempt to make coherent the main thrusts of our political history. That is democracy's virtue and, of course, its problem, sometimes, indeed, its dilemma.

Knowing that progress is the fruit of innovation, society must facilitate freedom—the opportunity for experimentation. It must at the same time protect itself against private gluttony and the use of freedom as merely an opportunity for individual imperiousness. Innovators' opportunities are dependent on the social cooperation that gives them freedom for experimentation, but they must protect themselves against the majority that reviles originals for their danger to the orderliness it's accustomed to. The doctrine of sanctity of individual belief is the heretic's main protection against martyrdom, yet the heretic's object is usually, perhaps always, a change in public policy; heresy will be for nothing unless it becomes cooperative public policy.

These are the general problems with which any democracy must of necessity deal. They can be put as axioms. The particular problems with which contemporary American democracy must deal are not at all so easily or quickly to be formulated. They are problems created by a social-economic-political situation radically unlike that in which the main terms of our democratic ideology and our institutions for reifying them were established.

II

I have been saying that democracy is integral to our whole progressive history of economic, intellectual, and political work. The histories of these kinds of work have come now to fruitions and germinations that will mark the end of a period and the beginning of another, as did, for example, the revolutions in economics, in thought, and in politics of the late eighteenth century. America's contribution to that progress has been very great. The question now is whether America will be willing to continue, whether America will undertake the political progress—the extension of democracy—that can make moral sense of our economic power and our understanding of the human condition.

If progress is the extension of individual freedom and the extension of social continuity and the extension of power on which both depend, then from the seventeenth century through the nineteenth century America was among the most progressive countries in the world, perhaps, indeed, the most progressive country in the world. Most Americans felt it: they felt themselves to be in league with the future, and they were exuberant. If the primary impediment to progress—to an increasing range of choices—is poverty, then America's primary contribution was the unprecedented mobility toward wealth it made possible. Many thought it the American vice, many thought it the American virtue, but everybody agreed that economic success was the preoccupation of the American character and opportunities to get there the essential obligation and accomplishment of the American system.

It is not less true for being now a truism that America is a migrant's country. What most have migrated from have been systems that perpetuate poverty and its constraints. What most have migrated to has been economic opportunity. Few can maintain complicated aspirations or consciousness of the complications of their distress. The good life seems to be the simple opposite of the lowest common denominator of our misery. Most come to America to get freedom from poverty. Wealth has appeared to us not as a liberation to extra-economic concerns, but as itself the final accomplishment. If poverty is hell, then wealth is heaven. We have been like the sick man who imagines that if he were only well he would be perpetually happy. For the sick man that is probably a useful illusion. So it has been for the American people. No country has accomplished more toward creating the situation in which people can be free. The appalling question our accomplishments have brought us to face is, "Free now to do what?" For three centuries our social life has been for the most part organized by a single aspiration. It worked. But now the brink of its realization has a double terror: success is not what we thought it would be—all that work, all that life, has meant much, much less than we dreamed: what aspirations now can give our lives, our work, meaning? We are living on leftover ideology. It has never been easy to make a new one. The present flowering of reactionary politics expresses the wish, the need, to believe that the now is no different from the then when we knew exactly where we were going. And we will shoot those who say no.

Democracy has always to do with two values: first, freedom; second, equality—the idea that everyone ought to have whatever it is that the society thinks of as the preeminent good. For three hundred years the preeminent good has seemed to us to be wealth, and freedom has meant to us freedom to get wealth, especially freedom from the imperious sociopolitical systems that depend on and sponsor mass poverty. Our feeling for the positive function of government was narrowed by the migrants' memory of the history of governments that had oppressed them. Monarchists assume that the government should own the people. The democratic breakthrough of the eighteenth century was in the idea that the people should own the government. But we could think of our ownership only as the power to keep government out of the way except as the guarantor of our privacy.

But there is no theoretical contradiction between democracy and governmental—that is to say, the people's—ownership of our economic institutions. Indeed, if the government's function is primarily to guarantee freedom, and our economic institutions are at once major regulators of our lives and major instruments for our liberation from the tyranny of nature, then it follows that our government must own our economic institutions. Either democracy is a good idea or it is not. Either the people are capable of owning their government—the institutions for directing their communal life—or they are not.

In the nineteenth century, the separation of political and economic institutions made sense. We were migrants fleeing governments that had always been instruments of privilege. But even if that had not been the case, the land, the opportunity, was so large, the government so small, and the population so dispersed, that private enterprise was the only kind there could have been if rapid expansion was to be our object. But that is no longer the case. Our democratic ideology was established when the family farm or the small shop was the essential economic unit. The essential economic unit is now the internationally organized corporation that operates on a scale of organized planning to which only governments are equal, unless we mean to make an economic class—this time the corporate managerial aristocracy—again the owners of society, the legitimate authority for directing the use of the society's powers; unless, that is, we mean to abandon democracy altogether.

Democracy and capitalism, it seems to me, have always been theoretically incompatible. Democracy enfranchises the concerted wills of the populace. Capitalism enfranchises the will of the wealthy: it says that the ownership of capital is the proper authority for decisions about what should be produced, in what quantity, and how. At least when not irresistibly pressed by the need for sustenance, labor can, of course, refuse employment and in that degree impose a check on capital's autonomy. But even that is only a negative check. Labor—those who are hired by capital and whose work-lives have the social purpose established by capital—cannot positively design the goals to which the society's resources of economic work will be given.

But though democracy and capitalism were always theoretically incompatible, they were not always practically so. When the private manager of capital planned no more than a few people's work, when the society's economic needs were rudimentary and obvious and thereby dictated what the manager of capital would undertake to produce, then private-enterprise capitalism was commensurate with our economic possibilities. The individualism in it as against the tyrannies we came from made it commensurate with our dreams of political freedom. But such is no longer the case. Private profit is the object of private capital, but the economic possibility is now universal economic well-being. Freedom from, rather than freedom for, individualistic economic work is the political option to which our progress has brought us. And the history of thought has brought us to no understanding more forcefully than to the understanding that the moral quality of an individual's life is a function of the moral possibilities our situations make available. That we adapt readily to the most disparate situations is at once the beauty and the menace in the complexity of our character. We can be Nazis or we can be anti-Nazis. We can now choose to create a situation in which people no longer need to regard one another as competitors for nature's limited supply of sustenance, in which at least the economic constraints upon benevolence and understanding have been eliminated, in which class or race or gender or nation can at last be in day-to-day reality the merely superficial impediments to human concert that they have for so long been in theory only. That we have for so long regarded one another as competitors primarily is the major impediment to our choosing the new situation. Perhaps we cannot because the present demands of progress are unbelievable to us, or perhaps believing them would make us seem to mock our past. That is not to say that there may not be fundamental, irreconcilable, and fatal enmities amongst us. But it will take us yet a lot of progress to find that out. The enmities that create our present jeopardy are obviously trivial. They are mostly economic, as are the major constraints upon most people's opportunity to discover what they would do with freedom. These constraints we could now eliminate if we would. That these are now the real options with which we are faced seems proof of a very great progress in the past. It does not, of course, prove progress inevitable in the future. We may indeed blow ourselves up rather than undertake the work of the modern opportunity for the integration of knowledge and people. The progress we have made does suggest, however, that its continuation is not impossible and may even be likely.

III

It is unfortunate, but it is not strange, that the general populace does not now demand political power for economic accomplishment commensurate with the economic institutions in which we live. Unless the situation is desperate, most people see change not as hopeful possibility, but as jeopardy for whatever contentment they've got. The general populace has less of felicity than it could have, but more than it had before. We are more likely to feel comfortable with accomplished than with potential progress. But if not strange, then much less readily to be explained is the fact that most of those who express most forcefully the profoundest dismay, even disgust, with the present terms of our social life appear to be as unwilling to handle the institutional instruments of progress as is the general populace itself. There is considerable radical dissent from the present political arrangement of our economic life, but very little assent to the radical reintegration of politics and economics.

It may, of course, indicate merely my own oversimplification of the issues, but it seems to me that the moral possibilities of our present situation are great and the direction necessary to their accomplishment clear. All the great moral systems, whether embodied in a politics or not, have benevolence and power as their commitments. The extension of benevolent relations amongst people is the primary object. Power—the ability to make the environment conform to one's wishes—is secondary, in that it will be admired or loathed depending on the relevance in the extension of benevolent relations it is understood to have. An essential problem for every morality is to work out some system for the integration of benevolence and power, some theory of the hierarchy of powers according to their usefulness in the extension of benevolence. The extension of technological power is the key fact of contemporary American life. And in America private wealth is the socially sanctioned, the socially sponsored, object of technological power, and competition is the socially sponsored means for getting it. But sympathetic cooperation is the action by which benevolence is known, and the multiplication of opportunities for sympathetic cooperation seems obviously necessary if benevolence is what we want. By the democratization of our economic institutions—that is, by making them directly the instruments of the public will—we could make a major step toward the moralizing of power and the empowering of benevolence. The maximum development of economic techniques depends now on our establishing either of two choices: either we can choose the political reorganization of our economic institutions so that the social effect of economic action will be the general welfare, or we can choose indifference to the general social consequence of economic development. If we choose the democratic reorganization of the economy, that will not only be consistent with a continuous direction of history, it will be itself an act of social benevolence, it will be an extension of benevolence decreasing the degree to which competitions for private economic gain are made the principal form of social action. By the elimination of poverty it will mean an extension of personal choice, and, by making cooperative public ownership the ground of economic action, it will enhance the likelihood that personal choice will be a moral opportunity, an opportunity consistent with the general welfare, or at least less likely to be inconsistent with the general welfare than competitors' choices would be.

This seems to me clear. It is also clear that public support of this view is small and dispersed. Those who hold to it will not be importantly influential unless and until the political status quo fails to maintain the level of economic satisfaction to which the populace has become habituated. It is reasonable to assume that such a failure is inherent in the way automation will be extended under the new status quo. In the meantime, many on the Left are devoting themselves to the reorganization of leftist thought. In my view a useful part of that work would be the development of a clearer picture than we now have of the relation of leftist thought to the anti-political traditions amongst those who share with the political Left a radical dissent from the status quo, and of the relation of both to the now more, now less liberal politics of the mainstream.

AFTERWORD

How shall we understand the difference between those of us who see the greatest goodness in wealth and market competition to accumulate it and those of us who see the greatest goodness in liberty, fraternity, and equality (to rely on one good old way of putting it)? How shall we understand this deep, deep division amongst us, this difference in our motives and our understandings on which our survival itself may well depend?

The difference could be quite plain and uncomplicated, the same difference in our depths as on our surfaces. Of our species having more than one orientation for managing life there is no question. Certainly there are at least these two: we try to dominate and we try to cooperate. All of us try both and develop systems for integrating them—we do this with allies, we do that with opponents, and we do still otherwise with those neither one nor the other. For some, though, contention for preeminence is the good way, the best way, the success-defining way, at once the most personally fulfilling way and the most socially fulfilling way. And for some others it is the other way around. There is no question that all of us have both enemies and allies and are capable of both the contentious and the cooperative. There is no question that all of us do some of both and develop systems for the integration of them that adaptation seems to require. Both ways are ours by nature.

And if both are ours by nature, it *could* be that it is one's nature to feel one way more deeply, feel it to be more fully satisfying, than the other way. That one or the other way *should* be more satisfying has been argued for a very long time. See *Gilgamesh* or see Homer, for example, about the excellence, the beauty, of dominance. Or see Plato's and Aristotle's laborious work to balance the two. Or, for the other side, the side that loves kindness best and may even hate the drive to dominance, see, for example, the stories about Jesus Christ.

So it could be that those who love dominance best—dominance and the privileges of wealth and the power to command that the dominant can amass—it *could* be that they are altogether in tune with their own deepest selves. Partisans of dominance are many. They may not speak for every one—they have passionate opponents—but they may be speaking well and truly for themselves.

But if that is so, that is not such good news even for the partisans of dominance themselves. For the history of their development of the social and technological means of dominance—governments and armies and corporations and weapons unto the nuclear—has brought us all to the very serious possibility of extinction. Extinction! The possibility is now so readily named that saying it blandly comes easily to us. We need to do something special to keep vital the assertion that extinction is not OK.

Unless, of course, extinction, at our own hand, is inevitable for us (and for all we will take down with us), and may even be imminent. In which case perhaps it is better just to get used to it.

It may be, though, that the passion for dominance is not the deepest passion even of its partisans—even its political and economic and military and philosophical, and just plain everyday partisans. It could be that the passion for dominance rises out of ambivalence and gets its awesome and very widely shared energy from the thwarting of a deeper desire, the desire for love, perhaps, and for the kindness that love loves, and for the beautiful radiance of mutuality's opened hearts.

Where might we find evidence that the love of mutuality's harmonies is deeper than the passion for dominance?

Well, perhaps in this way. It is clear to many people who take these things seriously (and there are quite a few scientists among them) that the developments of "growth" and armaments together (and separately: either one or the other could kill us all) are suicidal, and suicide is not fulfillment's climax, but frustration's. The partisans of dominance are, in their denial of the extinctions they are courting, defending either astonishing obtuseness or the drive toward suicide.

If it is a drive toward suicide, and from the unbearable thwarting of the deeper desire—the desire for love—that is good news, isn't it? Wouldn't you rather it were love than dominance that is our deeper need? Yes. But the thwarted need for love has killed many, hasn't it? Has led many to kill many, themselves included. If that is where we are going, how do we fix *that*? Perhaps we cannot.

Or perhaps the denial of the rush toward extinction that the passion for dominance drives has another base. Imagine parents whose delight in their children is excited by nothing so much as their children's drive to "succeed" and who see success only in dominance and alliance with the dominant. Then imagine asking those who have in that way "succeeded" to give up the delight in them—the love of them—that their "successes" have excited. Could the impossibility of that giving-up be enough to make one obtuse about even the eventual catastrophes the success might entail? Even if the obtuseness risked death? After all, people often risk death—in war, for example—for the sake of a chance at glory as those they have depended on for love (or for admiration or, at least, for respectful acceptance) see glory. And might not such a path to glory make many deaths together, including one's own, resolve an intolerable hidden confusion of need and pain and fear and resentment and an awful conglomeration of hurts to be avenged? Do you really want me to set out to kill and to take on, thus, my intended victims' rage to kill me? Just so that you will love or admire or at least respect me? And won't that sow in me some terrible dark seeds of rage: at you for requiring my awful danger, and at myself for my own cowardly acceptance of your cruel ideals?

Many of us—most of us, I suppose—get to stay out of the limelight of intense consideration of such things. It is safer and easier and less dramatic just to accept and honor the respectable mix of contentions and cooperations orthodox for our time and place. Those in power see to it that most of us have quite safe neighborhoods and enough of the necessities and the luxuries to keep things calm enough for preoccupation by the everyday's established balance of those to fight, those to befriend, and those to ignore. No big dangers, no big questions. So we may inch dumbly toward our system's imminent catastrophes.

Big financial crashes, though, spoil orthodoxy's dignity and thus its bargaining power. Then settled questions—settled balances—become unsettled. Disorder excites and radical rebalancings become thinkable, even necessary. Which rebalancings this time, though? Like Germany's in 1932 or like FDR's? Then their confrontation—another World War? Could be. Things could go something like that again. But mightn't there be many more Hiroshimas and Nagasakis this time? And which way would that danger draw us? To the suicide we were considering? Like Hitler's? Or, rather, to some more deeply united nations, some bill of human rights more fully realized, some great refusal in disgust with "free" trade's right freely to exploit life of all kinds? Or maybe some cracking of the shell that keeps alliance narrow, love timid, pride dangerous, skill shallow—and commerce king? Could be.

* * *

Capitalism has over the several centuries of its rise to dominance produced more affluence and spread affluence more broadly than the other systems have. See the miles and miles of our glassy cities, our manicured suburbs, our landscaped highways for getting between the two, usually just one of us at a time in a gleaming vehicle with the power of more than a hundred horses. And even the poor, now, have much that would have seemed affluence not so very long ago. But the poor are still many, and many are still very poor. Twenty percent of us in America, I'm told, cannot afford a healthy diet. Let that stand for all that the poor cannot afford—or add, if you'd rather, good health, good education, good housing, good work, and good governance. The Left finds that absurd. Outrageous. Disgusting. Great wealth and its ugly superfluities next to poverty and its clenching anxieties. When the plenty, shared, could be health to us all. Absurd.

For almost two centuries most on the Left have found it hard to believe—even impossible to believe—that clear delineation of our society's ugly wealth and unnecessary poverty will not excite us all to the changes that could create general well-being. But the delineation, no matter how clear, hasn't done that. Not enough, anyway, to persuade even the poor to develop the strength in their numbers. The constantly propagandized chance of individual wealth has kept capitalism's appeal lively, even for poor people. The Left's analysis of the majority's self-interest hasn't been as persuasive as capitalism's appeal to the individual's craving for compensatory redemption from the past's humiliations.

Over the last two decades, or so, there has been added, with increasing force, to the Left's sense of the absurd, the environmental devastation capitalist wealth-mongering is causing. Causing for everybody—the rich, too. It used to be the job of the Left's intellectuals to lay out for the poor to see where their self-interest lies. Now, given what capitalism is doing to the environment, it can be shown that all our interests are becoming homogenized: capitalism is going to kill us all. But there are many—maybe even majorities—not persuaded by that argument either. How is that? How shall we understand those of us who seem to be liking capitalism better than survival?

Not such an easy question. But oughtn't we to ask it? The first big question that capitalistical affluence raised was why there couldn't be enough of it to end poverty altogether, for everyone. The anticapitalists said that indeed there could be enough. Simple: take from the rich their disgusting superflux. No way! answered the capitalists. Unnecessary! Capitalism will universalize affluence all by itself. How? Easy! Growth! And capitalism itself is growth's greatest engine. For a long time that argument has satisfied many. (My sense is that of those many, many are lying. What they really want to preserve in preserving capitalism is exactly its guarantee that some will be richer than others, very much richer.)

Lately, though, the growth argument has come upon hard times of a new sort. It is exactly capitalism's greed for growth, we now say, that is destroying our Earth's ability to provide even the rudiments of what we need. How about breathable air and potable water for rudimentary needs we may soon have to make war to secure? It's growth that is going to shrink us! Really? Really! How's *that* for an irony?

So if the capitalists are right that affluence is our deepest desire and industrial/commercial growth is the way to get it for still more and more of us—though *still* more and more of us is what we are fast creating—and that growth as we now grow it is going to be the death of us—then the question of "deepest need" gets a considerable weight.

It doesn't seem to be the same question for all of us. In fact, many oppose capitalist growth. Indeed, many have spent and are spending their whole lives developing that opposition. They oppose capitalism's making so many poor. More and more nowadays they oppose capitalism's rush toward the destruction of life. And many have a very different idea than do the capitalists and their loyal subjects about the way to our profoundest fulfillment—of ourselves and of our relations to one another.

These last see neither affluence nor even survival itself as their sufficient goals. They have something else in mind. About that in a moment.

Just now, a bit more about those for whom the pursuit of affluence *is* life's most fulfilling labor, its accomplishment life's most fulfilling accomplishment. In the past, I have understood these affluentists (I will try that name for a while) as unwell—their affluentism a pathological condition—perhaps our species' most widespread pathology—a form, *very* widespread and *very* dangerous—of sado-masochism. Let our wars stand as the most horrendous symptom of both—both the sadism and the masochism. But because wars have winners, the sadism is the more obvious. The nuclear warriors, though, have been for some time in the process of proving their masochism: their definitive masochism, hence their sado-masochism as well. No?

That is how I have understood our affluentists, those of us now bringing to climax in corporate free-trade capitalism both their sadism and their masochism, their symptoms disguised by bathings in wealth.

What, then, about those among us devoted to peace and health and equality and freedom and harmony and the work that broadens and deepens these devotions? Am I entitled to think them (as I have thought them) the psycho-morally healthiest of our kind; those most profoundly in touch with their own deepest desires, the desires the fulfillment of which will bring the fullest, the profoundest well-being, self-realization, self-assent, happiness?

Well, surely it means something important about us that those most vividly devoted in this way are the ones whose birthdays our society dependably and energetically celebrates on a grand scale.

We make holidays too, though, we must note, of their death days. And their deaths were premature, terribly premature. They were, many of them, these great heroes and heroines of ours, murdered. By agents of the acquisitivist systems they devoted their lives to trying to change. And we have long known this about such lives: the more vividly they are so, the more likely they are to inspire the system they would transform to get somebody to murder them. And these heroes and heroines of ours, and those devoted to them, knew that, too. And went on with their work anyway. And accepted not only their own likely murder, but the murders of their allies and colleagues and followers as well. And does that mean that *they* are sado-masochists and their devotion to life as they think life beautiful a cover for *their* sado-masochism? Am I stuck with that implication of the sado-masochism I assign to the dominantists?

It could be. But are there grounds for thinking that that is not so, as I very much want to believe it is not, and feel it is not, and must face the possibility, therefore, that it is only the wish that leads to the belief and props it up?

This is hard. After all, when both sides of our deepest disagreements about where to go and how to get there—when both roads seem to be taking us to the same place, the same death, there is reason to suspect that under our deepest disagreement there may be a still deeper agreement, a still deeper drive. It could be that life is just too hard for *all* of us.

It could be. But isn't it so that if the partisans of equality and cooperation and kindness and the thrill of shared truth and of the knowledge of likeness beneath difference and of the strengths aglow in our mutualities and the warmths aglow in our sympathies and in our empathies and in the gifts that these excite and in the kinds of work they excite—and so on, until we get to the crux of it all, which is love—isn't it so that if the partisans of love (so at last most boldly to call them) had their way, life would get longer and, yes, happier, and more beautiful, all over the place? I think so. Don't you? And isn't there envy of the partisans of love in it when the partisans of greed lust after bombs?

* * *

If one loves, then one knows that love is possible. Being told that one is loved does not prove it. Falsity about love is common enough to prove *that*. How, then, does one become capable of doing it? (Capable of loving, I mean.) By being loved before one learned the logic of falsehood and doubt. I suppose that if one learned doubt first, one may never be able to unlearn it. Sight must be activated by light within days of birth or it can never be activated. I suppose the same is true about love. The sense of it must be activated early. If it is, then we can do love and then we can know love when we see it—when we feel it, that is. It is love that triggers love. The same is true of affection of all intensities and depths. The same is true of respect. And the same is true of malice. They—the scientists of such things—know that at the start it is unalloyed indifference that kills us. They say it withers the brain stem. Severe malice can kill, too, of course, but it has to be active. Active ambivalence will keep you alive: if alive is good, then ambivalence is better than indifference. Sadism is, after all, a form of intimacy, which enlivens. The degree of ambivalence by which one is nourished is probably the degree of it one will feel for others. Good luck can bring one more love, more affection, more respect than one was granted at the start, but one had to have enough to make one able to believe the good luck of more, should one get more. Too little at first will make the chance of more seem only a terrible taunt to excite hopes one survived by repressing. I think it a general rule that the safer our society makes us, the less our children will worry us and the more their needs will excite our affection and respect and kindness and broaden both their and our own readiness to like others, too; our readiness, indeed, to love life itself.

These axioms and many more like them give the grounds for the sense I make of the way things, politically speaking, are going. They give the grounds for the sense I have that our political economy's ugly cruelties are not just the clean and neat expression of an adaptive orientation exhaustively fundamental to some of us, but foreign to others. We are of a kind, I think, and are made deeply different by the deeply different circumstances that embolden love, or don't.

What people do and say does not give us to *know* what they feel. We are certain there are mysteries between motives and actions, hardly less our own motives and actions than others'. We can't *know*, but we can feel as if we do. That we call faith. The tough fact is that many acts of faith are nonsense and give faith a bad name.

Do you remember the character Crook in Dickens' *Bleak House*? He is a junk dealer who collects especially the discarded records of court proceedings—lies, mostly. Such stuff has taught him to trust nobody. *Nobody.* So he would not learn to read. How could he *know* that anybody would teach him right? Sitting before his fire of discarded court records one winter night, Crook himself bursts into smoke and flames and is in a minute gone. Puff! Spontaneous combustion, Dickens calls it. So goes life with faith in no one. Crook was right, of course. All *might* teach him wrong. Certainly many do. And he couldn't *know* that any didn't. Luckily, though, we can learn faith in others before we learn about the rigors of knowing. With luck, we can wait to learn that later.

There are people who test one's hopeful faith that their cruelties and indifferences are not simple expressions of their natures but contortions wrought by their own sufferings. That is why I make so much of the logic that calls them sado-masochists. Sado-masochists could have been lovers, I say, but didn't get the chance and hope only for the intimacies of revenge.

Where's the consolation in that? Well, if it is true that safety makes loving more likely and we can nourish our talents for extending and deepening safety and with each extension and each deepening tilt our ambivalence toward trusting, hence toward affection and respect and kindness, hence toward love, even (of life itself, even), well, that ought to be somewhat more inspiriting of us leftists than seeing the looming doom* as nothing but the fulfillment of our basic competitivist destructiveness: bringing extinction in the way that getting very big and strong has been thought to have done it for dinosaurs, for example.

---

* I indulge myself in the playful "looming doom," here, not because I am sure that no doom is looming but because our time's terrible possibilities are too terrible for me to feel them whole or say them straight.